T0212780

Lecture Notes of the Institute for Computer Sciences, Social Informatics and Telecommunications Engineering 155

More information about this series at http://www.springer.com/series/8197

Nathalie Mitton · Melike Erol Kantarci
Antoine Gallais · Symeon Papavassiliou (Eds.)

Ad Hoc Networks

7th International Conference, AdHocHets 2015
San Remo, Italy, September 1–2, 2015
Proceedings

 Springer

Editors
Nathalie Mitton
INRIA Lille-Nord Europe
Villeneuve d Ascq
France

Antoine Gallais
Université de Strasbourg
Strasbourg
France

Melike Erol Kantarci
Clarkson University
POTSDAM
USA

Symeon Papavassiliou
National Technical University
Athens
Greece

ISSN 1867-8211   ISSN 1867-822X   (electronic)
Lecture Notes of the Institute for Computer Sciences, Social Informatics
and Telecommunications Engineering
ISBN 978-3-319-25066-3   ISBN 978-3-319-25067-0   (eBook)
DOI 10.1007/978-3-319-25067-0

Library of Congress Control Number: 2015949927

Springer Cham Heidelberg New York Dordrecht London
© Institute for Computer Sciences, Social Informatics and Telecommunications Engineering 2015

Printed on acid-free paper

Springer International Publishing AG Switzerland is part of Springer Science+Business Media
(www.springer.com)

Preface

Ad hoc networks, which include a variety of autonomous networks for specific purposes, are used in a wide range of applications. These networks were originally envisioned as collections of autonomous mobile or stationary nodes that dynamically self-configure into a wireless network without relying on any existing network infrastructure or centralized administration. With the significant advances in the last decade, the concept of ad hoc networks now covers an even broader scope, referring to many types of autonomous wireless networks designed and deployed for a specific task or function, such as wireless sensor networks, vehicular networks, mobile robot networks, home networks, and so on. Also, new challenges arise with the interconnection of these heterogeneous networks and transversal aspects such as energy, security, privacy, etc. While it is essential to advance theoretical research on fundamental and practical research on efficient policies, algorithms, and protocols, it is also critical to develop useful applications, experimental prototypes, and real-world deployments to an achieve immediate impact on society for the success of this wireless networking paradigm.

The annual International Conference on Ad Hoc Networks (AdHocNets) aims at providing a forum to bring together researchers from academia as well as practitioners from industry and government to meet and exchange ideas and recent research work on all aspects of ad hoc networks. As the seventh edition of this event, AdHocNets 2015 was successfully held in San, Remo, during September 1-2, 2015. We received high-quality submissions from many parts of the world, including Europe, North America, South America, and Asia. After a rigorous review process, 17 regular and three invited papers were included in the technical program. The technical program also included two keynote talks and five technical sessions, which presented recent advances in various aspects of ad hoc networks. In particular, the program featured two keynotes addressed by Prof. Mario Gerla from UCLA and Dr. Thomas Watteyne from Inria, France. This volume of LNICST includes all the technical papers that were presented at AdHocNets 2015. We hope that it will become a useful reference for researchers and practitioners working in the area of ad hoc networks.

September 2015   Nathalie Mitton

Organization

AdHocNets 2015 was organized by the EAI in cooperation with ICST.

Steering Committee

Imrich Chlamtac	Create-Net, Italy (Chair)
Jun Zheng	Southeast University, China
Shiwen Mao	Auburn University, USA

Organizing Committee

General Chair

Nathalie Mitton	Inria, France

TPC Co-chairs

Melike Erol-Kantarci	Clarkson University, NY, USA
Antoine Gallais	Université de Strasbourg, France
Symeon Papavassiliou	National Technical University of Athens, Greece

Publicity Co-chairs

Riccardo Petrolo	Inria, France
Eirini Eleni Tsiropoulou	NTUA, Greece
Miroslav Botta	Brno University, Czech Republic

Workshop Co-chairs

John Soldatos	AIT, Greece
Gregor Schiele	DERI, Ireland

Web and Publication Chair

Raffaele Gravina	University of Calabria, Italy

Conference Manager

Ruzanna Najaryan	EAI

Technical Program Committee

Mouhamed Abdulla	
Kemal Akkaya	Florida International University
Evangelos Anifantis	National Technical University of Athens
Paolo Bellavista	University of Bologna, Italy
Claude Chaudet	Institut Telecom / Telecom ParisTech/LTCI CNRS
Stefano Chessa	Department of Computer Science, University of Pisa
Melike Erol Kantarci	University of Ottawa
Antoine Gallais	University of Strasbourg
Raffaele Gravina	University of Calabria
Francesca Guerriero	University of Calabria
Essia Hamouda	University of California, Riverside
Ibrahim Korpeoglu	Bilkent University
Srdjan Krco	DunavNET
Jelena Misic	Ryerson University
Vojislav Misic	Ryerson University
Nathalie Mitton	Inria
Ruzanna Najaryan	EAI
Symeon Papavassiliou	NTUA
Sushmita Ruj	Indian Statistical Institute, Kolkata
Pratap Kumar Sahu	University of Montreal
Ramon Sanchez-Iborra	Universidad Politecnica de Cartagena
Loren Schwiebert	Wayne State University
Fatih Senel	Antalya International University
Houbing Song	West Virginia University & West Virginia Center of Excellence for Cyber-Physical Systems
Mujdat Soyturk	Istanbul Technical University
Aaron Striegel	University of Notre Dame
Fabrice Theoleyre	University of Strasbourg - CNRS
Manabu Tsukada	University of Tokyo
Damla Turgut	University of Central Florida
Jana Vlnkova	EAI

Contents

Physical Layer

MAC and Routing

Mobility in Networks

Self-Organization, Virtualization and Localization

Cloud, Virtualization and Prototypage

Security and Fault Tolerance in Wireless Mobile Networks

Physical Layer

Evaluation of Different Signal Propagation Models for a Mixed Indoor-Outdoor Scenario Using Empirical Data

Oleksandr Artemenko, Adarsh Harishchandra Nayak,
Sanjeeth Baptist Menezes, and Andreas Mitschele-Thiel

Integrated Communication Systems Group, Technische Universität Ilmenau,
98693 Ilmenau, Germany
{Oleksandr.Artemenko,Adarsh.Nayak,Sanjeeth.Menezes,Mitsch}@tu-ilmenau.de

Abstract. In this paper, we are choosing a suitable indoor-outdoor propagation model out of the existing models by considering path loss and distance as parameters. Path loss is calculated empirically by placing emitter nodes inside a building. A receiver placed outdoors is represented by a Quadrocopter (QC) that receives beacon messages from indoor nodes. As per our analysis, Stanford University Interim (SUI) model, COST-231 Hata model, Green-Obaidat model, Free Space model, Log-Distance Path Loss model and Electronic Communication Committee 33 (ECC-33) models are chosen and evaluated using empirical data collected in a real environment. The aim is to determine if the analytically chosen models fit our scenario by estimating the minimal standard deviation from the empirical data.

Keywords: Path loss, Signal propagation models, Signal strength, Experiment.

1 Introduction

Network planning is quite important in outdoor and indoor scenarios and the tools that are developed are to help operators to optimize their networks. The tools help in determining the best parameters like the position of the emitter nodes, the signal strength, and the suitable transmission channels. For these parameters to work efficiently in the chosen environment, it is also important to choose the best suited signal propagation model [1]. The propagation mechanisms are examined to help the development of propagation prediction models and to enhance the understanding of electromagnetic wave propagation phenomena involved when dealing with radio transmission in mobile and personal communication environments.

Evidently, the radio propagation phenomena are by themselves not new and do not depend on the environment considered. However, considering all the existing radio propagation phenomena, the most important one must be identified and investigated to improve the modeling of the mobile radio communication

© Institute for Computer Sciences, Social Informatics and Telecommunications Engineering 2015
N. Mitton et al. (Eds.): AdHocNets 2015, LNICST 155, pp. 3–14, 2015.
DOI: 10.1007/978-3-319-25067-0_1

channel or of the prediction of radio coverage and signal quality in radio communication systems. The most important radio propagation phenomena depend on the environment and differ whether we consider a flat terrain, or houses in a suburban area, or buildings in the city center. Propagation models are efficient only when the most dominant phenomena are taken into account and in how much detail do they need to be considered will also differ whether we are interested in modeling the average signal strength, or the path loss, or the power density, or any other signal characteristics.

The propagation environment causes difficulties in the investigation of the wireless signal propagation. Here, the most important aspects are as follows: (i) the distance between the base station and receiver range from several meters to several kilometers, (ii) walls inside the building have sizes ranging from very small to very large in comparison to the signal wavelength and affect the propagation of radio waves, (iii) the knowledge of the signal propagation environment is usually not known [1].

Since a suitable propagation model is important to work in a mixed indoor-outdoor environment we select few of the existing signal propagation models by considering the parameters for our scenario. The literature study suggests models which work either in the indoor or outdoor environment. By comparing other existing models, we propose to provide a model which is nearer in approximation in terms of minimum root mean squared error (RMSE) in comparison to the log-distance path loss model, in the frequency range of 2400 MHz and applicable in a mixed indoor-outdoor scenario. The latter considers that the emitter and the receiver are separated by one or multiple walls.

The remainder of this paper is organized as follows. In Section II, we briefly describe the criteria to select the signal propagation models for our scenario and provide detailed explanation of our analytically chosen models. In Section III, we present the evaluation scenario. Section IV gives the analysis of results. In Section V, the conclusion are drawn.

2   State of the Art

Path loss or path attenuation is reduction in the power density of an electromagnetic wave as it propagates through space [14]. The signal propagation models are designed keeping in mind the path attenuation factor, base station antenna height, mobile station antenna height, distance and operating frequency. Several other factors also contribute to the design of the signal propagation model. For example, such models can help to find the best position of the emitters, the optimal radiated power and the best propagation channel. A overview of the existing and the most well-known signal propagation models is provided in Table 1. Next, we highlight the models selected for further evaluation.

The following models are chosen as they fall in the frequency range of approximately 2400 MHz and the characteristics of these models are in accordance with our indoor-outdoor scenario.

Table 1. Existing Signal Propagation Models.

Title	Signal Model	Frequency Range [MHz]	Environment
Free Space Propagation [8]	$L = 32.44 + 20log_{10}d + 20log_{10}f$	NA	Free Space
SUI [4]	$L = A + 10\gamma log_{10}(\frac{d}{d_0}) + X_f + X_h + S$	2500-2700	Indoor/Outdoor
ECC 33 [3]	$L = A_{fs} + A_{bm} - G_t - G_r$ $A_{fs} = 92.4 + 20log_{10}d + 20log_{10}f$ $A_{bm} = 20.41 + 9.83log_{10}d + 7.894log_{10}f + 9.56(log_{10}f)^2$ $G_t = log_{10}\frac{h_b}{200}[13.958 + 5.98log_{10}d]^2$ $G_r = [42.57 + 13.7log_{10}f][log_{10}h_m - 0.585]$	3500	Indoor/Outdoor
Log-distance Path Loss Model [8]	$P_r(d) = P_r(d) + X_\sigma$ $P_r(d) = P_{r0} - 10\gamma log_{10}d + X_\sigma$	NA	Indoor/Outdoor
COST-231 Hata Model [6]	$L50 = 46.3 + 33.9log_{10}f - 13.82log_{10}h_b - ah_m + (44.9 - 6.55log_{10}h_b)log_{10}d + c_m$	500-2000	Indoor/Outdoor
Ericsson-9999 Model [10]	$PL_U = a_0 + a_1log_{10}d + a_2log_{10}h_b + a_3log_{10}h_blog_{10}d - 3.2(log_{10}(11.75h_r)^2) + g(f)$ $g(f) = 44.49log_{10}f - 4.78(log_{10}f)^2$	3500	Indoor/Outdoor
Hata Model [14]	$L50(urban) = 69.55 + 26.16log_{10}f_c - 13.82log_{10}h_t - a(h_r) + (44.9 - 6.55log_{10}h_t)log_{10}d$	150-1800	Indoor/Outdoor
Okumura Model [7]	$L50 = L_f + Amu(f, d) - G(H_t) - G(H_r) - G_{area}$	150-1920	Indoor/Outdoor
Walfisch and Bertoni Model [15]	$S = L0Q^2L_{rts}$	800-2000	Indoor/Outdoor
Walfisch and Ikegami Model [16]	$L_b = L0 + L_{rts} + Lmsd$	800-2000	Indoor/Outdoor
Clutter Factor Model [16]	$L = 40logD - 20logH_m - 20logH_b$	30-88	Indoor/Outdoor
Okumura Hata Model [17]	$L = A + BlogD - E, L = A + BlogD - C$	150-1500	Indoor/Outdoor
Obaidat-Green model [18]	$L_{fs} = 40log_{10}d + 20log_{10}f - 20log_{10}h_th_r$	2400	Outdoor

Table 2. Weather and experiment setup.

Parameter	Value/Name
Air temperature	$7^\circ C$
Humidity	75, %
Speed of wind	5, m/s
Air pressure	1008, mb
Building size	30×20 m^2
Number of nodes	11
Measured data sequences	>20000
Measured parameter	RSS

Wall Attenuation Model. In order to predict received signal strength between emitters and receivers, we employ the wall attenuation model [19]. In this model, received power $P_r(d)$ (in dBm) at a distance d (in meters) from the transmitter is given by:

$$P_r(d) = \bar{P}_r(d) + X_\sigma = P_{r0} - 10\gamma log_{10}d + X_\sigma,$$

where P_{r0} is the signal strength 1 meter from the transmitter, γ is the path loss exponent and X_σ represents a Gaussian random variable with zero mean and standard deviation of σ dBm [8]. In the equation above, $\bar{P}_r(d)$ represents the mean (expected) signal strength d meters from the transmitter, while $P_r(d)$ denotes a random outcome. This model takes into account the different obstacles present in multiple transmitter-receiver paths with the same separation. This phenomenon referred to as log-normal shadowing. For example, Seidel et al. report the results of modeling two office buildings at 914 MHz, with best fits (γ, σ) corresponding to (3.27, 11.2) and (3.25, 5.2) for single-floor measurements [13]. Other installations that have also been shown to follow this model can be found in [8,11,12]. This equation can also be extended with a wall attenuation factor W:

$$P_r(d) = P_{r0} - 10\gamma log_{10}d - W.$$

The parameter γ defines the statistical model and is viewed as heavily dependent on the environment. Measurements in the literature have reported empirical values for γ in the range between 1.8 (lightly obstructed environments with corridors) and 5 (multi-floored buildings), while values for γ usually fall into the interval (4, 12) dBm [8]. According to [19], the following parameters are representing the best fit for this model applied in a mixed indoor-outdoor scenario:

$$P_{r0} = -40dBm, W = 4.8dBm, \gamma = 3.32.$$

Free Space Model. Free Space Model is also considered to be the benchmark model for our scenario. In this model, the received power is a function of transmitted power, antenna gain and distance between the transmitter and the receiver. The basic idea is that the received power decreases as the square of the distance between the transmitter and the receiver subjected to the assumption that there is one single path between the transmitter and the receiver. The received signal power in a free space at a distance d from the transmitter is [8]

$$P_r(d) = P_t G_t G_r (\tfrac{\lambda}{4\pi d})^2,$$

where, P_t is the transmitted signal power, P_r is the received signal power, G_t is the transmitter antenna gain, G_r is the receiver antenna gain, λ is the wavelength. It is common to select $G_t = G_r = 1$. It can be expressed in dBm as:

$$L = 32.44 + 20log_{10}d + 20log_{10}f[dBm].$$

Stanford University Interim (SUI). IEEE 802.16 Broadband Wireless Access working group proposed the standards for the frequency band below 11 GHz containing the channel model developed by Stanford University, namely the SUI model. The correction parameters are allowed to extend this model up to 3.5 GHz band. In the USA, this model is defined for the Multipoint Microwave Distribution System (MMDS) for the frequency band from 2.5 GHz to 2.7 GHz [3].

The base station antenna height of SUI model can be used from 10 m to 80 m. Receiver antenna height is from 2 m to 10 m. The cell radius is from 0.1 km to

Table 3. Parameters for different terrains (SUI model).

Constants	Terrain A	Terrain B	Terrain C
a	4.6	4	3.6
b	0.0075	0.0065	0.005
c	12.6	17.1	20

8 km. The SUI model describes three types of terrain: A, B and C. There is no declaration about any particular environment. Terrain A can be used for hilly areas with moderate or very dense vegetation. This terrain presents the highest path loss. Terrain B is characterized with either mostly flat terrains with moderate to heavy tree densities or hilly terrains with light tree densities. This is the intermediate path loss scheme. Terrain C is associated with minimum path loss and applies to flat terrains with light tree densities. The basic path loss expression of the SUI model with correction factors is presented as [4,5]:

$$L = A + 10\gamma log_{10}\frac{d}{d0} + X_f + X_h + S \text{ for } d > d_0,$$

where d is the distance between emitter and receiver [m], $d_0 = 100$ m; λ is the wavelength [m]; X_f is the correction for frequency above 2 GHz; X_h is the correction for receiving antenna height, S is the correction for shadowing in the range between 8.2 and 10.6 [4] [dBm], γ is the path loss exponent. The parameter A and γ are defined as:

$$A = 20log_{10}\frac{4\pi d0}{\lambda},$$

$$\gamma = a - bh_b + \frac{c}{h_b},$$

where, the parameter h_b is the base station antenna height in the range between 10 m and 80 m. The constants a, b, and c depend upon the type of terrain and are given in Table 3. As a result, the value of parameter $\gamma = 2$ corresponds to the free space propagation in an urban area, $3 < \gamma < 5$ to an urban non-line-of-sight environment, and $\gamma > 5$ to an indoor propagation.

The frequency correction factor X_f and the correction for the receiver antenna height X_h are defined as follows:

$$X_f = 6.0log_{10}\frac{f}{2000}$$

$$X_h = 10.8log_{10}\frac{h_r}{2000}, \text{ for terrain types A and B}$$

$$X_h = -20.0log_{10}\frac{h_r}{2000}, \text{ for terrain type C,}$$

where, f is the operating frequency in MHz, and h_r is the receiver antenna height in meters. For the above correction factors this model is extensively used for the path loss prediction of all three terrain types in rural, urban and suburban environments.

Electronic Communication Committee 33 (ECC-33) Model. The ECC 33 path loss model, which is developed by Electronic Communication Committee (ECC), is extrapolated from original measurements by Okumura [7]. The model is defined as [3]:

$$PL(dBm) = A_{fs} + A_{bm} - G_t - G_r,$$

where A_{fs} is the free space attenuation, A_{bm} is the basic median path loss, G_t is the base station height gain factor and G_t is the receiving antenna height gain factor. These parameters are individually defined as:

$$A_{fs} = 92.4 + 20log_{10}d + 20log_{10}f$$

$$A_{bm} = 20.41 + 9.83log_{10}d + 7.894log_{10}f + 9.56[log_{10}f]^2$$

$$G_t = log_{10}\frac{h_b}{200}[13.98 + 5.8(log_{10}d)^2]$$

$$G_r = [42.57 + 13.7log_{10}f][log_{10}h_m - 0.585],$$

where d is the distance between the base station and the mobile [km], h_b is the base station antenna height [m] and h_m is the mobile antenna height [m].

COST-231 Hata Model. A model that is widely used for predicting path loss in mobile wireless systems is the COST-231 Hata model [6]. It was devised as an extension to the Hata-Okumura model [7]. The COST-231 Hata model is designed to be used in the frequency band from 500 MHz to 2000 MHz. It also contains corrections for urban, suburban and rural (flat) environments. Although its frequency range is outside of the one used in our measurements, its simplicity and the flexibility have motivated many researchers to widely use it for the path loss prediction in frequencies above 2000 MHz. The basic equation for path loss in dBm is [8]:

$$L = 46.3 + 33.9log_{10}f - 13.82log_{10}h_b - ah_m + (44.9 - 6.55log_{10}(h_b))log_{10}d + c_m,$$

where, f is the frequency in MHz, d is the distance between antennas in km, and h_b is the transmitter antenna height above ground level in meters. The parameter c_m is defined as 0 dBm for suburban or open environments and 3 dBm for urban environments. The parameter ah_m is defined for urban environments as [9]:

$$ah_m = 3.20(log_{10}(11.75h_r))^2 - 4.97, for f > 400MHz,$$

and for suburban or rural (flat) environments as:

$$ah_m = (1.1log_{10}f - 0.7)h_r - (1.56log_{10}f - 0.8),$$

where, h_r is the antenna height above ground level. Observation reveals that the path loss exponent of the predictions made by COST-231 Hata model is given by:

$$n_{COST} = \frac{(44.9 - 6.55log_{10}(h_b))}{10}.$$

Green-Obaidat Model. This model was first described by Green and Obaidat [18] in 2002. It considers the path loss accounting due to Fresnel zone with near earth antenna height (i.e. typically between 1 and 2 meters) [18]. The proposed path loss for near ground antennas is as follows:

$$P_{LOSS} = 40log_{10}d + 20log_{10}f - 20log_{10}h_th_r,$$

where f is the frequency in GHz, h_th_r represent the antenna heights for the transmitter and the receiver correspondingly, and d is the overall distance. This equation can further be simplified for use in 2.4 GHz IEEE 802.11 frequency as:

$$P_{LOSS} = 7.6 + 40log_{10}d - 20log10h_th_r.$$

Next, the above models will be evaluated according to our empirical data.

3   Evaluation

For the evaluation of our scenario, we consider the following environment. Our experiment took place at Leonardo Da Vinci building in the TU Ilmenau campus. The building plan and the placement of nodes is shown in Fig. 1. A total of 11 nodes were used in the experiment from which ten nodes were represented by netbooks as well as smartphones and were placed inside the building; and one node represented by a quadrocopter (QC) that was placed inside to perform indoor measurements and outside to perform measurement of a mixed indoor-outdoor signal propagation. In Fig. 1, the nodes in black represent the netbooks and the nodes in yellow represent the smartphones. Outdoor measurements were taken both in front and rear (South and North correspondingly) of the building by placing the quadrocopter at distances of 5, 10, 12, 15, 20 meters in the front, and 5, 10, 16, 20, 25, 30, 35, 40, 50, 55 meters in the rear. Since some models require reference measurements at distance $d = 1$ m, these measurements have been carried out indoors (the average value is $P_{r0} = 37$ dBm). For further indoor measurements, the nodes were placed equidistant at intervals of 0.9 meters. The technical specifications of the QC are given in Table 4.

Table 5 gives a description of the propagation parameters used for the evaluation of results. These parameters have been used to find the best fit for every

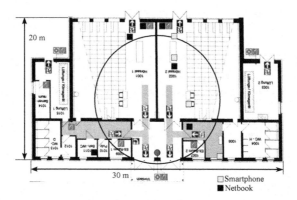

Fig. 1. The floor-plan of the chosen building. Positions of the smartphones and net-books are marked accordingly.

Table 4. Technical parameters of quadrocopter.

Technical Characteristic	Model or Parameter
Processor	600MHz Cortex A8
RAM	256MB
Gyroscope/Acceleration Sensor	MPU6050
Magnetic Field Sensor	HMC5883L
GPS Receiver	UBLOX6
Barometric Pressure Sensor	MS5611
Ultrasonic Sensor	MaxSonar I2CXL
Operating System	Gentoo Linux
Flight and Measurement Software	PengPilot (github.com/PenguPilot)

signal propagation model described above. We used the brute force method to go through all possible constellations of the values for the path loss exponent γ and the intercept (intercept has been applied for the log-distance and wall attenuation models only). For every combination of γ and intercept, an RMSE value has been calculated as an indication of correspondence to our empirical data. The smaller an RMSE value is, the more precisely a model fits to our scenario.

4   Evaluation Results

Using the data obtained our setup, we evaluated the path loss in dBm with respect to the distance between the emitter nodes and the QC. In Fig. 2, we plot the average signal strength measurements for different distance values using outdoor measurements only. Whereas, Fig. 3 incorporates both indoor and outdoor measurements.

Table 5. Propagation parameters for the evaluation.

Parameters	Values
Frequency	2.4 GHz
distance $d0$	1 m
Receiving antenna height	0.15 m
Wavelength λ	0.12 m
Transmitting antenna height	1.2 m
Path loss exponent γ	[1, 5]
Intercept	[0, 100] dBm

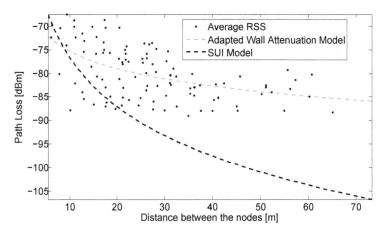

Fig. 2. Received signal strength vs. distance considering outdoor measurements only.

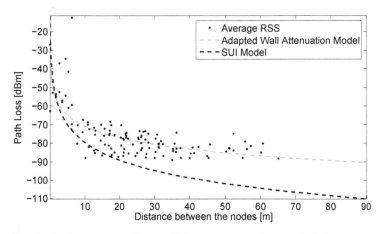

Fig. 3. Received signal strength vs. distance considering both indoor and outdoor measurements.

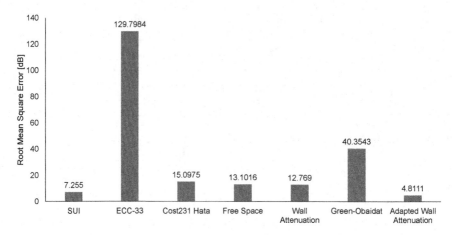

Fig. 4. Comparison of chosen models considering outdoor measurements only.

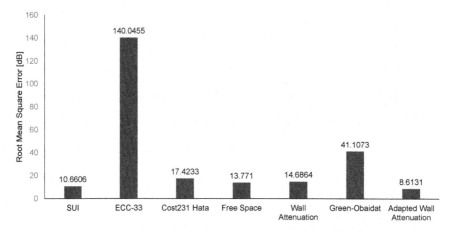

Fig. 5. Comparison of chosen models considering both indoor and outdoor measurements.

The upper line in Fig. 2 and 3 represents the adapted wall attenuation model. The line below represents the SUI model for the path loss exponent that produces the minimum error. It is obvious in both figures that the SUI model, presenting the second best result in this work, deviates significantly from the cloud of measurements. The wall attenuation model provides the smallest RMSE using the path loss exponent $\gamma = 2.05121$ and the sum of transmitted power and wall attenuation factor at 50.3292 dBm. The RMSE for the various models chosen is shown in Fig. 4 which represents the RMSE for the measurements taken with QC being outside of the building and Fig. 5 represents the RMSE for all measurements. In both figures, the adapted wall attenuation model outperforms its opponents presenting RMSE values 4.8 and 8.6 considering outdoor measurements and all measurements correspondingly. Considering high heterogeneity of data applied for the calculation of the RMSE using measurements from both indoor and outdoor environments, we can explain the enormous degradation and almost doubled value of the RMSE compared to the results achieved with outdoor measurements only.

5   Conclusion

As per the analysis of the chosen models, we obtained the minimum root mean squared error using the adapted wall attenuation model. The SUI model, the Free Space Model and the COST-231 Hata model provide the next best possible choice with respect to the minimum error. Hence for the chosen set of parameters and for the chosen mixed indoor-outdoor environment, the adapted wall attenuation model provides a closer approximation of the RMSE in comparison to other models.

Comparing the obtained set of values for the adapted wall attenuation model ($P_{r0} = 37$ dBm, $W = 13.3$ dBm, $\gamma = 2.05$) with the one of the original model from [19] ($P_{r0} = 40$ dBm, $W = 4.8$ dBm, $\gamma = 3.32$), we can conclude the following:

- The obtained RMSE for the model with the adjusted parameters is significantly better than the original one (the corresponding ratio is 2.6).
- Similar environmental conditions do not guarantee similar behavior of the signal propagation.
- A calibration of parameters can improve the accuracy of the model significantly. However, such a calibration represents an overhead and needs to be periodically repeated for the same area. This is partially due to the fact that the environmental conditions like temperature, light, open and closed doors and windows of the building can have a considerable impact on the resulting signal propagation.

References

1. Cichon, D.J., Krner, T.: Propagation Prediction Models. Prentice Hall (2002)
2. Saunders, S.R., Arago N-Zavala, A.: Antennas and propagation for wireless communication systems, 2nd edn. John Wiley and Sons, Ltd. (2007)
3. Abhayawardhana, V.S., Wassell, I.J., Crosby, D., Sellars, M.P., Brown, M.G.: Comparison of empirical propagation path loss models for fixed wireless access systems. In: Vehicular Technology Conference, 30 May-1 June, vol. 1, pp. 73–77. IEEE (2005)
4. Erceg, V., Hari, K.V.S., et al.: Channel models for fixed wireless applications, tech. rep., IEEE 802.16 Broadband wireless access working group, January 2001
5. Erceg, V., Greenstein, L.J., et al.: An empirically based path loss model for wireless channels in suburban environments. IEEE Journal on Selected Areas of Communications 17, 1205–1211 (1999)
6. COST Action 231, Digital mobile radio towards future generation systems, final report, tech. rep., European Communities, EUR 18957 (1999)

7. Okumura, T., Ohmori, E., Fukuda, K.: Field strength and its variability in VHF and UHF land mobile service. Review Electrical Communication Laboratory 16(9–10), 825–873 (1968)
8. Rappaport, T.S.: Wireless communication Principles and practice, 2nd edn. Prentice-Hall (2001)
9. Anderson, H.R.: Fixed Broadband Wireless System Design. John Wiley and Co. (2003)
10. Milanovic, J., Rimac-Drlje, S., Bejuk, K.: Comparison of propagation model accuracy for WiMAX on 3.5GHz. In: 14th IEEE International Conference on Electronic Circuits and Systems, Morocco, pp. 111–114 (2007)
11. Hashemi, H.: The Indoor Radio Propagation Channel. Proceedings of IEE 81(7), 943–968 (1993)
12. Molkdar, D.: Review on Radio Propagation into and within Buildings. IEE Proceedings-H 138(1), 61–73 (1991)
13. Seidel, S.Y., Rappaport, T.S.: 914 MHz Path Loss Prediction Models for Indoor Wireless Communications in Multifloored Buildings. IEEE Transactions on Antennas and Propagation 40(2), 207–217 (1992)
14. Hata, M.: Empirical Formula for Propagation Loss in Land Mobile radio Service. IEEE Transactions on Vehicular Technology (1980)
15. Walfisch, J., Bertoni, H.L.: A Theoretical Model of UHF Propagation in Urban Environments. IEEE Transactions on Antennas and Propagation (1988)
16. Low, K.: Comparison of urban propagation models with CW measurements. In: IEEE Vehicular Technology Society 42nd VTS Conference. Frontiers of Technology, pp. 936–942
17. Leppnen, R., Lhteenmki, J., Tallqvist, S.: Radiowave propagation at 900 and 1800 MHz bands in wooded environments. COST 231 TD(92)112, Helsinki (1992)
18. Green, D.B., Obaidat, A.S.: An accurate line of sight propagation performance model for ad-hoc 802.11 wireless LAN (WLAN) devices. In: IEEE International Conference on Communications, ICC 2002, vol. 5 (2002)
19. Faria, D.B.: Modeling Signal Attenuation in IEEE 802.11 Wireless LANs - Vol. 1. Technical Report TR-KP06-0118, Kiwi Project, Stanford University, January 2006

Setting Radio Transmission Range Using Target Problem to Improve Communication Reachability and Power Saving

Ryo Hamamoto[1], Chisa Takano[1], Hiroyasu Obata[1],
Masaki Aida[2], and Kenji Ishida[1]

[1] Graduate School of Information Sciences, Hiroshima City University,
3-4-1 Ozuka-Higashi, Asa-Minami-Ku, Hiroshima, 731-3194 Japan,
ryo@net.info.hiroshima-cu.ac.jp {takano,obata,ishida}@hiroshima-cu.ac.jp
[2] Graduate School of System Design, Tokyo Metropolitan University,
Hino-shi, Tokyo, 191-0065 Japan
aida@tmu.ac.jp

Abstract. Ad hoc networks can be composed entirely of mobile wireless terminals, and do not require permanent network infrastructure such as access points. They are considered a useful network configuration technology for various situations. For example, they are used to construct sensor networks in which distributed, inexpensive sensors monitor environmental conditions such as temperature and humidity. Further, ad hoc networks can be implemented after severe disasters that have disabled other network infrastructures. In general, ad hoc network terminals are battery powered. Therefore, extending network lifetime by reducing terminal power consumption is an important issue in ad hoc network management. One method for reducing power consumption involves reducing the radio transmission range of each terminal. However, reducing the radio transmission range causes degradation in the reachability of each terminal. In this paper, we propose a method to set ad hoc network radio transmission ranges using a *Target problem*, to reduce power consumption and increase each terminal's reachability. Next, we evaluate our method using various routing protocols, and define the applicability of our proposed method for each protocol. Simulation results show that the proposal improves communication reachability and power savings in ad hoc networks with normally distributed terminals, when the Destination-Sequenced Distance-Vector (DSDV) routing protocol is used.

Keywords: ad hoc network, power saving, reachability, target problem.

1 Introduction

Ad hoc networks [1] are used in many situations because they can be constructed autonomously, without network infrastructures such as access points (APs). In times of peace, for example, ad hoc networks are used to configure sensor networks [2] for environmental monitoring; they are also used in geocast communications systems [3], which distribute data among all terminals in a geographic area. Moreover, they are employed in vehicle-to-vehicle (V2V) communications [4] to

© Institute for Computer Sciences, Social Informatics and Telecommunications Engineering 2015
N. Mitton et al. (Eds.): AdHocNets 2015, LNICST 155, pp. 15–28, 2015.
DOI: 10.1007/978-3-319-25067-0_2

deliver information regarding traffic congestion and accidents. In contrast to ad hoc networks, infrastructure mode networks may suffer severe damage during large-scale disasters such as tsunamis or earthquakes. In these situations, infrastructure mode networks may lose their ability to communicate. However, ad hoc networks can communicate because they are not dependent on network infrastructures [5].

In general, terminals in an ad hoc network (such as smartphones and tablets) are battery powered. Terminals in an ad hoc network send data packets and also act as packet relay nodes. Thus, compared to an infrastructure mode network, power consumption must be suppressed as much as possible. Ad hoc network terminals are unable to work rapidly if their power consumption is reduced. As a result, the network structure becomes extremely sparse, and the terminal's reachability is impeded. Therefore, extending network lifetime by reducing terminal power consumption is an important issue in ad hoc network management. As a possible solution, the power consumption of terminals can be restrained by reducing their radio transmission range; however, this solution degrades reachability. Some studies have proposed and evaluated various transmission range management methods [6,7]. If a normal terminal distribution is followed, however, these approaches may not work effectively. In this paper, we propose a method to set the radio transmission range using a *Target Problem* [8]; this method reduces power consumption and increases terminal reachability in ad hoc networks with normally distributed terminals. Moreover, we evaluate the total goodput using 2 routing protocols (Destination-Sequenced Distance-Vector: DSDV [9], Ad hoc On-demand Distance Vector: AODV [10]), and we define the applicability of our proposed method for each routing protocol. Simulation results show that when the DSDV routing protocol is used, the proposed method improves both communication reachability and power savings in ad hoc networks with normally distributed terminals. The remainder of this paper is constructed as follows: Section 2 describes related works. Section 3 provides an overview of the target problem and the method of setting the radio transmission range based on the target problem; subsequently, we evaluate our proposed method in Sect. 4. Finally, Sect. 5 summarizes our paper and discusses future studies.

2   Related Works

In this section, we provide an overview of ad hoc networks and their applications. Furthermore, we discuss the power consumption and reachability issues of ad hoc networks.

2.1   Overview of the Ad Hoc Network

There are two forms of wireless local-area networks (WLANs) based on IEEE 802.11 [11] infrastructure mode and ad hoc mode. In infrastructure mode, WLAN systems contain access points (APs) connected to outside networks via Ethernet, and a number of terminals located within the radio transmission range of the

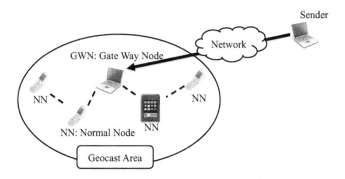

Fig. 1. Overview of geocast communication.

APs. Conversely, networks using ad hoc mode can be configured autonomously using wireless terminals such as laptops and tablets, without network infrastructure such as APs. Moreover, ad hoc mode networks can be configured rapidly and inexpensively. In this paper, we focus on ad hoc mode. In ad hoc networks, there are 2 communication methods, referred to as single-hop and multi-hop. In single-hop communication, each terminal communicates directly (1 hop). Thus, the sender must increase transmission power if the distance between the sender and receiver is relatively long. Therefore, single-hop communication is not suitable for extending ad hoc network lifetime. Conversely, in multi-hop communication, the sender and receiver are not required to communicate directly; packets can be relayed by terminals in between the sender and receiver. In other words, terminals in multi-hop communication networks can receive packets from neighboring terminals. Thus, multi-hop communication is suitable for extending the lifetime of ad hoc networks.

Geocast communications are examples of ad hoc networks. Here, we explain geocast communication, in which data is sent only to terminals in a specified area (referred to as the geocast area: GA) using the terminal's location information. Figure 1 shows components in a geocast communication system. Here, we explain the geocast communication process, using Fig. 1. First, there are 2 types of terminals in a GA gateway nodes (GWNs) and normal nodes (NNs). The GWN is a terminal that connects the GA to other networks outside of the GA. Only the GWN receives information from outside networks; the received information is delivered to the NNs in the GA by the GWN. In geocast communication, a terminal outside of the GA (Sender in Fig. 1) sends information to the GWN of the GA, in order to communicate with an NN inside the GA. The GWN sends its received information to NNs in the transmission area of the GWN, and the NN can also send its received data to other NNs.

We describe the following examples of geocast communication applications:

1. Send warning messages in the event of a disaster
2. Delivery of traffic information such as traffic congestion and accidents using V2V.
3. Delivery of information for residents in a specific area

2.2 Power Consumption and Reachability Issues of Ad Hoc Networks

In this section, we describe the power consumption and the reachability issues of ad hoc networks. Note that we assume the sending of emergency evacuation information during a disaster. In emergency situations, the information from the GWN must be received by all NNs that exist in the GA, because users are sending urgent information. That is, all NNs in the GA must be able to communicate with the GWN using single-hop or multi-hop communication. However, the transmission range of the terminals may be not sufficient if it was set haphazardly; in this case, an NN may not be able to connect to an NN that is communicating with the GWN. As a result, the NN is isolated from the GWN (isolated terminal). The isolated terminal cannot receive information from the GWN, and cannot send the information outside of the GA.

One solution for this issue is to extend the radio transmission range. Using this solution, it is possible to create an environment in which all NNs can transmit and receive information. However, terminals in the ad hoc network are, in general, battery powered. In addition to transmitting and receiving packets, terminals in an ad hoc network relay packets for other terminals. Thus, terminals consume more battery power if power consumption is not suppressed as much as possible. Terminal batteries are rapidly depleted, and network lifetime is shortened (by increasing the number of the terminals in which battery depletion is occurring). In particular, having access to the latest information is urgently required during a disaster. Therefore, sufficient network lifetime is required to obtain the latest information. To extend the network's lifetime, its power consumption must be reduced. Consequently, there is the trade-off between the creating an environment in which all terminals can transmit and receive information, and maintaining sufficient battery power. However, both *network power savings* and *communication reachability* are important goals in the management of geocast communications for ad hoc networks. In order to solve this issue, various studies have proposed transmission range management methods. For example, [6] shows the optimum transmission range in chain networks, and [7] suggests the designing method of transmission range based on the energy efficiency in simple network model. If a normal terminal distribution is followed, however, these approaches may not work effectively.

3 Setting the Radio Transmission Range Based on the Target Problem

In this section, we provide an overview of the 2 dimensional target problem [8]. Furthermore, we describe the method of setting the radio transmission range based on the target problem, to improve power savings and terminal reachability in ad hoc networks.

3.1 Overview of the 2 Dimensional Target Problem and Its Application to Single-Hop Communication

The nodes appear equivalent to the arrows that an archer shoots at a target. The hit points have a probabilistic characteristic. The 2 dimensional target problem considers the distribution of hit points. Random variables X_i $(i = 1, 2, \cdots, n)$ are independent of each other, and the normal distribution has variance σ_i^2 and average μ_i. Random variable Z is defined as Eq. (1):

$$Z = \sum_{i=1}^{n} \left(\frac{X_i - \mu_i}{\sigma_i} \right)^2 \tag{1}$$

Z has χ^2 distribution for which flexibility is n. This indicates that the sum of the squares of independent random variables that follow standard normal distribution $N(0,1)$ has a χ^2 distribution. In other words, the distribution of the squared sums of the distances between the hit points and the origin of the space has a χ^2 distribution. In the 2 dimensional target problem, distribution of the distances is important. We consider the χ distribution as the square root distribution of the χ^2 distribution. That is, the square root of the squared sum of distances from the origin to the hit point. Thus, the distribution of the distances from the origin indicates a χ distribution if flexibility n yields each component of the Cartesian coordinates (Fig. 2). Therefore, in the 2 dimensional target problem, the arrow's hit probability takes a χ distribution if the size of the target is known and the neighboring distribution of the hit points forms a normal distribution. As an example, we assume a target with a radius of R, whose origin is the center of a 2 dimensional plane. Hit probability $F(R)$ has a χ distribution; its flexibility is 2 when the neighboring distribution of hit points follows a 2 dimensional $N(0, \sigma^2)$. In other words, it follows a Rayleigh distribution as below:

$$F(R) = 1 - \exp\left(-\frac{R^2}{2\sigma^2} \right) \tag{2}$$

Moreover, the probability that the hit point is outside of the target (miss probability) $Y(R)$ is expressed by the complementary distribution of Eq. (2) $(1 - F(R))$:

$$Y(R) = \exp\left(-\frac{R^2}{2\sigma^2} \right) \tag{3}$$

Next, we explain the application of the target problem in geocast communication systems. We assume that the GWN's transmission range is the radius of the target, and that the GWN is located at the center of a GA (origin $(0,0)$). The probability $Y(R)$ that an NN in the GA cannot connect to the

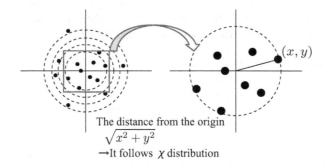

The distance from the origin

$$\sqrt{x^2 + y^2}$$

→It follows χ distribution

Fig. 2. Relationship between the distance from the origin and the χ distribution in the 2 dimensional target problem

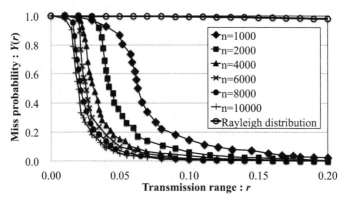

Fig. 3. Relationship between the transmission range r and miss probability for each n ($\sigma = 1.0$).

GWN with a single hop is estimated by Eq. (3). Therefore, NNs are placed according to a 2 dimensional normal distribution and the GWN is placed in the center of a geocast area, and the miss probability $Y(R)$ that the NN cannot connect to the GWN with a single hop follows the complementary distribution of a Rayleigh distribution. In the 2 dimensional normal distribution, the NNs are concentrated near the GWN (the GWN is placed where NN density is high). As a specific example, the GWN may be placed in an evacuation center when a disaster occurs. Moreover, when the GWN is placed in a location that will be used as a landmark for users, such as an aircraft [12], many users who can see the GWN move toward it. As a result, the distribution of the users follows a normal distribution.

3.2 Miss Probability Estimation Method in Multi-hop Communication

To facilitate geocast communication in an ad hoc network, it is preferable for the NNs and the GWN to be connected using multi-hop, from the viewpoint of

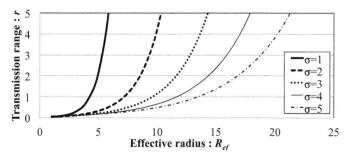

Fig. 4. Relationship between the transmission range r and effective radius R_{ef} for each σ $(n = 1,000)$.

reducing network power requirements. Based on the results from the single-hop environment in the previous section, we model the existence probability of an isolated node (miss probability) in the communication area of the GWN for a multi-hop environment. This problem is a kind of the connectivity problem [13]. Note that the network model is a unit disk graph (UDG), which is a type of intersection graph containing equal-radius circles. Moreover, the GWN is the nearest terminal from the origin.. In this section, as a preliminary experiment, we investigated the relationship between multi-hop miss probability and transmission range, for varying numbers of terminals. We assumed a 2 dimensional plane, and terminals were distributed according to 2 dimensional $N(0, \sigma)$. The numbers of terminals n were set to $(1,000, 2,000, 4,000, 6,000, 8,000, 10,000)$. In this paper, we shows the results of $\sigma = 1.0$ as an example. Experimental results contain the averages of 30 trials. Figure 3 shows the relationship between the transmission range of each terminal in the multi-hop environment r and the miss probability of terminal $Y(r)$, and Fig. 3 also shows the relationship between r and the complementary Rayleigh distribution. In Fig.3, the vertical axis denotes $Y(r)$ and the horizontal axis denotes r. From Fig.3, $Y(r)$ does not indicate the complementary Rayleigh distribution, regardless of the number of terminals n.

Next, we investigated the relationship between the effective radius R_{ef} and transmission range of each terminal r. R_{ef} can be obtained by adding r and the distance of the farthest terminal that the GWN can connect with using multi-hop. Moreover, it meets $R_{ef} \geq r$. The relationship between R_{ef} and r is obtained as follows. First, we established the transmission range of the GWN in the single-hop environment R as R_{ef}. Next, we compared the miss probability of r in the multi-hop environment and the miss probability of R in the single-hop environment. Then, we investigated the relationship between R_{ef} and r, to determine if the miss probability had the same value. As an example, Figure 4 shows the relationship between R_{ef} and r when n is $1,000$. Note that σ was set to $(1.0, 2.0, 3.0, 4.0, \text{ and } 5.0)$. As shown in Fig. 4, R_{ef} has an exponential relation with r as Eq. (4):

$$r = \alpha \exp(\beta R_{ef}) \tag{4}$$

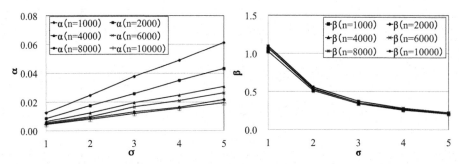

Fig. 5. Relationship between α and σ.   **Fig. 6.** Relationship between β and σ.

Table 1. Value of $\phi(n)$.

n	1,000	2,000	4,000	6,000	8,000	10,000
$\phi(n)$	0.0123	0.0087	0.0062	0.0053	0.0043	0.0039

We then investigated the relationship between α and σ. Figure 5 is the relationship between α and σ. As shown in Fig. 5, a proportionality relation exists between α and σ ($\alpha = \phi(n)\sigma$). Table 1 shows the value of $\phi(n)$. From Table 1, $\phi(n)$ is described as Eq. (5):

$$\phi(n) = 0.03786n^{0.496} \tag{5}$$

Thus, α can be presented as follows:

$$\alpha = \frac{0.03786\sigma}{\sqrt{n}} \tag{6}$$

Next, Fig. 6 shows the relationship between β and σ. As the figure shows, β is inversely proportional to the σ regardless of n. Moreover, β can be written using σ as follows:

$$\beta = \sigma^{-1} \tag{7}$$

From Eq. (6) and Eq. (7), r is presented using R_{ef} as follows:

$$r = 0.3786\frac{\sigma}{\sqrt{n}}\exp(R_{ef}\sigma^{-1}) \tag{8}$$

By substituting R_{ef}, which was obtained from Eq. (8) for Eq. (3), the existence probability of an isolated terminal (miss probability) in a multi-hop environment for each r can be obtained as follows:

$$Y(R_{ef}(r)) = \exp\left(-\frac{(\log(\sqrt{n}r\sigma^{-1})+1)^2}{2}\right) \tag{9}$$

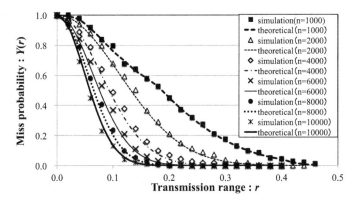

Fig. 7. Comparison of simulation values and theoretical values from Eq. (9) ($\sigma = 1.0$).

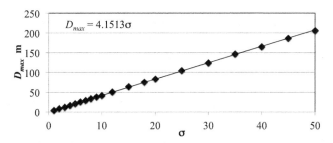

Fig. 8. Relationship between σ and the distance of the farthest node from the GWN.

In other words, the minimum transmission range that satisfies the existence probability of an isolated terminal P can be estimated by Eq. (9). Note that we refer to P as an acceptable miss probability in Sec. 4.

Subsequently, we compared the theoretical formula Eq. (9) and the simulated miss probability values in the multi-hop environment. Figure 7 shows the relationship between r and the miss probability in the multi-hop environment. Note that the values of n and σ are the same as they were in the preliminary experiment. In Fig. 7, the vertical axis shows the miss probability and the horizontal axis shows r. As shown in Fig. 7, Eq. (9) outputs almost the same miss probability as the simulation value. Therefore, Eq. (9) can estimate the miss probability in a multi-hop environment for each r. Here, Fig. 8 shows the relationship between σ and the distance D_{max} between the GWN and the node farthest from the GWN. As shown in Fig. 8, the relationship between σ and D_{max} is obtained as follows:

$$D_{max} = 4\sigma \tag{10}$$

Therefore, σ can be obtained by Eq. (10).

4   Evaluation

In this section, we describe the evaluations of our proposed method using ns2 [14]. We focused on the total goodput and total power consumption. Note that the main purpose of the evaluations was to show the effectiveness of our proposed model equation (Eq. (9)). Therefore, both the number of terminals and σ are known by terminals in our evaluations.

In our evaluation, we assumed a 2 dimensional plane. The sink node was placed at $(0,0)$, and wireless terminals (senders) were distributed according to 2 dimensional $N(0, \sigma^2)$; the number of senders was 100. This network used an IEEE802.11b (PHY) wireless LAN environment, and UDP (User Datagram Protocol) (with a segment size of 128 byte [15]) for the transport protocol [15]. Moreover, each sender generated 60 seconds of constant bit rate (CBR) traffic (1 Kbps). The routing protocol used DSDV [9] and AODV [10]. We assumed that none of the terminals moved. In this evaluation, terminals consumed battery power when they were connected to the GWN in the multi-hop environment, and power consumption was a normalized value. In the power consumption model for our evaluation, the amount of electricity used by the terminal for the transmission range r was proportional to the square of r [16], and terminals used electricity equal to 0.001 when r was 0.01. That is, terminal power consumption was increased 4 times when r was doubled. Moreover, total power consumption was the sum of the power consumption for terminals that could communicate with the GWN, using multi-hop in one unit time. In addition, the acceptable miss probability P was 0.1% (to obtain r which satisfied P, we calculate $Y(R_{ef}(r)) = 0.001$); the simulation results contain the averages of 20 trials.

Figure 9 shows the relationship between σ and the total goodput for each r when the DSDV routing protocol was used. In Fig. 9, the vertical and horizontal axes represent the total goodput and σ, respectively. Note that "proposed" in Fig. 9 is the transmission range set by Eq. (9), and proposed meets P. As

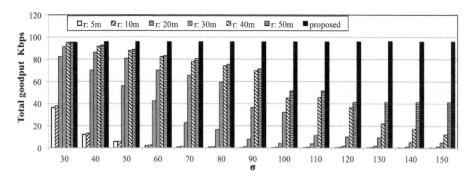

Fig. 9. Total goodput for each σ ($n = 100$, DSDV).

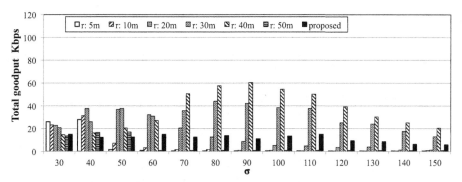

Fig. 10. Total goodput for each σ ($n = 100$, AODV).

shown in Fig. 9, when r m was fixed, the total goodput decreased if σ increased. This occurred because terminals were widely distributed across the area when σ increased. Therefore, the number of terminals that could not connect to the GWN increased if r was fixed. On the other hand, total goodput in each σ was highest when r was set to the proposed m. Our method set the transmission range for each σ in order to meet P. As a result, the proposed method improved communication reachability when DSDV was used as the routing protocol.

Figure 10 shows the relationship between σ and the total goodput for each r when AODV was used. In the figure, the vertical and horizontal axes represent total goodput and σ, respectively. Fig. 10 also represents the proposed transmission range, which was set by Eq. (9). The figure also shows that total goodput was lower than the results produced using DSDV. This decrease was caused by the placement of terminals, and the fact that AODV is a reactive protocol. In our evaluations, terminals were distributed according to a 2 dimensional $N(0, \sigma)$. That is, terminals were concentrated near the sink node. Here, a path for the sink node was generated according to the routing table, which was constructed by exchanging distance vectors with broadcasts in DSDV. Moreover, the topology near the sink node was constructed in a similar manner to a mesh network. Even if a node near the sink lost information it received from a node, it was possible to obtain that information from another neighboring node. Conversely, in AODV, a sender broadcasts a route request (RREQ) packet and receives a route reply (RREP) packet from the sink or other terminals that have already found a path to the sink during the routing path configuration process. In our evaluations, however, terminals were distributed according to a 2 dimensional $N(0, \sigma)$. Therefore, frame collisions that included AODV control packets occurred frequently near the sink. Moreover, CSMA/CA congestion frequently occurred when terminals were densely located, and a significant amount of time was required to exchange AODV control packets. As a result, goodput decreased when AODV was used for the routing protocol. For this reason, network performance decreases when the transmission range is expanded and terminals are densely distributed (similar to a normal distribution), and reactive routing protocols such as AODV are used. This is known as a type of exposed node prob-

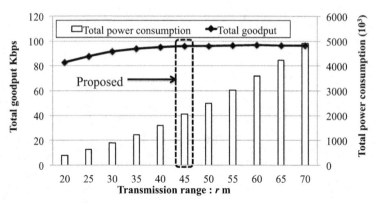

Fig. 11. Relationship between the transmission range r and both the total power consumption and total goodput ($\sigma = 30.0$, DSDV).

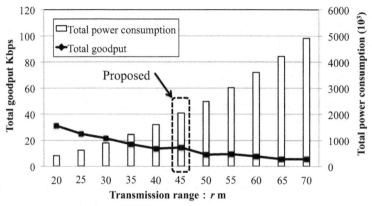

Fig. 12. Relationship between the transmission range r and both the total power consumption and total goodput ($\sigma = 30.0$, AODV).

lem [17]. Therefore, the use of AODV is unsuitable for setting the communication radius using our proposed method.

Next, Fig. 11 shows the relationship between r and both the total power consumption and total goodput when σ is set to 30 and DSDV is used. In Fig. 11, r is shown within the 25 m ranges before and after proposed (approximately 45.4 m). Total goodput was improved along with the increase in power consumption (until proposed was reached). However, total goodput was not improved to the same extent when the transmission range extended beyond proposed; only the total power consumption increased. Therefore, the transmission range that was obtained by the proposed method improved both communication reachability and terminal power savings when the DSDV routing protocol was used. Finally, Fig. 12 shows the results of a similar experiment using AODV. In this experiment, goodput was improved by using transmission ranges narrower than the proposed range. This is because the exposed node problem is restrained by reducing the number of adjacent terminals for each node, which is achieved by narrowing the communication radius. As a result, the exchange of AODV control packets is achieved easily. From the viewpoint of increasing ad hoc network uptime, setting the terminal transmission range using the target problem was very effective. Further, by using simulation experiments, we demonstrated that our method can improve communication reachability when DSDV is used for the routing protocol.

5   Conclusion

In this study, we proposed a method to set the radio transmission range using a target problem, in order to improve both the communication reachability and power savings for each terminal. We evaluated our method using ns2, from the viewpoint of both the total goodput and total power consumption. Moreover, we compared the results obtained by our proposed method and results obtained by setting a fixed value for the communication range. From the simulation results, we demonstrated that setting the communication range using our method can provide significant improvements in goodput and power savings when DSDV is used as the routing protocol. Furthermore, when AODV was used as the routing protocol, our method caused total goodput to decrease drastically. Future works will include the following evaluations.

1. Evaluations considering the joining and leaving of terminals
2. Evaluations considering more realistic power consumption model

Acknowledgment. The authors would like to thank Mr. Takuya Sakamoto and Ms. Miki Tomomune for their constructive contributions. This work was partly supported by JSPS KAKENHI Grant Numbers 26420367, 26280032, 15K00431.

References

1. Perkins, C.E. (ed.): Ad Hoc Networking. Addition Wesley (2000)
2. Akyildiz, I.F., Su, W., Sankarasubramaniam, Y., Cayirc, E.: A Survey on sensor networks. IEEE Commun. Mag. 40(8), 102–114 (2002)
3. Maihöfer, C.: A survey of geocast routing protocols. IEEE Commun. Surveys & Tutorials 6(2), 32–42 (2009)
4. Al-Sultan, S., Al-Doori, M.M., Al-Bayatti, A.H., Zedan, H.: A comprehensive survey on vehicular ad hoc network. Journal of Network and Computer Applications 37, 380–392 (2014)
5. Reina, D.G., Toral, S.L., Barrero, F., Bessis, N., Asimakopoulou, E.: Evaluation of ad hoc networks in disaster scenarios. In: Proc. 3rd International Conference on INCoS2011, pp. 759–764 (2011)
6. Chen, P., O'Dea, B., Callaway, E.: Energy efficient system design with optimum transmission range for wireless ad hoc networks. In: Proc. IEEE ICC 2002, vol. 2, pp. 945–952 (2002)
7. Deng, J., Han, Y.S., Chen, P.-N., Varshney, P.K.: Optimum transmission range for wireless ad hoc networks based on energy efficiency. IEEE Trans. commun. 55(9), 1772–1782 (2007)

8. Johnson, N.L., Kemp, A.W., Kotz, S.: Univariate discrete distributions. Series in Probability and Statistics (2005)
9. Perkins, C.E., Bhagwat, P.: Highly dynamic destination-sequenced distance-vector routing (DSDV) for mobile computers. In: Proc. ACM SIGCOMM 1994, pp. 234–244 (1994)
10. Perkins, C.E., Royer, E.M.: Ad-hoc on-demand distance vector routing. In: Proc. 2nd IEEE workshop on Mobile Computing Systems and Applications, pp. 90–100 (1999)
11. IEEE 802.11 Working Group, Part 11: Wireless LAN medium access control (MAC) and physical layer (PHY) specifications. ANSI/IEEE Std. 802.11 (1999)
12. Suzuki, H., Kaneko, Y., Mase, K., Yamazaki, S., Makino, H.: An ad hoc network in the sky, SKYMESH, for large-scale disaster recovery. In: Proc. 64th IEEE VTC-Fall, pp. 1–5 (2006)
13. Schiller, E., Starzetz, P., Theoleyre, F., Duda, A.: Properties of greedy geographical routing in spontaneous wireless mesh networks. In: Proc. IEEE GLOBECOM 2007, pp. 4941–4945 (2007)
14. Network Simulator - ns (version 2). http://www.isi.edu/nsnam/ns/ (2015)
15. Kominami, D., Sugano, M., Murata, M., Hatauchi, T.: Robust and resilient data collection protocols for multihop wireless sensor networks. IEICE Trans. Commun. E95-B(9), 2740–2750 (2012)
16. Takada, J., Promwong, S., Hachitani, W.: Extension of Friis' transmission formula for ultra wideband systems. IEICE technical report, WBS2003-8 (2003)
17. Thorpe, C., Murphy, L.: A survey of adaptive carrier sensing mechanisms for IEEE 802.11 wireless networks. IEEE Commun. Surveys & Tutorials 16(3), 1266–1293 (2014)

Optimizing the Placement of ITAPs in Wireless Mesh Networks by Implementing HC and SA Algorithms

Liqaa Nawaf, Christine Mumford, and Stuart Allen

Cardiff University, Computer Science, Cardiff, UK
{NawafLF,MumfordCL,AllenSM}@cardiff.ac.uk

Abstract. In this paper, we present novel heuristic improvement (move) operators for the design of Wireless Mesh Networks (WMN), and demonstrate their efficiency within simple Hill Climbing (HC) and Simulated Annealing (SA) frameworks. The management cost of Internet Transit Access Points (ITAPs) in WMN is significant, so it is crucial to minimize the number of ITAPs required whilst maintaining an acceptable quality of service (QoS). Using a single objective method, we investigate algorithms to make informed placement decisions based on the grid size, wireless range connectivity, wireless link capacity and user demands. The experimental results showed the efficiency of the proposed combination of move operators.

Keywords: wireless mesh network, move operators, optimization.

1   Introduction

Wireless Mesh Networks (WMNs) are a promising approach to provide ubiquitous broadband internet access due to their great potential in supporting multimedia applications. WMNs, an emerging technology, may bring the dream of a seamlessly connected world into reality. In a WMN, a limited number of Internet Transit Access Points (ITAPs) serve as gateways or bridges to the Internet, and are deployed across a community. Individual houses within the community are equipped with antennae and low cost routers (namely, mesh routers) which perform two roles: 1) to service the traffic in and out of the house to the individual laptops and other devices (that is, to the mesh clients), and 2) to provide a link in a multi-hop wireless backbone that is formed between the houses to cooperatively route traffic throughout the neighbourhood, communicating with the Internet through the ITAPs. Such a multi-hop structure dramatically reduces the number of ITAPs needed, which can result in massive savings in cost. The networking infrastructure is decentralized and simplified because each node need only transmit as far as the next node. An ITAP will share its Internet connection wirelessly with all houses in its vicinity. Those houses then share the connection wirelessly with the nodes closest to them. Large or small networks can be created in this way to serve small rural communities, or millions of residents in a city. In this paper, we address the ITAP placement problem, which involves determining the numbers and locations of ITAPs that are required to service the needs of a community. This situation is easily modelled using graph theory. In wireless

© Institute for Computer Sciences, Social Informatics and Telecommunications Engineering 2015
N. Mitton et al. (Eds.): AdHocNets 2015, LNICST 155, pp. 29–41, 2015.
Doi: 10.1007/978-3-319-25067-0_3

neighbourhood networks, a set of Houses and set of ITAPs are designed and deployed. Fixed capacities are associated with each house and ITAP and with all connecting edges in the network.

The focus of our present paper is to demonstrate the effectiveness of our novel move operators on a simple ideal link model with a single objective. Our simple ideal link model is taken from [3]. To the best of our knowledge, our proposed move operators have not previously been applied to WMNs. We show that, by using a suitable combination of move operators to place the ITAPs, rapid improvements can be made to the underlying WMN. The remainder of this paper is structured as follows: we discuss related work in section 2. Section 3 outlines the ideal link model, and section 4 formulates the associated integer linear program. In section 5, our heuristic algorithms are described, and the experimental methodology and results are presented in section 6. Finally, conclusions are drawn in section 7.

2   Related Work

[1] Addresses the problem of ITAP (gateway) placement, consisting of placing a minimum number of ITAPs so that Quality of Service (QoS) requirements are satisfied. In a wireless mesh network, traffic is aggregated and forwarded towards the ITAPs. The authors formulate the ITAP placement problem given by integer linear programming (ILP) and show that the problem of finding a minimum number of ITAPs is NP-Hard. In practice, an LP solver, such as CPLEX, can only handle small sized networks under the proposed model due to the rapid increase in the number of variables and constraints with increasing network size. The authors proposed an algorithm that produces recursive approximations of the Minimum Dominating Set problem. When compared to other algorithms, their approach reduced the number of ITAPs by up to 50%, whilst at the same time exhibiting smooth and consistent performance when subject to different QoS constraints. From [1] it is clear that CPLEX is too slow to use on large instances, and some experimental work we undertook (not reported here) also supports this conclusion. In [2]the fundamental issue is the placement of mesh routers in a local network that has one ITAP, and to find the minimal configuration of mesh routers so as to satisfy the network coverage, connectivity, and Internet traffic demand. The rate of the increase with respect to the number of ITAPs increases with the network size, which indicates that the traffic density has significant impact on the number of required ITAPs in the larger size of networks. Chandra et al. [3] developed algorithms to place ITAPs in multi-hop wireless network to minimize the number of ITAPs while satisfying users' bandwidth requirements. They formed the ITAP placement problems as linear programs and presented several greedy-based approximation algorithms. The placement of ITAPs is based on neighbourhood layout, user demand, and wireless link characteristics. In [4] the authors observe that the transmission rate and the channel utilization required to satisfy the WMN's demand clearly depend on device technologies, but in particular

on the distance between the mesh client and the ITAPs to which it is connected; hence, the allocation mechanism influences the number of mesh clients that have the opportunity to exploit the available bandwidth. The authors in [5] minimize the network installation cost while providing full coverage to wireless mesh clients. In this type of network architecture, a limited number of ITAPs wirelessly connected to the wired realm can potentially provide low cost internet connectivity to a large number of mesh routers. The authors of [5] and [6], also supported by our experimental work, indicate that the heuristics can provide close to optimal solutions even for large instances. Jangeun Jun and Mihail L. Sichitu [7] discuss the problem of the capacity of WMNs and the fairness of multi-hop networks; for example, as more nodes are installed, the reliability and network coverage increase.

The obtained numerical results of [8] show that directional antennas can greatly enhance the performance of WMNs, thus enabling high throughput services. The cause of the problems of wireless network performance can be traced back to the original design assumptions. The authors [9] believe that a well-planned and optimized wireless network can often provide extra capacity with the same infrastructure cost; for instance, this may result from more efficient use of radio frequencies. Another way to achieve a better network performance is to optimize the placement and characteristics of ITAPs before network deployment. A careful placement of ITAPs, may lead to less congestion, low delay and eventually better throughput if the distances and the links capacity are taken into account. The authors [10] considered neighbourhood search-based methods as more powerful methods than ad hoc methods for achieving near optimal placements of mesh router nodes. Their experimental evaluation demonstrated an excellent performance of a swap-based movement neighbourhood search. In [11] the neighbourhoods are based on reversing segments of routes (sub-routes) and exchanging segments between routes. The authors demonstrated that their Variable Neighbourhood Search is very competitive compared with previously published state-of-the-art heuristic algorithms. In [12] the authors considered three different types of movements (Random, Radius and Swap). Their results showed a very good performance of combination movement for Router Nodes placement problem in WMNs. In [13] they propose a grid-based ITAPs (called Gateways there) deployment method using a cross-layer throughput optimization, and prove that the achieved throughput using this method is a constant times of the optimal.

From the literature review, we observe that local search algorithms with suitable heuristic move operators can produce acceptable results on instances that are too large for solutions by exact methods. In this paper, we propose a new two phase approach for solving the network optimization problem, in which the underlying framework iterates between the two phases. The first phase focusses on improving the QoS that can be obtained from deploying a fixed number of ITAPs by moving individual ITAPs from one place to another. The second phase then attempts to reduce the number of ITAPs required, whilst still maintaining adequate QoS. To effectively support different goals of the two phases, a mix of operators is required. In our experimental work, we demonstrate the effectiveness of combining our new operators in suitable proportions. We compare hill climbing (HC) and simulated annealing (SA) as heuristic drivers for two phase approach.

3   Network Model

We use the ideal link model proposed in [3], and aim to minimize the number of required ITAPs, while satisfying users' bandwidth requirements. Our algorithms are applied to place ITAPs in different locations, and the network flow algorithm of Ford-Fulkerson [14] is then used to ensure that demand is satisfied for a specific WMN configuration. Before the application of Ford-Fulkerson, however, it is necessary to transform the WMN into an equivalent single source, single sink model. Once this has been done, the Ford-Fulkerson Algorithm can be used to compute the maximum flow capacity of the edges in the network flow, and hence whether not or a given WMN configuration is able to support the required user demand.

In more detail, a set of houses $H=\{h_1,\ldots h_n\}$ is given in the network, along with a set (I) of locations at which ITAPs can be installed. Each house has a traffic demand, wh, and we say a house is served if this traffic can be successfully transmitted to an active ITAP (possibly by a sequence of hops). Traffic from each house can be routed along multiple paths simultaneously, hence the problem can be modelled using max flow algorithms. We construct a graph with HUI as nodes, with edges joining each pair that are within wireless range. The capacity of each edge, Cap_e, is the data rate that can be sustained on that link, and each node has a capacity Cap_h, or $Cap_h = Cap_e$, which denotes their ability to process and forward data. Each ITAP also has a capacity limit, based on its connection to the Internet and its processing speed, where the Cap_i denotes the capacity of ITAP. To complete the graph, we add a source (joined by edges of capacity Cap_e to each house) and a sink (joined by edges of capacity Cap_e to each ITAP).

4   Integer Linear Program Formulation

In this section, we describe the ideal link model of [3]; it is defined by the equations and inequalities listed below. For each edge e and house h, we have a variable $x_{e,h}$ to indicate the amount of flow from h to the ITAPs that is routed through e. For each ITAP$_i$,, a variable y_i indicates the number of ITAPs opened at the location i (more precisely, y_i is the number of ITAPs opened at locations in the equivalence class i). As defined previously in the present paper, Cap_e, Cap_h, and Cap_i denote the capacity of the edge e, house h, and ITAP$_i$, respectively; wh denotes the traffic demand generated from house h.

The first constraint, equation (1) formulates the flow conservation constraint, namely, for every house except the house originating the flow, the total amount of flow entering the house is equal to the total amount of flow exiting it. The inequality, equation (2) formulates the constraint that each house has wh amount of flow to send, and the third constraint indicates that a house does not receive flow sent by itself. The next three inequalities of the integer program capture the capacity constraints on the edges, houses, and ITAPs. Equation (7) says that no house is allowed to send any traffic to an ITAP unless the ITAP is open. Notice that this inequality is redundant and follows from the ITAP capacity constraint and the assumption that y_i is an integer.

Minimize $\sum_{i \in x} y_i$

Subject
$$\sum_{e=(v,h')} x_{e,h} = \sum_{e=(h',v)} x_{e,h} \quad \forall h, h' \in H, \ h' \neq h \qquad (1)$$

$$\sum_{e=(h,v)} x_{e,h} \geq wh \qquad \qquad \forall h \in H \qquad (2)$$

$$\sum_{e=(v,h)} x_{e,h} = 0 \qquad \qquad \forall h \in H \qquad (3)$$

$$\sum_h x_{e,h} \leq Cap_e \qquad \qquad \forall e \in E(G) \qquad (4)$$

$$\sum_{h',e=(v,h)} x_{e,h'} \leq Cap_h \qquad \qquad \forall h \in H \qquad (5)$$

$$\sum_{h',e=(v,i)} x_{e,h'} \leq Cap_i \, y_i \qquad \qquad \forall i \in I \qquad (6)$$

$$\sum_{e=(v,i)} x_{e,h} \leq wh \, y_i \qquad \qquad \forall i \in I, \ h \in H \qquad (7)$$

$$x_{e,h} \geq 0 \qquad \qquad \forall e \in E(G), h \in H \qquad (8)$$

$$y_i \in \{0,1,2,...\} \qquad \qquad \forall i \in I$$

To generate the maximum flow of edges, a graph (G) is constructed consisting of nodes and edges (X, Y) between them. Every house node is directly connected to the source node and every ITAP node is directly connected to the sink node. Let graph Gp be the sub-graph of G with the same capacities as G.

House h node;

- For each house h in graph G replace it with two nodes h_in and h_out and connect those nodes using directed edges.
- Add edges between h_in and h_out nodes to graph Gp.
- Source is connected directly to every (h_in) in the Graph.

Edge (X, Y) in G;

- Add edge (X , Y) to graph Gp.
- Add some capacities to the edges.

ITAPi in G;

- For each ITAP in graph G replace it with two nodes $ITAP\_in$ and $ITAP\_out$ and connect those nodes using directed edges.
- Add edges between $ITAP\_in$ and $ITAP\_out$ nodes to graph Gp.
- Sink is connected to each ITAP.
- The connection of edges for the graph Gp would be starting from the source node and go through h_in, h_out, $ITAP\_in$ and $ITAP\_out$ then to the sink node, to compute the maximum flow of the network, as shown below in figure 1.

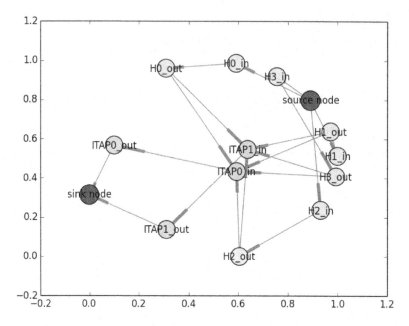

Fig. 1. The model of 4 houses and 2 ITAPs with source and sink.

5 Our Heuristic Algorithms

We experiment with Hill Climbing and Simulated Annealing algorithms to provide simple frameworks for experimenting with our proposed move operators: Swap, Reallocate, Delete and Add. Each one of these moves is designed to work on different aspects of the candidate WMN configuration, and our goal is to use combinations of our moves to sample the search space efficiently and effectively. The "Swap" exchanges the numbers of ITAPs from two locations, while "Reallocate" moves a single ITAP from one location to another. The "Delete" removes an ITAP from a given location, and "Add" increments the number of ITAPs at a given location.

Our approach to WMN design requires two phases: 1) Optimizing the placement of a fixed number of ITAPs to maximize the network flow, and 2) Using the excess network capacity provided by Phase 1, minimizing the number of ITAPs. In the first phase, we employ only the reallocate and swap move, which does not change the number of ITAPs, but can relocate them to give a better value of maximum flow, following the application of the Ford-Fulkerson algorithm. The second phase is aimed at minimizing the number of ITAPs, which is the main objective. In the second phase, we use all four of our moves.

We represent a solution by a vector $s_1, s_2, ..., s_n$ where s_i is the number of ITAPs to be installed at location $_i$. A move modifies a solution s to a new solution s' as follows;

- Swap; select i and j at random with i≠j, and set
  s'[i], s'[j] =s[j], s[i]

- Reallocate; select i and j at random with i≠j and s[i]>0, and set
  s'[i] = s'[i] -1
  s'[j] = s'[j] +1
- Delete; select j at random with s[j]>0, and set
  s'[j] = s[j] -1
- Add; select j at random, and set
  s'[j] = s[j] +1

5.1   Hill Climbing

Hill climbing (HC) starts with a sub-optimal solution to a problem (that is, starting at the base of a hill) and then attempts to repeatedly improve the solution in small steps (neighbourhood moves) until some condition is maximized (the top of the hill is reached). HC Algorithm will simply accept neighbour solutions that are better than the current solution; when HC cannot find any better neighbours, it stops. HC usually does not find a global optimum; more likely, it gets stuck in a local optimum.

5.2   Simulated Annealing

Simulated Annealing (SA) is similar to HC, but a little more sophisticated. It has been used successfully in solving many combinatorial optimization problems, and is better at avoiding local optima than HC if it is well implemented. SA was originally inspired by the slow cooling of metals to form crystalline structures of minimum energy, and Metropolis et al. (1953)[15] first introduced these principles into numerical minimization. Like HC, SA is launched with a starting configuration, s_0, and then works through a large number of neighbourhood moves (s to s') in an attempt to produce better solutions. Unlike HC, however, the acceptance criterion for s' is less strict, allowing the algorithm to jump out of local optima. If the new solution, s', is better than our old solution, s, it is accepted unconditionally. If, however, the new solution is worse, then it is accepted with a certain probability, related firstly to how much worse it is; and secondly, to how high the current "temperature" of our system is. At high temperatures, the system is more likely to accept solutions that are worse. In practice, a simulated annealing implementation is typically constructed within two nested loops. In the outer loop, the temperature is reduced gradually, and within the inner loop many perturbations of s to s' are tried. At each step, s' faces an acceptance test, based on $\Delta = \text{Cost}(s') - \text{Cost}(s)$. The new solution, s', is accepted with a probability of 1, if $\text{Cost}(s') < \text{Cost}(s)$ (just like HC), and with a probability of $e^{-\Delta/T}$ otherwise, where T is the current temperature. In our system, we set the initial temperature, $T_0 = 2$.

5.3   Implementation of HC and SA in the Ideal Link Model

We evaluate the performance of HC and SA Algorithm using various levels of wireless range connectivity in the context of maximizing throughput and reducing the number of ITAPs. In Figure 2, we provide a framework that covers our HC and SA algorithms.

Algorithm 1. Framework for our Hill Climbing and Simulated Annealing Approaches

---

Our objective function is to maximize the throughput in Phase 1, and to minimize the number of ITAPs in Phase 2.

    Generate an initial solution *s* randomly
    {Set initial Temperature, T_0–SA only}
    *{While $T > T_{min}$ **Do** – SA only}*
        While number of iterations < max iterations **Do**
            Generate a new solution *s'* within the neighbourhood of *s*(*s'* ∈ *N*(*s*))
            $\Delta \leftarrow Cost(s') - Cost(s)$
            If acceptance criterion is passed (see text) for HC or SA, *s* ← *s'*

Phase 1:
            For Each possible ITAP Location
            Select one move randomly
            Apply Swap OR Reallocate move to the ITAPs
            Evaluate the amount the throughput
        End for
Phase 2:
            For Each possible ITAP Location
            Select one move randomly
            Apply Swap OR Reallocate OR Delete OR Add move to the ITAPs
            Evaluate the number of unsatisfied houses and number of ITAPs
        End For
        End While
    {Reduce T – SA only}
    *{**End While** – SA only}*
        Return *s*

Fig. 2. General Pseudo Code Outline of our Heuristic Methods

The cost function plays a key role in any optimization problem. It is through its calculation that one can measure the quality of any solution. Hence, its correct definition is essential for the behaviour of any search algorithm. Our aim is to minimize the required number of ITAPs, whilst still maintaining adequate QoS which maximize the number of houses served. To formulate this using a single cost function, we instead consider minimizing a weighted sum of the number of ITAPs and the unserved houses.

$$E(s) = Fw * \sum_{i \in h} Wh - \sum_{i \in I} F + Iw \sum_{i \in x} S \qquad (9)$$

In equation (9), variable $E(s)$ which represents the cost function; Fw indicates the flow weight of the house (more precisely, Fw represents the flow cost of each house). Wh indicates the traffic demand generated from house h, and let F denote the amount of traffic routed to ITAPi in this solution where $i \in$ multiset of ITAPs, we have a variable Iw that indicate the weight of the ITAPs. For each ITAPi we have a variable S which represents the solution (number of ITAPs opened at locations i) S may be written: $S = (s_1, s_2, ..., s_n)$ for some variables s_i.

6   Experimental Methodology and Results

The initial temperature of the SA is ($T_0 = 2$) and then the temperature is gradually reduced using a cooling schedule. To test our approach effectively, we generated a wide range of instances for our experiments, based on a random uniform distribution of nodes. We varied the number of houses, the number of ITAPs, the number of ITAP locations and the grid size. For instances with the same number of houses, those houses are placed at the same locations for each instance.   Each experiment, runs five ranges three times and reports the average and best result with the runtime as shown in tables below. For experiments 1-10, only Phase 1 is applied, which attempts to maximize the throughput (traffic flow) by moving ITAPS from one place to another, without changing the number of ITAPs. The aim is to demonstrate the effectiveness of the two moves in improving the throughput for a range of instances with different characteristics (such as ITAP capacity and number of ITAP locations, etc.). For these experiments, only the swap and reallocate move are needed.   For experiments 11-14, we apply both phases of the HC and SA algorithms, using all four move operators. The main goal here is to minimize the number of ITAPs.

6.1   Performance and Evaluation

We illustrate the numerical results obtained to minimize the number of ITAPs using combinations of different move operators in the HC and SA algorithms. In tables 1–6. Table 1, shows a comparison of the individual move operators, such as Swap move and Reallocate move, and we can observe that the reallocate move outperforms the swap move but takes longer. Nevertheless, using swap move reduces the chance of being trapped in local optimum [16], hence both moves are used together to improve the throughput and running time, as shown in Table 2.   It can be observed from the results that there is improvement in the throughput when the number of ITAP locations and wireless range connectivity are increased. It is important to note that the throughput probability is determined by the WRC, distribution number of ITAP Location and the network size, as shown in Table 2.   We find that HC works well in small and simple instances (in table 2, EXP. 1, 2, 8 and 9) but does not work as well as the SA on large instances (EXP. 3-7 and 10). The results for experiments 11 – 14 in Tables (3 – 6) show that less ITAPs are required to satisfy the demands using the first and second phases together. However, the cost function that we use for these experiments shows that there is a trade-off between minimizing ITAPs and unsatisfied houses. Table 3 illustrates our evaluation of the combination of move operators with the SA algorithm as good and efficient in satisfying the houses demand with less ITAPs, which is near to the optimal solutions as shown in Figure 3 for experiment 12. Thus, the cost function in SA surpasses HC and yields excellent solutions by effective combinations of different move operators, as shown in Tables (3 and 5). However, in Tables (4 and 6), using swap and reallocate move only demonstrates no improvement in minimizing the number of ITAPs.

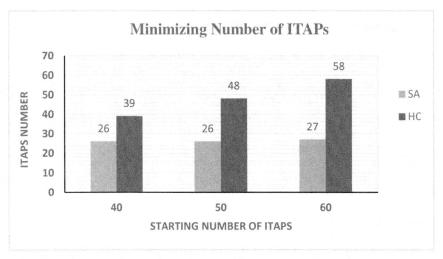

Fig. 3. Result of experiment 12 starting with different number of ITAPs (40, 50 and 60)

Table 1. Throughput value for Reaallocate and Swap move individually

EXP	#House	#ITAP	#ITAP-Location	ITAP-Cap	Grid-Area	WRC	W-Link	#Iterations	Cost-Real HC(RT/sec)	Cost-Swap HC(RT/sec)	Cost-Real SA(RT/sec)	Cost-Swap SA(RT/sec)
1	100	10	10	10	100*100	25	5	500	100(7)	100(3)	100(69)	100(67)
3	500	50	50	20	500*500	25	20	500	360(625)	348(615)	366(669)	365(663)
5	500	50	50	20	500*500	25	15	1000	364(1289)	354(1265)	366(1356)	366(1345)
8	500	50	100	20	500*500	30	15	500	495(1071)	494(1040)	495(1073)	495(1060)
10	500	50	100	20	1000*1000	50	15	500	434(892)	430(866)	469(935)	461(922)

Table 2. Throughput value and running time of Experiments 1- 10

EXP	#House	#ITAP	#ITAP-Location	ITAP-Cap	Grid-Area	WRC	W-Link	#Iterations	Cost HC(RT/sec)	Cost SA(RT/sec)
1	100	10	10	10	100*100	25	5	500	100(6)	100(66)
2	500	50	10	10	100*100	25	5	1000	500(173)	500(3623)
3	500	50	50	20	500*500	25	20	500	360(623)	366(665)
4	500	50	70	20	500*500	25	15	500	395(762)	402(797)
5	500	50	50	20	500*500	25	15	1000	362(1267)	366(1332)
6	500	50	100	20	500*500	25	20	500	431(862)	466(935)
7	500	50	100	20	500*500	25	15	1000	440(1712)	467(1852)
8	500	50	100	20	500*500	30	15	500	495(1027)	495(1045)
9	500	50	50	20	500*500	35	15	500	500(1000)	500(1029)
10	500	50	100	20	1000*1000	50	15	500	432(841)	463(889)

Table 3. Cost function of Experiment (11-14) using all move operators with different number of ITAPs in SA Algorithm.

EXP	#House	#ITAP-Location	ITAP-Cap	Grid-Area	WRC	W-Link	#Iterations	Cost-min(Avg)	RT/sec	Satisfied House	#ITAP End(start)
11	500	10	10	100*100	25	5	500	500(500)	1759	500	50(50)
12	500	100	20	500*500	30	15	1000	415(425)	2152	495	26(50)
13	500	50	20	500*500	35	15	3000	250(250	6099	500	25(50)
14	1000	100	20	500*500	35	15	1000	500(500)	9006	1000	50(50)
11	500	10	10	100*100	25	5	500	500(500)	1755	500	50(40)
12	500	100	20	500*500	30	15	1000	415(423)	2161	495	26(40)
13	500	50	20	500*500	35	15	3000	250(250)	6167	500	25(40)
14	1000	100	20	500*500	35	15	1000	500(500)	9080	1000	50(40)
11	500	10	10	100*100	25	5	500	500(500)	1697	500	50(60)
12	500	50	20	500*500	30	15	1000	425(441)	2131	495	27(60)
13	500	50	20	500*500	35	15	3000	250(250)	5962	500	25(60)
14	1000	100	20	500*500	35	15	1000	500(500)	8569	1000	50(60)

Table 4. Cost function of Experiment (11-14) using Swap & Reallocate move operators only in SA Algorithm.

EXP	#House	#ITAP-Location	ITAP-Cap	Grid-Area	WRC	W-Link	#Iterations	Cost-min(Avg)	RT/sec	Satisfied-House	#ITAP End(start)
11	500	10	10	100*100	25	5	500	500(500)	1811	500	50(50)
12	500	100	20	500*500	30	15	1000	748(1039)	1391	492	50(50)
13	500	50	20	500*500	35	15	3000	500(500)	6168	500	50(50)
14	1000	100	20	500*500	35	15	1000	500(500)	6203	1000	50(50)

Table 5. Cost function of Experiment (11-14) using all move operators with different number of ITAPs in HC Algorithm.

EXP	#House	#ITAP-Location	ITAP-Cap	Grid-Area	WRC	W-Link	#Iterations	Cost-min(Avg)	RT/sec	Satisfied-House	#ITAP End(start)
11	500	10	10	100*100	25	5	500	500(500)	175	500	50(50)
12	500	100	20	500*500	30	15	1000	635(667)	1545	495	48(50)
13	500	50	20	500*500	35	15	3000	470(496)	741	500	47(50)
14	1000	100	20	500*500	35	15	1000	500(500)	2152	1000	50(50)
11	500	10	10	100*100	25	5	500	3200(3380)	153	410	41(40)
12	500	100	20	500*500	30	15	1000	545(733)	1421	495	39(40)
13	500	50	20	500*500	35	15	3000	370(396)	2747	500	37(40)
14	1000	100	20	500*500	35	15	1000	5380(6234)	3723	840	42(40)
11	500	10	10	100*100	25	5	500	590(596)	237	500	59(60)
12	500	50	20	500*500	30	15	1000	735(755)	1555	495	58(60)
13	500	50	20	500*500	35	15	3000	580(594)	1050	500	58(60)
14	1000	100	20	500*500	35	15	1000	600(600)	5320	1000	60(60)

Table 6. Cost function of Experiment (11-14) using Swap & Reallocate move operators only in HC Algorithm.

EXP	#House	#ITAP-Location	ITAP-Cap	Grid-Area	WRC	W-Link	#Iterations	Cost-min(Avg)	RT/sec	Satisfied-House	#ITAP End(start)
11	500	10	10	100*100	25	5	500	500(500)	291	500	50(50)
12	500	100	20	500*500	30	15	1000	655(661)	2050	495	50(50)
13	500	50	20	500*500	35	15	3000	500(500)	2644	500	50(50)
14	1000	100	20	500*500	35	15	1000	500(500)	8518	1000	50(50)

7   Conclusion

This paper has presented a new two phase approach for solving the network optimization problem, and new heuristic move operators. We have demonstrated that the approach is highly successful for optimizing ITAP placements in WMNs. We verify from our result that our reallocate move always showed a better performance than the swap move, but it is slower. Our results show that our SA produces better results than our HC, but it takes slightly longer to run. Therefore, our implementations of SA algorithms produce near optimum solutions. The experimental evaluation shows the efficiency of a combination of all four move operators and it provides a better solution for the placement of ITAPs in WMNs. We will next look into bandwidth allocation for the house demand in order to achieve a good trade-off between fairness and throughput.

These abbreviations are used in the above tables;

EXP= Experiment

ITAP-Cap= ITAP Capacity/ Mbps

WRC= Wireless Range Connectivity/ M

W-Link= Wireless Link's Capacity/ Mbps

Cost= Cost Function

RT= Running Time/ Seconds

Real= Reallocate Move

References

1. Aoun, B., Boutaba, R., Member, S., Iraqi, Y., Kenward, G.: Gateway Placement Optimization in Wireless Mesh Networks With QoS Constraints. IEEE J. Sel. Areas Commun. 24(11), 2127–2136 (2006)
2. Wang, J., Xie, B., Cai, K., Agrawal, D.P.: Efficient mesh router placement in wireless mesh networks. In: 2007 IEEE Internatonal Conference on Mobile Adhoc and Sensor Systems, pp. 1–9 (2007)
3. Chandra, R., Qiu, L., Jain, K., Mahdian, M.: Optimizing the placement of internet TAPs in wireless neighborhood networks. In: Proceedings of the 12th IEEE International Conference on Network Protocols, ICNP 2004, pp. 271–282 (2004)
4. Martignon, F., Paris, S., Filippini, I., Capone, A.: Efficient Bandwidth Allocation in Wireless Community Networks (2011)
5. Amaldi, E., Capone, A., Cesana, M., Filippini, I., Malucelli, F.: Optimization models and methods for planning wireless mesh networks. Comput. Networks 52(11), 2159–2171 (2008)
6. Allen, S.M., Cooper, I.M., Whitaker, R.M.: Optimising multi-rate link scheduling for wireless mesh networks. Comput. Commun. 35(16), 2014–2024 (2012)
7. Jun, J., Sichitu, M.L.: The Nominal Capacity of Wireless Mesh Networks. IEEE Wirel. Commun. 10, 8–14 (2003)
8. Capone, A., Filippini, I., Martignon, F.: Joint routing and scheduling optimization in wireless mesh networks with directional antennas. In: 2008 IEEE International Conference on Communications, pp. 2951–2957 (2008)
9. Benyamina, D., Ha, A., Gendreau, M.: Wireless Mesh Networks Design — A Survey. IEEE Communications Surveys & Tutorials 14(2), 299–310 (2012)

10. Xhafa, F., Sanchez, C., Barolli, L.: Ad hoc and neighborhood search methods for place-ment of mesh routers in wireless mesh networks. In: 2009 29th IEEE Int. Conf. Distrib. Comput. Syst. Work., pp. 400–405, June 2009
11. Fleszar, K., Osman, I.H., Hindi, K.S.: A variable neighbourhood search algorithm for the open vehicle routing problem. Eur. J. Oper. Res. 195(3), 803–809 (2009)
12. Xhafa, F., Sanchez, C., Barolli, L., Miho, R.: An annealing approach to router nodes placement problem in wireless mesh networks. In: 2010 Int. Conf. Complex, Intell. Softw. Intensive Syst, pp. 245–252, February 2010
13. Li, F., Wang, Y., Li, X.-Y., Nusairat, A., Wu, Y.: Gateway Placement for Throughput Op-timization in Wireless Mesh Networks. Mob. Networks Appl. 13(1–2), 198–211 (2008)
14. Cormen, T.H., Leiserson, C.E., Rivest, R.L.: Introduction to Algorithms, 2nd edn., vol. 7 (2001)
15. Rosenbluth, M.N., Teller, A.H., Metropolis, N., Rosenbluth, A.W.: Equation of state Cal-culations by Fast Computing Machines. J. Chem. Physic 21(6) (1953)
16. Manuscript, A.: NIH Public Access 21(suppl. 1), 1–19 (2006)

Service Differentiation and Resource Allocation in SC-FDMA Wireless Networks through User-Centric Distributed Non-Cooperative Multilateral Bargaining

Eirini Eleni Tsiropoulou, Ioannis Ziras, and Symeon Papavassiliou

School of Electrical & Computer Engineering
National Technical University of Athens (NTUA)
9 Iroon Polytechniou str. Zografou 15773, Athens, Greece
eetsirop@netmode.ntua.gr; el06083@central.ntua.gr;
papavass@mail.ntua.gr

Abstract. In this paper service differentiation is provided through user-centric distributed non-cooperative multilateral bargaining for resource allocation in the uplink of multi-service SC-FDMA wireless network. Initially, a well-designed utility function is formulated to appropriately represent users' diverse QoS prerequisites with respect to their requested service. The subcarriers allocation problem is solved based on a multilateral bargaining model, where users are able to select different discount factors to enter the bargaining game, thus better expressing their different needs in system resources. The subcarriers mapping is realized based on the localized SC-FDMA method where the subcarriers are sequentially allocated to the users. Given the subcarriers assignment, an optimization problem with respect to users' uplink transmission power is formulated and solved, in order to determine the optimal power allocation per subcarrier assigned to each user. Finally, the performance of the proposed framework is evaluated via modeling and simulation and extensive numerical results are presented.

Keywords: Resource allocation, SC-FDMA, Service differentiation, Utility function, Multilateral bargaining, User-centric approach.

1   Introduction

Single carrier frequency division multiple access (SC-FDMA), which utilizes single carrier modulation and frequency domain equalization, is the primary multiple access scheme for the uplink of the 4G wireless communication systems, where the total bandwidth is divided into orthogonal subcarriers in order to be allocated to multiple users [1]. In this paper, we adopt the localized subcarrier mapping method, i.e. L-FDMA, where the subcarriers are allocated to a user in a consecutive manner.

Considerable research efforts have been devoted to the resource allocation problem in the uplink of SC-FDMA wireless networks. Among the key elements that need to be considered and controlled in such environments are users' occupied subcarriers and their corresponding uplink transmission power. Given the inherent difficulty to

© Institute for Computer Sciences, Social Informatics and Telecommunications Engineering 2015
N. Mitton et al. (Eds.): AdHocNets 2015, LNICST 155, pp. 42–54, 2015.
Doi: 10.1007/978-3-319-25067-0_4

jointly allocate a continuous resource, i.e. user's uplink transmission power and a discrete resource, i.e. user's occupied subcarriers, there have been proposed various heuristic subcarrier allocation methods, while equal-bit-equal-power (EBEP) allocation or the water-filling method have been primarily adopted to allocate users' uplink transmission power [1]. Aiming at considering users' specific Quality of Service (QoS) prerequisites, the authors in [2] present two heuristic subcarriers allocation algorithms, i.e. Low Complexity Delay Algorithm (LC-DA) and Proportional Fairness Delay Algorithm (PF-DA), considering delay and fairness constraints, respectively. LC-DA algorithm assigns each subcarrier to a user, if the constraints of maximum delay and minimum throughput are satisfied for all users, while considering the adjacency restriction for each users' allocated subcarriers. On the other hand, PF-DA algorithm adopts the proportion between the current throughput to the total throughput, instead of using the marginal utility, as in LC-DA algorithm, and it does not assign the subcarriers in order, but it gives higher priority to the users with the most critical delay requirement. In [3], the authors target at the maximization of users' sum-rate, where each user has a personal minimum rate constraint, which is imposed by his requested service. Specifically, they allocate the subcarriers to the users based on the maximum marginal weighted rate, while satisfying the adjacency restriction of the subcarriers and exploiting a linear estimate of the average number of subcarriers allocated to each user. In [4], an enhanced greedy subcarrier allocation algorithm is proposed, which in the first step allows N users with the higher priority to select first their initial subcarriers and then all users compete for the rest subcarriers, which are allocated based on the maximum marginal proportional fairness value. All the above subcarrier allocation algorithms adopt EBEP allocation with respect to power, i.e. user's uplink maximum transmission power is equally distributed among user's occupied subcarriers [5].

1.1 Paper Contribution and Outline

In this paper, we propose a user-centric distributed non-cooperative subcarriers and users' uplink transmission power allocation, while supporting service differentiation. Towards allocating the subcarriers to the users, we adopt a multilateral bargaining model, i.e. Rubinstein's bargaining model, to obtain a feasible and stable subcarriers allocation, in terms of the number of subcarriers allocated per user [6]. The use of multilateral model of bargaining has been demonstrated as an efficient approach for energy-efficiency subcarrier allocation in SC-FDMA wireless networks supporting single service. The main novelty of this paper and key difference with respect to our previous work [7], is that users are allowed to select a preferable value of the discount factor to compete the rest of the users during the bargaining process, while in [7] all users were assumed to utilize the same factor, a fact that was not allowing the provisioning of service differentiation. The specific value of the discount factor reflects users' necessity to occupy subcarriers considering their requested service, possibly taking into account the differences in QoS prerequisites. Within the multilateral bargaining process, the game is sequentially played among users. Users that enter first the bargaining process are a priori favored compared to the rest of the users. Additionally, a user that adopts high value of the discount factor has also privilege compared to the rest of the users. Therefore, based on users' requested service appropriate value of the discount factor can be selected, so as to competitively request system's resources.

Initially, each user adopts a general and realistic utility function, which represents user's service QoS-aware performance efficiency as a tradeoff between the number of user's reliably transmitted bits and the corresponding consumed power (Section 2.1). The joint subcarriers and user's uplink transmission power allocation problem is formulated as a user-centric distributed non-cooperative optimization problem aiming at maximizing each user's overall utility (Section 2.2). The N-person multilateral bargaining model with various values of users' discount factors is proposed towards allocating the subcarriers to the users while considering the specific QoS characteristics of users' requested services (Section 3). Given the subcarriers allocation, a power control optimization problem is formulated and solved. Thus, user's optimal uplink transmission power per each occupied subcarrier is determined, instead of simply adopting the EBEP allocation or the waterfilling method to allocate users' uplink transmission power (Section 4). An iterative, distributed and low-complexity algorithm is proposed to converge to a stable subcarriers and uplink transmission power allocation (Section 5). Finally, the performance of the proposed approach is evaluated in detail and its operational characteristics are illustrated through analytical numerical results (Section 6), while Section 7 concludes the paper.

2   System Model and Background Information

The uplink of a single-cell SC-FDMA infrastructure wireless network, consisting of N continuously backlogged users is considered, where N denotes their corresponding set. The system bandwidth B Hz is divided into a set $\mathbb{S}_{sub} = \{ s_i^j / i \in \mathsf{N} = \{1,2,...,i,...,N\}, j = 1,2,...,K_i \}$, where K_i denotes the number of subcarriers occupied by user i and $\mathbb{S}_i = \{ s_i^j / j = 1,2,...,K_i \}$ refers to the corresponding set. Each user $i \in \mathsf{N}$ is characterized by a subcarrier gain G_{i,s_i^j}, an uplink transmission power P_{i,s_i^j} for that subcarrier, its maximum value P_i^{Max}, which is imposed by the physical and technical limitations, and a corresponding signal-to-interference ratio (SIR) γ_{i,s_i^j}, which is given by:

$$\gamma_{i,s_i^j} = \frac{P_{i,s_i^j} G_{i,s_i^j}}{\sigma_{s_i^j}^2} \tag{1}$$

where $\sigma_{s_i^j}^2$ denotes the noise power of subcarrier s. Based on the above, the overall number of subcarriers in the system is $S = \sum_{i=1}^{N} K_i$ and for each user the inequality

$\sum_{j=1}^{K_i} P_{i,s_i^j} \leq P_i^{Max}$ should hold true.

2.1 Utility Function and Multiple Services

This paper aims at devising a user-centric and distributed joint subcarriers and users' uplink transmission power allocation in SC-FDMA wireless networks, via utilizing an N-person multilateral bargaining model with different users' adopted discount factors. Before presenting the formulation of the actual Multi-Service User-centric Distributed non-cooperative BArgaining model for Resource allocation problem (MUD-BAR problem) in Section 2.2, for completeness purposes in the following we present user's adopted utility function, as well as the corresponding QoS requirements imposed by the different type of services.

Initially, aiming at aligning users' diverse and multiple QoS prerequisites under a common optimization framework, the concept of a well-designed utility function has been adopted, which represents users' satisfaction related to the allocated resources, i.e. subcarriers and uplink transmission power and correspondingly their QoS demands fulfillment. In wireless networks, a user ideally would prefer to transmit with low uplink transmission power P_{i,s_i^j} and achieve high throughput. Therefore, user's satisfaction at each of his occupied subcarrier $s_i^j \in \mathbb{S}_i \subseteq \mathbb{S}_{sub}$ can be expressed by the following utility function.

$$U_{i,s_i^j}(P_{i,s_i^j}) = \frac{R_{service} f\left(\gamma_{i,s_i^j}\right)}{P_{i,s_i^j}} \tag{2}$$

where $R_{service}$ is user's fixed designed transmission rate, depending on user's requested service and $f\left(\gamma_{i,s_i^j}\right)$ is his efficiency function representing the probability of a successful packet transmission for user i at subcarrier s_i^j. The efficiency function is an increasing and sigmoidal function of his SIR γ_{i,s_i^j} [7].

In next generation wireless networks, new applications and services, such as pervasive 3D multimedia, HDTV, VoIP, gaming, e-health, etc are emerging, where each type of service imposes different QoS prerequisites. In this context, mobile users are expected to have different targeted throughput, thus requesting different amount of resources. Service differentiation can be achieved via assigning different numbers of subcarriers to different users, according to their demands and requirement. In a holistic and uniform way, users' various demands on system resources are captured and expressed in their overall utility function, which can be expressed as:

$$U_i(\mathbf{P}_{i,s_i^j} = \left[P_{i,s_i^j}, ..., P_{i,s_i^{K_i}}\right], K_i) = \sum_{j=1}^{K_i} U_{i,s_i^j}(P_{i,s_i^j}) \tag{3}$$

for user $i \in \mathbb{N}$, where K_i denotes the number of subcarriers allocated to user i.

2.2   Multi-service User-Centric Distributed Non-cooperative BArgaining Model for Resource Allocation (MUD-BAR) Problem Formulation

Let $G = \left[N, \{ \mathbb{S}_i, P_i \}, \{ U_i \left(P_{i,s_i^j}, K_i \right) \} \right]$ denote the MUD-BAR optimization problem in SC-FDMA wireless networks. The goal of each user is to maximize his utility via selecting an appropriate number of subcarriers K_i and a corresponding strategy of uplink transmission power P_{i,s_i^j} for each of his occupied subcarriers $s_i^j \in \mathbb{S}_i \subseteq \mathbb{S}_{sub}$. Therefore, the joint subcarriers and uplink transmission power allocation problem can be formulated as a maximization problem of each user's i, $i \in N$ overall utility function.

$$
\max_{\substack{P_{i,s_i^j} \in P_i \\ 0 \prec K_i \leq S}} U_i(P_{i,s_i^j} = \left[P_{i,s_i^j}, \dots, P_{i,s_i^{K_i}} \right], K_i) = \sum_{j=1}^{K_i} U_{i,s_i^j} (P_{i,s_i^j})
$$

$$
s.t. \ \sum_{j=1}^{K_i} P_{i,s_i^j} \leq P_i^{Max}, i \in N, \ S = \sum_{i=1}^{N} K_i \tag{4}
$$

where $P_i = [0, P_i^{Max}]$ denotes the set of user's $i \in N$ feasible uplink transmission power, which is a compact and convex set with maximum and minimum constraints.

As it is analytically discussed in [8] solving a standard form of the optimization problem (4) is extremely complex due to the following reasons: (i) the extremely large search space that is created by the N users and the S subcarriers, which should be adjacently allocated to each user the localized subcarrier mapping method, i.e. L-FDMA is adopted, and ii) the objective function in (4) is formulated as a complex form dependent on a discrete (i.e. subcarriers) and a continuous (i.e. uplink transmission power) resource, while an additional power constraint for each user, i.e. $P_i = [0, P_i^{Max}]$ should be considered. Thus, the straightforward solution of the optimization problem presented in (4) is clearly not practical and we need a different approach of treating this problem. Our proposed methodology involves reformulating the problem and solving it in a two-step approach. In the first step, the multilateral bargaining model is adopted towards determining subcarriers allocation. Each user is able to select a different value of the discount factor to enter the bargaining process, thus representing his priority and necessity to occupy a corresponding number of subcarriers considering his requested type of service. Then, in the second step, given the subcarriers allocation, an optimal power assignment to the allocated subcarriers is realized towards achieving energy-efficiency.

3   Multilateral Bargaining Model with Different Discount Factors towards Subcarriers Allocation

In SC-FDMA multi-service wireless networks, each user makes a resource request, in terms of number of subcarriers and uplink transmission power. In typical centralized systems, the base station is used to process users' requests, determine how many subcarriers should be allocated to each user, as well as his corresponding uplink transmission power and broadcast this allocation to the users. However, this approach causes an overall delay to the resource allocation process. To eliminate typical problems associated with the centralized nature of such an approach in this paper a user-centric distributed non-cooperative subcarriers allocation algorithm is designed instead, in order to complete the subcarriers assignment to the users in a distributed manner. The solution to this problem may be found from the Rubinstein bargaining game [6], where users adopt different values of the discount factor to express their different needs of system resources with respect to their requested service. Next, a subcarriers allocation scheme based on game theory is presented. First, the three-player version of the subcarriers allocation game is given. Then, the subcarriers allocation scheme is extended to N players/users.

The three-user sequential subcarriers allocation game belongs to the general category of bargaining games [9], where all the users must agree on how to share the total number of subcarriers. The fundamental concept of this game is that users must either accept the offer made by the other user, considering how the available subcarriers should be allocated, or reject it by making a counter offer in turns. An acceptance of an offer by all users ends the game, whereas a rejection by at least one user continues it. In [7], it has been shown shown that if the three users are discounted by a common factor δ, then the partitioning of the total number of subcarriers is given as:

$$K^{\cdot} = \left(\left[\frac{1-\delta}{1-\delta^3} S \right], \left[\frac{\delta(1-\delta)}{1-\delta^3} S \right], \left[\frac{\delta^2(1-\delta)}{1-\delta^3} S \right] \right) \tag{5}$$

where $[\cdot]$ is the round process.

In the following, let δ_1, δ_2, δ_3 denote the three users' different discount factors. For each user $i = \{1,2,3\}$ we define the bargaining operator Δ_i, as follows: $\delta_{ii} = 1$, $\delta_{jj} = \delta_j$, $\delta_{ij} = 1-\delta_j$, $\delta_{others} = 0$, where i: row and j: column. Thus, we have:

$$\Delta_1 = \begin{bmatrix} 1 & 1-\delta_2 & 1-\delta_3 \\ 0 & \delta_2 & 0 \\ 0 & 0 & \delta_3 \end{bmatrix}, \Delta_2 = \begin{bmatrix} \delta_1 & 0 & 0 \\ 1-\delta_1 & 1 & 1-\delta_3 \\ 0 & 0 & \delta_3 \end{bmatrix}, \Delta_3 = \begin{bmatrix} \delta_1 & 0 & 0 \\ 0 & \delta_2 & 0 \\ 1-\delta_1 & 1-\delta_2 & 1 \end{bmatrix}$$

Then, the overall bargaining operator $\Delta = \Delta_1 \Delta_2 \Delta_3$ of the trilateral game is calculated by: $\Delta = \prod_{i=1}^{3} \Delta_i$. The characteristic polynomial for Δ is determined as: $c(\lambda) = \det(\lambda I - \Delta)$ and its first order derivative $\left. \frac{\partial c(\lambda)}{\partial \lambda} \right|_{\lambda_{\max}=1}$ is evaluated at $\lambda_{\max} = 1$ (Perron – Frobenius theorem [10]). The overall bargaining operator Δ is partitioned accordingly, $\Delta = (\delta_{ij})_{3\times 3} = \begin{bmatrix} \Delta_{11} & \Delta_{12} \\ \Delta_{21} & \Delta_{22} \end{bmatrix}$, where Δ_{11} is a scalar and Δ_{22} is a square matrix of size (3-1). We define the share function $sf(\delta_2, \delta_3) \equiv \det(I - \Delta_{22})$, which is independent of first user's discount factor δ_1 and we conclude to the unique efficient bargaining outcome $K^* = \left[K_1^*, K_2^*, K_3^* \right]$, which is given by:

$$K_i^* = \left[\frac{\delta_i^{i-1} s f_i \left(\delta_{\neq i} \right)}{\left. \frac{\partial c(\lambda)}{\partial \lambda} \right|_{\lambda_{max}=1}} S \right] \tag{6}$$

and more specifically it can be written as:

$$K^* = \begin{bmatrix} K_1^* \\ K_2^* \\ K_3^* \end{bmatrix} = \begin{bmatrix} \dfrac{(1-\delta_2)(1-\delta_3)(1+\delta_3+\delta_2\delta_3)}{(1-\delta_1\delta_2\delta_3)^2 + \delta_1\delta_3(\delta_2-\delta_3) + \delta_1\delta_2(\delta_3-\delta_1) + \delta_2\delta_3(\delta_1-\delta_2)} S \\ \dfrac{\delta_2(1-\delta_1)(1-\delta_3)(1+\delta_1+\delta_1\delta_3)}{(1-\delta_1\delta_2\delta_3)^2 + \delta_1\delta_3(\delta_2-\delta_3) + \delta_1\delta_2(\delta_3-\delta_1) + \delta_2\delta_3(\delta_1-\delta_2)} S \\ \dfrac{\delta_3^2(1-\delta_1)(1-\delta_2)(1+\delta_2+\delta_1\delta_2)}{(1-\delta_1\delta_2\delta_3)^2 + \delta_1\delta_3(\delta_2-\delta_3) + \delta_1\delta_2(\delta_3-\delta_1) + \delta_2\delta_3(\delta_1-\delta_2)} S \end{bmatrix}$$

The N-users subcarriers allocation game is a generalization of the three-users case which was analytically presented above, with N users arranged in a fixed order, say *1, 2, 3,...,N*. The N-users subcarriers allocation based on multilateral bargaining model concludes to a partitioning of the total number of subcarriers, where the subcarriers' partition for each user $i \in N$ is given by (6) via utilizing subscripts' rotation in the equation (6) for *i=1, 2, 3, ..., N*. Furthermore given the number of subcarriers that are occupied by each user, the users are assigned only sequential subcarriers to transmit, i.e. L-FDMA. That is, *user 1* is sequentially assigned the first K_1^* subcarriers, *user 2* is assigned sequentially the next set of K_2^* subcarriers, etc.

4   Power Allocation towards Energy-Efficiency

Given the subcarriers allocation that is already performed in the previous section, each user has determined the number and IDs of his occupied subcarriers. Therefore, the goal of this section is to determine an optimal uplink transmission power allocation per each user's occupied subcarrier. Thus, we formulate a pure power control optimization problem considering each user's utility per each of his allocated subcarriers.

$$\max_{P_{i,s_i^j} K_i^* \in P_i} U_{i,s_i^j} \left(P_{i,s_i^j} \right)$$

$$s.t. \quad \sum_{j=1}^{K_i^*} P_{i,s_i^j} \leq P_i^{Max} \tag{7}$$

In [7], it has already been proven that the power control optimization problem presented in (7) has a unique and stable solution in users' uplink transmission powers, which is given by

$$P_{i,s_i^j}^* = \min\left\{ \frac{\gamma_{i,s_i^j}^* \sigma_{s_i^j}^2}{G_{i,s_i^j}}, \left(P_i^{Max} - \sum_{\substack{u \neq j \\ u=1,...,K_i^*}} P_{i,s_i^u} \right) \right\} \tag{8}$$

Based on the above, a more efficient users' uplink transmission power allocation is achieved compared to the EBEP allocation or the waterfilling method, which a priori allocate users' maximum uplink transmission power [1].

5   MUD-BAR Algorithm

In this section, we present an iterative distributed and low-complexity algorithm, towards determining users' subcarriers and uplink transmission power allocation. The first part allocates and assigns the subcarriers to all users, and the second part, given the subcarriers allocation and mapping, determines the optimal users' power allocation.

MUD-BAR Algorithm

Step 1: Subcarriers Allocation

At the beginning of time slot t, the subcarriers allocation $K^* = \left(K_1^*, K_2^*,..., K_i^*,..., K_N^* \right)$ is determined via equation (6), based on the proposed multilateral bargaining model, where users adopt different values of discount factors, i.e. $\delta_1, \delta_2,..., \delta_N$, based on the QoS prerequisites that their requested service imposes.

Step 2: L-FDMA Subcarriers Mapping

Given the subcarriers allocation in Step 1, users occupy sequential subcarriers. Thus, the user with number ID *1* occupies and transmits to the first K_1^* subcarriers, the user with number ID *2* occupies the following K_2^* subcarriers and so on till all users are exhausted.

Step 3: Optimal Uplink Transmission Power Allocation

   Given the subcarriers allocation and the assignment to the users, each user i, $i \in \mathbb{N}$ computes his uplink transmission power based on equation (8) for each of his assigned subcarrier $s_i^j \in \mathbb{S}_i^*$. Set $k=0$.

Step 4: Set $k:=k+1$, delete the subcarrier s in the set of user's i available subcarriers, i.e. $K_i^{*(k+1)} = K_i^{*(k)} - \left\{ s_i^j \right\}$, renew user's i maximum transmission power, i.e. $P_i^{Max(k+1)} = P_i^{Max(k)} - P_{i,s_i^j}^*$, and if $P_i^{Max(k+1)} \neq 0$ or $\mathbb{S}_i^* \neq \varnothing$ go to step 3, otherwise stop.

It should be noted that MUD-BAR algorithm refers to closed forms to determine subcarriers and uplink transmission power allocation, thus its complexity is low.

6   Numerical Results

In this section, we provide some numerical results illustrating the operations and features of the proposed framework and the MUD-BAR algorithm. We assume that the total bandwidth B is divided into $S=256$ subcarriers and $N=30$ users reside within the cell. We assume two different types of service, i.e. type I and type II, where type I service is more demanding in terms of achievable throughput. Users are able to adopt different values of discount factor $\delta_i \in (0,1]$ based on the type of service that they request and are placed in equal distance from the base station (i.e. $d_i=450m$) in order to have a common basis of comparison among them. We model users' path gains as $G_{i,s_i^j} = \Lambda_{i,s_i^j}/d_i^a$, where d_i is the distance of user i from the base station, a is the distance loss exponent, and Λ_{i,s_i^j} is a log-normal distributed random variable with standard deviation $8dB$, which represents the multi-path fading effect. Moreover, we set users' maximum uplink transmission power to $P_i^{Max} = 2\ Watts$ and $\sigma_{s_i^j}^2 = 5 \cdot 10^{-15}$.

Users' efficiency function is given by: $f\left(\gamma_{i,s_i^j}\right) = \left(1-\exp\left(-\gamma_{i,s_i^j}\right)\right)^M$, where $M=80$.

Fig. 1 illustrates the number of subcarriers allocated to each of the $N=30$ users residing in the cell under three different scenarios: (i) common discount factor ($\delta=0.9$), (ii) different discount factors among users based on the type of service that they request: (a) $\delta_I=0.85$, $\delta_{II}=0.95$ and (b) $\delta_I=0.89$, $\delta_{II}=0.99$. Considering the first scenario, we observe that the first users inserted in the bargaining rounds are favored compared to the rest and a larger portion of the subcarriers is allocated to them. Thus, aiming at a fair allocation among the users, a discount factor δ close to one is a more appropriate choice. However, considering the two other scenarios, we observe that users' QoS prerequisites and their need to occupy a corresponding number of subcarriers based on the type of service that they request can be mapped to an appropriate selection of discount factor's value. More specifically, by observing the (ii-a) scenario, we conclude that the first 15 users are favored in terms of number of subcarriers due to the fact that they enter early the bargaining process, even if they have selected lower discount factor compared to the latter 15 users. On the other hand, the scenario (ii-b) clearly shows that users' privilege in occupying more subcarriers due to their early insertion to the bargaining process can be limited if they select a lower value of discount factor compared to the rest of the users. Thus, we conclude that the order of user's entry in the bargaining process, as well as the value of the discount factor, strongly affect the number of subcarriers that are allocated to each user. Therefore, the results demonstrated that a user who requests a demanding service in terms of throughput, e.g. type I service should enter early the bargaining process and adopt a high value of discount factor.

Fig. 2 and Fig. 3 illustrate the number of subcarriers and users' total uplink transmission power at the stable point of MUD-BAR algorithm, where each user adopts a different value for the discount factor, i.e. $\delta_{i+1} = \delta_i + 0.007$, $\delta_1 = 0.777$. The results reveal that the first users inserted in the bargaining process occupy a large number of subcarriers, even if they have low discount factor. Moreover, the latter users are also being allocated a large portion of subcarriers, due to the high value of their discount factor. Also, users' uplink transmission power follows the same trend as subcarriers allocation, due to the fact that the users who occupied more subcarriers, they transmit with corresponding higher total uplink transmission power. Furthermore, none of the users exhausts his maximum uplink transmission power, thus the proposed power allocation is more energy-efficient compared to the EBEP allocation and the waterfilling method, which allocate users' maximum power to their occupied subcarriers.

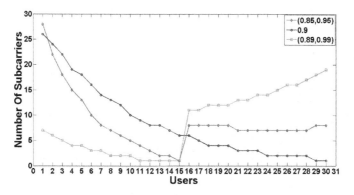

Fig. 1. Subcarriers allocation under 3 different scenarios: i) common $\delta=0.9$, ii-a) $\delta_I=0.85$, $\delta_{II}=0.95$ and ii-b) $\delta_I=0.89$, $\delta_{II}=0.99$.

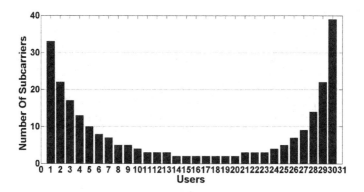

Fig. 2. Subcarriers allocation for increasing discount factor: $\delta_{i+1} = \delta_i + 0.007$, $\delta_1 = 0.777$.

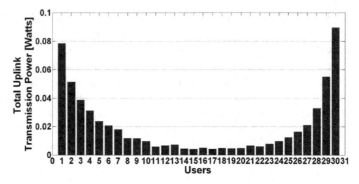

Fig. 3. Users' total uplink transmission power allocation for increasing discount factor: $\delta_{i+1}=\delta_i+0.007$, $\delta_1=0.777$.

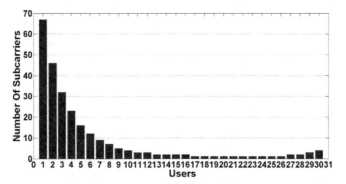

Fig. 4. Subcarriers allocation for increasing discount factor: $\delta_{i+1}=\delta_i+0.007$, $\delta_1=0.700$.

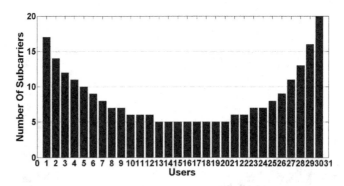

Fig. 5. Subcarriers allocation for smaller range of increasing discount factor: $\delta_{i+1}=\delta_i+0.003$, $\delta_1=0.893$.

Therefore, we conclude that users who request demanding services can either enter early the bargaining process or alternatively select a high value of discount factor δ.

Fig. 4 illustrates subcarriers allocation to each of the $N=30$ users, while the initial value of the discount factor for the first user entered the bargaining process is set to

δ_1=0.700 and we keep the same step for the discount factors of the rest of the users, i.e. δ_{step}=0.007. The results reveal that the latter users that entered the bargaining process do not have enough competitive value of their discount factor and they are also unfavored in terms of their order in the bargaining process, thus they obtain less subcarriers compared to the first users. This scenario could be applied in the case of the first users request a demanding service.

Finally, Fig. 5 presents subcarriers allocation to the users, while considering a smaller range of users' discount factors (δ_1=0.893 and δ_{step}=0.003). Based on the results, we observe that we obtain a more fair and balanced subcarriers allocation among users.

7   Concluding Remarks

In this paper, we introduced a user-centric distributed non-cooperative multilateral bargaining model for resource allocation in order to support service differentiation in multi-service wireless networks. The main novelty of the proposed framework is that the mobile users are able to select different discount factors to enter the multilateral bargaining process, thus better representing their needs in occupying system resources. Following this initial subcarrier allocation, an optimal users' uplink transmission power allocation is proposed per each user's allocated subcarrier towards achieving an energy-efficient resource allocation. The proposed power allocation does not exhaust users' maximum uplink transmission power, compared to equal-bit-equal-power (EBEP) allocation and the waterfilling method, which have been widely utilized in the recent literature.

Based on the promising results of the proposed approach, part of our current and future work is to extend and apply the proposed framework in multi-service and multi-tier wireless networks, e.g. two-tier femtocell networks. In addition the proposed model can be examined in the context of the 5G wireless networks – specifically in M2M and D2D communication networks – where cellular users and machines / devices will be able to adopt different values of the discount factor, so as to express their priority in occupying a corresponding portion of resources.

Acknowledgments. This research is co-financed by the European Union (European Social Fund) and Hellenic national funds through the Operational Program 'Education and Lifelong Learning' (NSRF 2007-2013).

References

1. Rumney, M.: 3GPP LTE: Introducing single-carrier FDMA. Agilent Technology, Tech. Rep., January 2008
2. Delgado, O., Jaumard, B.: Scheduling and resource allocation in LTE uplink with a delay requirement. In: 8th Annual Communication Networks and Services Research Conference (CNSR), pp. 268–275, May 2010

3. Marsch, P., Fettweis, G.: Uplink CoMP under a Constrained Backhaul and Imperfect Channel Knowledge. IEEE Transactions on Wireless Communications 10(6), 1730–1742 (2011)
4. Zhang, M., Zhu, Y.: An Enhanced Greedy Resource Allocation Algorithm for Localized SC-FDMA Systems. IEEE Communications Letters 17(7), 1479–1482 (2013)
5. Myung, H.G., Goodman, D.J.: Single Carrier FDMA: A New Air Interface for Long Term Evolution. Wiley (2008)
6. Rubinstein, A.: Perfect Equilibrium in a Bargaining Model. Econometrica, Econometric Society 50(1), 97–109 (1982)
7. Tsiropoulou, E.E., Kapoukakis, A., Papavassiliou, S.: Energy-efficient subcarrier allocation in SC-FDMA wireless networks based on multilateral model of bargaining. In: IFIP Networking 2013, Brooklyn (2013)
8. Wong, I.C., Oteri, O., McCoy, W.: Optimal Resource Allocation in Uplink SC-FDMA Systems. IEEE Transactions on Wireless Communications 8(5), 2161–2165 (2009)
9. Asheim, G.B.: A unique solution to n-person sequential bargaining. Games and Economic Behavior 4(2), 169–181 (1992)

MAC and Routing

Minimum Spanning Tree Topology in Real Zigbee-Arduino Sensor Network

Mourad Ouadou[1], Ouadoudi Zytoune[1], Yassin El Hillali[2], Atika Menhaj-Rivenq[2], and Driss Aboutajdine[1]

[1] LRIT, Associated Unit to CNRST (URAC 29), Faculty of Science, MohammedV University, Rabat, Morocco
[2] IEMN-DOAE, University of Valenciennes, Campus Mont Houy, Aulnoy-les-Valenciennes, France

Abstract. In this paper, we present a real indoor application for improved "Cluster Tree" network using Zigbee sensor nodes integrated with "Arduino" microcontrollers where the main goal is to study the efficiency of our improved clustering topology based on Minimum Spanning Tree (MST) construction under real conditions. Our system is based on many sensor nodes deployed all over a building to monitor temperature and humidity and detect any brutal temperature increase. These nodes are based on simple , cheap and easily programmed equipment. while several simulations using NS-2 and other simulators has been conducted in many other works to study the efficiency of a network based on MST, our application tests this topology in real conditions to ensure it effectiveness in a Zigbee network. Our developed system provides an easy interface for programming and displaying results. All sensed data is sent to the coordinator which forwards it to the user's pc to be viewed by the user. This paper also presents some performances of this discussed topology obtained by real conditions tests.

Keywords: Minimum Spanning Tree, Zigbee, Arduino, Hardware architecture, Temperature-Humidity sensing.

1 Introduction

Nowadays, we assist to great emergence of wireless sensor networks. This type of networks are applied in many fields such industrial and personal like home automation. These networks are self-organizing and consist of a large number of autonomous sensor nodes with low resources that transmit sensed data to the sink or base station [1]. Most of these networks intend to optimize the use of limited energy contained in each node, as well as other tasks like collection, routing and data aggregation to obtain high performances. Among the most emerging application fields for wireless sensor networks we find the indoor sensor networks. In fact, we focus in this work especially on improving the performances of this type of networks aimed for home automation and industrial monitoring by testing a a topology that has demonstrated its effectiveness in simulation in

© Institute for Computer Sciences, Social Informatics and Telecommunications Engineering 2015
N. Mitton et al. (Eds.): AdHocNets 2015, LNICST 155, pp. 57–68, 2015.
DOI: 10.1007/978-3-319-25067-0_5

real indoor conditions. For this type of applications, many previous works have demonstrated that conventional wireless standards such as Bluetooth or WLAN [2,3] are not suitable to be used in this type of networks. The first standard taking into consideration the new constraints of the indoor sensor networks, is the 802.15.4 standard. Other reason why we selected ZigBee is because it has been shown that ZigBee network noise is the least compared with other wireless networks in term of SNR [4,5] us referred in figure 1. In fact, in an indoor environment, noise has a strong presence especially in industrial buildings where machines cause high levels of it.

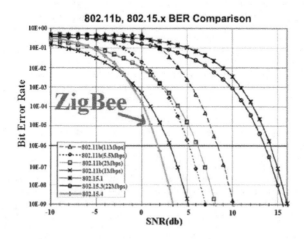

Fig. 1. 802.15.4 performance based on SNR.

Several works has been conducted in improving routing,topology control and data aggregation using simulation tools such as ns-2 [6,7], aimed to improve the efficiency of sensor networks. However in this paper, we focus more on the hardware aspect by presenting a real architecture of the network which allowed us to obtain satisfying results on two aspects: Energy saving and Reliability of data processing. In fact a combination between a Zigbee sensor node and the Arduino platform has allowed a very good reliability of the network as shown in the experimental results. This paper is organized us follows, we first present some concepts in a preliminary notes chapter, then we continue with the second chapter where we present our hardware architecture and system overview. In the third chapter we talk about network organization and communication before presenting in the last chapter our experimental results. At the end of paper we conclude and present our perspectives for future works.

2   Preliminary Notes

2.1   Arduino Open Source

The Arduino platform consists on an open source hardware and software. It is an open-source physical computing platform based on a simple microcontroller board, and a development environment for writing software for the board [8]. Arduino module is a printed board, generally built around an Atmel AVR microcontroller and additional components that facilitate programming and interfacing with other circuits. Each module has at least one linear regulator 5 V and a 16 MHz crystal oscillator. Some of the reason for which we choose the Arduino platform is that Arduino boards are relatively inexpensive compared to other microcontroller platforms and the programming environment is easy-to-use. For our sensor nodes, we used "Arduino Due" microcontroller board based on the Atmel SAM3X8E ARM Cortex-M3. It is the first Arduino board based on a 32-bit ARM core microcontroller. It has 54 digital input/output, 12 analog inputs, 4 UARTs, a 84 MHz clock, an USB OTG capable connection, 2 DAC, 2 TWI, an SPI header, a JTAG header, a reset button and erase buttons.

2.2 Minimum Spanning Tree

A minimum spanning tree (MST) of an undirected graph is a graph that spans all the nodes as vertices and contains no cycles [9]. In application for the sensor networks, several algorithms for routing and topology control based on MST have been developed. This algorithms use few methods that allow the construction of MST based topology as "Relax" algorithm, "Adjust weight" algorithm, "Adjust tree" algorithm, "STP tree based" algorithm and others. In general, spanning tree algorithms have shown to be energy efficient for different extreme sensor network conditions. For our network, we used an improved "Adjust Tree" algorithm for MST topology building for our network. This algorithm calculates the cost between two relations and continues until all the possible pairs have calculated there costs. It sorts all edges in the increasing order, and considers all these edges for inclusion in the tree. It initially has all vertices but no edges. An edge is included into the tree if and only if its addition does not create a cycle in the already constructed tree.

2.3 Temperature and Humidity Sensing

In many indoor systems, especially in industrial field, the temperature-humidity control is crucial. In fact, it is essential in the industry to control those parameters to ensure the safety of equipment and staff. This type of sensors provides temperature information to the controller so it can make some urgent decisions like over-temperature shutdown. it exists a lot of kinds of passive and active temperature sensors that can be used to measure system temperature. We used the "Aosong dht22" temperature-humidity based on Polymer capacitor. It uses exclusive digital-signal-collecting-technique and humidity sensing technology, assuring its reliability and stability. Its sensing elements are connected with 8-bit single-chip computer [10].

3   System and Hardware Overview

3.1   System Overview

The system we present in this paper is an energy independent indoor sensor network designed for an automation system in order to monitor temperature and humidity inside buildings. In this system, sensors needs a battery and the communication protocols have to be energy efficient. This system uses 802.15.4 standard to perform communications between the different components of this network. Our system is based as shown in figure 2 by a set of sensor nodes. These nodes are divided into three main categories:

Sensing Unit. This unit is composed by a big number of sensor nodes. This unit provides the task of sensing and routing. These nodes are composed into two kinds, routers and end devices. As presented in 802.15.4 standard [11], the "end devices" are only programmed to sense and send data to the next hope toward control unit, the "routers" are programmed to receive data and decide which node it has to be sent for the next hop toward the control unit.

Control Unit. This unit is composed by a coordinator node connected to user's pc. The coordinator has the main task of organizing the network and communications. It has the capability to add or remove any node from the Zigbee network, allow address to the nodes and create and control the topology. From the user's pc, we can make some occasional modifications wich are transmitted to the coordinator. This modifications can be in some cases a network re-building using a different topology.

3.2   Hardware Architecture

There is a large amount of works on developing sensor nodes and new communication devices. Many sensor nodes were developed by the researchers [12,13,14], and others are commercial.

Sensor node architecture depends on many components that goes into the constitution of the node. In table 1, we present a comparison between the most used Zigbee sensor nodes. The two main components in a Zigbee sensor node are the microcontroller and the RF module. The microcontroller defines the programming environment, meanwhile the choice of RF module has a major

Table 1. Comparison between some Zigbee sensor nodes

Commercial nodes	Microcontroller	RF Module	Comsumption	Indoor Range
Texas Instruments	CC2530	SmartRF05EB	24-29 mA	108 ft
Microchip	PIC24	MRF24J40	19-23 mA	110 ft
Digi	Arduino	Xbee	40-50 mA	100 ft
MEMSIC	ATmega128L	Micaz	11-19.7 mA	82 ft

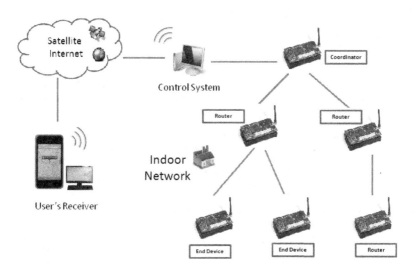

Fig. 2. System overview.

influence on the energy consumption and the organization of network since it defines the distance range for transmitting for indoor and outdoor areas. Our sensor network is composed by 13 sensor nodes composed each one by a circuit board attached to many components.

The principal component attached to our circuit is the MRF24J40MA showed in figure 3. All sensor nodes, except the coordinator uses this RF transceiver. The coordinator uses the MRF24J40MD which has a higher range. In fact, according to our tests, the range of the MRF24J40MD can reach 250 feet in a indoor area. This distance is more than enough for the coordinator in a building to be located a little far from the rest of the network, near to the user's pc.

We also used the "Aodong Dht22" temperature-humidity sensor based on Polymer capacitor. It uses exclusive digital-signal-collecting-technique and humidity sensing technology, assuring its reliability and stability. All nodes, including the coordinator are equipped by those sensors. The node includes also a 8-bit switch. The switch enabled us to allow a mac address to the different nodes manually. To build this nodes, we designed a circuit board wish design is shown in figure 3 in order to connect all components to the "Arduino Due" card.

This circuit board that includes all the components listed above is integrated to the Arduino circuit. We show in figure 4 one of the sensor modules that includes other electronic components: An 9A103G network resistor for the switch, one 10K resistor for the sensor, 2 capacitors and one reset button.

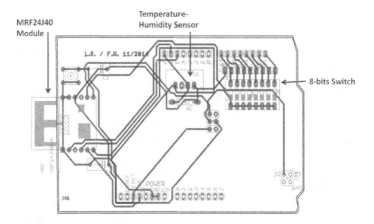

Fig. 3. Circuit board for sensor node

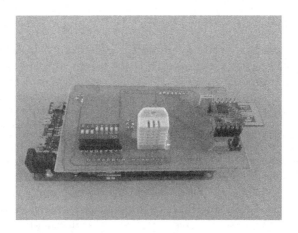

Fig. 4. MRF24j40Ma/Arduino sensor node

4   Software and Network Presentation

4.1   Software Interface

As seen in previous chapter, the sensor node's architecture in our system is based on Arduino microcontrollers, thus we used Arduino software for programming the MRF24J40 sensor nodes. In 802.15.4 standard, two types of zigbee devices are defined: Full-function device (FFD) and Reduced-function device (RFD). Note that, as explained in the next chapter, our topology is based on Cluster-tree. So we used 2 Arduino program files: Coordinator.ino, Non-Coordianator.ino. In the figure 5 we present the Arduino programming interface.

Fig. 5. Arduino programming environment

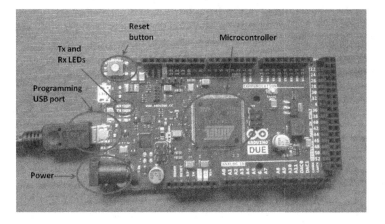

Fig. 6. "Arduino Due" principal components for programming

First, the code has to be uploaded to Arduino card. For uploading the code we use the programming port in figure 6. The Coordinator code has to be uploaded in the Arduino card that will be connected to the MRF24j40MD RF module. The non-coordinator code has to be uploaded to the other circuit boards that include the MRF24j40MA RF modules. When uploading the code in the Arduino board, the Tx and Rx LED are on. After that, we can disconnect the Arduino card from the PC, attach it to the circuit board including the Zigbee module, and connect the whole node to power input also shown in figure 6.

Once the reset button is pressed, the node self initializes and starts transmitting data according to steps explained in the next chapter.

All data sent by the sensor nodes in the network are received at the coordinator. The coordinator send the received data to the control system machine as shown in the system overview chapter. The control system's interface shows the coordinator's running interface. When the coordinator starts running, it initializes the "PAN ID", defines itself as coordinator using the "RXMCR" register of MRF device, assigns a 16 bits address to itself and starts waiting for other nodes the send "join request". Once a join request is received in the channel, the coordinator checks that the RF module of the node is the MRF24J40MA, and assign an address and the PAN ID to the device, and add it in to the network topology. A "request response" is then sent to the device. Once this steps performed successfully, the coordinator starts receiving data from the added node. This operation is then repeated for all the sensor nodes that request joining the network.

4.2   Network Deployment

In this section, we present how the sensor network is organized. The network topology used is the "Cluster Tree" from 802.15.4 standard. To obtain our topology, we made some modifications on the tree construction algorithm in order to create a minimum spanning tree where the leaves are "end devices", and the other nodes are "routers". The nodes sends a "Hello Packet" to the coordinator including the MAC address obtained from the 8-bits switch and their positions in the building. To create and control the topology, as we mentioned before, the improved adjust algorithm is used to create a minimum spanning tree. we Suppose a graph $G = (V, E)$ representing the network, where vertices V represents sensor nodes and edges E represent the link between two connected nodes [15]. In figure 7, we present the flowchart of the operations at the coordinator and the end devices. Note that the router have a similar functioning except the difference that it can receive packets from children nodes and send it to parent node.

To test the performance of your system, we deployed our network in an indoor environment. Figure 8 shows how network is deployed and topology is constructed inside the building of Faculty of Sciences of Rabat where we realized our network.

5   Experimental Results

As mentioned in sections before, we performed a field test for temperature and humidity sensing using MRF24J40-Arduino sensor network inside the building of Faculty of Sciences of Rabat. Our system was programmed in order to sense temperature and humidity for all nodes every minute. The coordinator sends obtained data from other nodes to user's pc. We show in figure 9 the results obtained in the user's PC that shows all the operations happening at the coordinator.

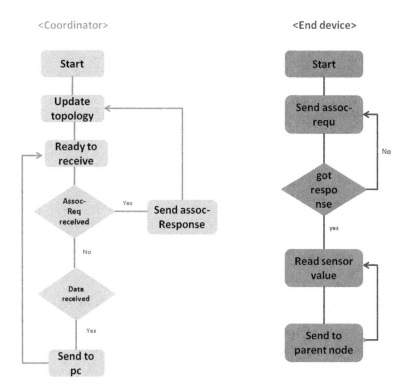

Fig. 7. Coordinator and End Device flowcharts

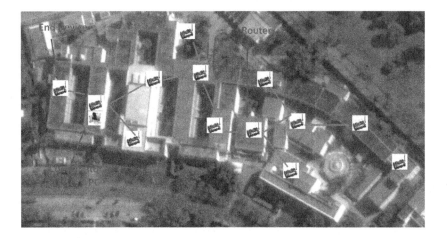

Fig. 8. Sensor network deployment in Faculty of Sciences of Rabat building

For the main performance results, we can view in figure 10 the packet loss ratio in the network according to the number of sensor nodes in the network for

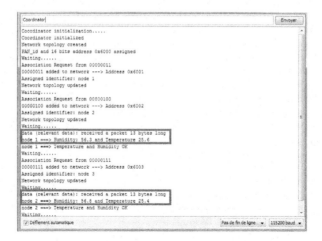

Fig. 9. "Coordinator operations at user's PC interface

typical Cluster Tree and Minimum Spanning Tree Cluster topologies. Our first tests started with 5 nodes and then we started adding nodes to reach 9 and then 13 by testing network performances. Our improved MST topology shows better results in terms of packet delivery ratio than the typical Cluser tree topology.

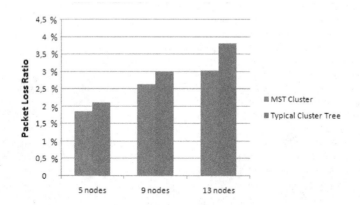

Fig. 10. Packet loss ratio

We also compared the average of power consumption in the network as shown in figure 11 by summing the energy consumption for all sensor nodes. Once again our improved topology shows better results for our network which means longer lifetime duration for our network.

In summary, the results show satisfactory performance of the network using our improved MST topology in real indoor Zigbee conditions in term of function-

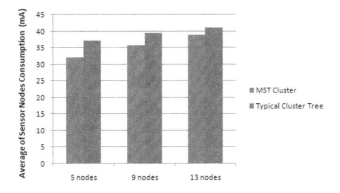

Fig. 11. Average power consumption

ality, packet deliverance and power consumption. In fact, the packets containing sensed data are routed quickly to the coordinator node, wish allows us to follow in real time the evolution of the temperature and humidity inside the building. The interface allows to visualize at the same time the evolution of the temperature in the building and the network status by showing the nodes joining our personal area network. The average of energy consumption, which represents a major issue for energy independent sensor networks, has been reduced by about 11 per cent compared to typical cluster tree topology in our tests, which is considered an important gain in term of network's lifetime.

6   Conclusion and Perspectives

In this paper, we presented how we built a prototype of a zigbee sensor network based based on minimum spanning tree clustering using MRF24J modules and "Arduino microcontrollers" to test performance of this topology. We presented the architecture and components of the nodes and how the easy programmed nodes are deployed to build a efficient sensor network for home automation. We made several tests that showed the reliability of our system based on easy interface for temperature-humidity monitoring. The tests showed also satisfactory results for our system in therm of functionality and network performances as packet delivery ratio and energy consumption. Extensions of our current work includes adding new technologies for energy harvesting in order to prolong network's lifetime.

References

1. Ulema, M.M.: Coll. Wireless sensor networks: architectures, protocols, and management. In: Network Operations and Management Symposium (2004)
2. Bargh, M.S., De Groote, R.: Indoor localization based on response rate of bluetooth inquiries. In: Proceedings of MELT 2008, pp. 49–54 (2008)

3. Gomez, C., Paradells, J.: Wireless home automation networks: a survey of architectures and technologies. IEEE Communications Magazine 48, 92–101 (2010)
4. Shuaib, K., Alnuaimi, M., Boulmalf, M., Jawhar, I., Sallabi, F., Lakas, A.: Performance Evaluation of IEEE 802. Journal of Communications 2 (2007)
5. Alnuaimi, M., Shuaib, K., Jawhar, I.: Performance evaluation of IEEE 802.15.4 physical layer using MatLab/Simulink. In: Innovations in Information Technology (2006)
6. Melodia, T., Pompili, D., Akyildiz, I.F.: On the interdependence of distributed topology control and geographical routing in ad hoc and sensor networks. IEEE Journal on Selected Areas in Communications 23(3), 520–532 (2005)
7. Li, M., Li, Z., Vasilakos, A.V.: A Survey on Topology Control in Wireless Sensor Networks: Taxonomy, Comparative Study, and Open Issues. Proceedings of the IEEE 101(12), 2538–2557 (2013)
8. Schubert, T.W., D'Ausilio, A., Canto, R.: Using Arduino microcontroller boards to measure response latencies. Behavior research methods. Springer (2013)
9. Javier, F., Martnez, O., Stojmenovic, I., Garca- Nocetti, F., Solano-Gonzlez, J.: Finding minimum transmission radii for preserving connectivity and constructing minimal spanning trees in ad hoc and sensor networks. Journal of Parallel and Distrubuted Computing 65, 132–141 (2005)
10. Liu, T.: Digital-output relative humidity and temperature sensor/module DHT22. Aosong Electronics Co.,Ltd.
11. Microchip Technology Inc . MRF24J40 Data Sheet, IEEE 802.15.4, 2.4 GHz RF Transceiver (2010)
12. Otto, C., Milenkovic, A., Sanders, C., Jovanov, E.: System Architecture of a Wireless Body Area Sensor Network for Ubiquitous Health Monitoring (2006)
13. Zulkifli, N.S.A., Harun, F.K.C., Azahar, N.S.: XBee wireless sensor networks for heart rate monitoring in sport training. In: 2012 International Conference on Biomedical Engineering (ICoBE), pp. 441–444 (2012)
14. Boonsawat, V., Ekchamanonta, J., Bumrungkhet, K., Kittipiyakul, S.: Xbee wireless sensor networks for temperature monitoring. In: ECTI-CARD (2010)
15. Khan, M., Pandurangan, G., Kumar, V.S.A.: Distributed Algorithms for Constructing Approximate Minimum Spanning Trees in Wireless Sensor Networks. IEEE Transactions on Parallel and Distributed Systems 20(1), 124–139 (2009)

SLACK-MAC: Adaptive MAC Protocol for Low Duty-Cycle Wireless Sensor Networks

Affoua Thérèse Aby[1,2], Alexandre Guitton[1,2],
Pascal Lafourcade[3,2], and Michel Misson[3,2]

[1] Université Blaise Pascal, LIMOS, BP 10448, F-63000 Clermont-Ferrand, France
[2] CNRS, UMR 6158, LIMOS, F-63173 Aubière, France
[3] Université d'Auvergne, LIMOS, BP 10448, F-63000 Clermont-Ferrand, France
{aby,guitton,lafourcade,misson}@sancy.univ-bpclermont.fr

Abstract. Wireless sensor networks (WSNs) are increasingly used in environmental monitoring applications. They are designed to operate for several months by featuring low activity cycles, in order to save energy. In this paper, we propose a MAC protocol for such WSNs with duty-cycles of 1%. Initially, nodes are activated randomly and independently, then they use the knowledge of previous successful frame exchanges to compute their next activation times. We study the choice of the history size, and we compare the performance of our protocol with other protocols from the literature. We show that with a limited history size of only six entries, we significantly improve the performance of existing protocols, while keeping the advantages of fully asynchronous protocols.

Keywords: WSN; adaptive; asynchronous MAC protocol; duty-cycle.

1 Introduction

Environmental monitoring applications, such as the monitoring of volcanoes [1], bird nests [2], fields [3], or bridges [4], are increasingly using Wireless Sensor Networks (WSNs). In such applications, wireless sensor nodes are deployed in the environment, where they perform periodic measurements and communicate the collected data to a sink in a multi-hop manner.

Energy-efficient protocols are designed to increase the lifetime of such WSNs. These protocols deactivate the radio module of nodes most of the time, as it is the node hardware component having the largest energy consumption. The MAC protocol is responsible for allowing nodes to communicate in the rare periods when the radio module of both node and neighbor are active.

In this paper, we propose the SLACK-MAC (Self-adaptive Low Activity Cycle Knowledge-based MAC) protocol. SLACK-MAC is an asynchronous protocol where nodes activate their radio modules randomly. The idea behind SLACK-MAC is inspired by the routing protocol proposed in [5], where authors proposed the SR3 protocol, which is an improvement over a biased random walk based on a reputation mechanism. In SLACK-MAC, nodes communicate opportunistically and consider discrete time. Nodes record a history of previous successful communications with neighbors, and use this history to determine the time of the next activation of their radio module.

© Institute for Computer Sciences, Social Informatics and Telecommunications Engineering 2015
N. Mitton et al. (Eds.): AdHocNets 2015, LNICST 155, pp. 69–81, 2015.
DOI: 10.1007/978-3-319-25067-0_6

This history increases the probability to select a recent successful time of activation among all possible times during each cycle. Thus, nodes adapt their activation times depending on their neighborhood. We show in this paper that this behavior improves the probability of successful communications, which in turn improves the performance in terms of delivery rate and delay.

The remainder of this paper is as follows. Section 2 presents the main existing MAC protocols for low duty-cycles. Section 3 describes the SLACK-MAC protocol, and justifies our choice of parameters. Section 4 compares the performance of existing protocols with the performance of SLACK-MAC. Finally, Section 5 concludes our work.

2   State of the Art

Most energy-efficient MAC protocols for WSNs are based on sequences of active and inactive periods, called *duty-cycle*. Indeed, as the radio module of a node is the component having the largest energy consumption, energy can be saved by deactivating it periodically. MAC protocols based on duty-cycles can be classified depending on whether the activities of nodes are synchronized or not.

2.1   Synchronous MAC Protocols

In synchronous duty-cycle MAC protocols, nodes share a common time (through synchronization) and agree on a common schedule for their activities and inactivities. Generally, all nodes are either simultaneously active or simultaneously inactive.

The IEEE 802.15.4 standard [6] in beacon-enabled mode is one of the most largely used synchronous MAC protocols. Full-function devices send periodic beacons, with period BI (for Beacon Interval). Reduced-function devices start their activities at the beacon reception, and are allowed to communicate during a period SD (for Superframe Duration). The communication is performed using the slotted CSMA/CA (Carrier-Sense Multiple Access with Collision Avoidance) mechanism, which is designed to consume low energy for channel sensing. After this period, nodes go back to sleep until the next beacon. The ratio SD/BI defines the duty-cycle of nodes.

Several other protocols have been proposed for the same purpose, such as D-MAC [7], DW-MAC [8], Speed-MAC [9], TreeMAC [10], MC-LMAC [11], SEA-MAC [12] and others [13,14,15]. As in IEEE 802.15.4, these protocols generally have three types of periods: a *synchronization period*, which ensures that all nodes share a common time, a *communication period*, where nodes can communicate efficiently, and an *inactive period*, where nodes save energy.

Synchronous duty-cycle MAC protocols have two main drawbacks. The first drawback is the overhead of the mandatory synchronization period. The second drawback is the high contention for the channel when all nodes are active simultaneously. In this paper, we focus on asynchronous duty-cycle MAC protocols.

2.2   Asynchronous MAC Protocols

Asynchronous duty-cycle MAC protocols do not need to synchronize nodes. Notice that generally, asynchronous MAC protocols yield large delays, but have a low energy consumption. In the following, we describe the two main categories of asynchronous protocols: sender-initiated protocols and receiver-initiated protocols.

Sender-Initiated Protocols. The first asynchronous MAC protocol for WSNs was B-MAC [16], which is based on LPL (Low Power Listening). In B-MAC, the source sends a long preamble before each frame, and receivers wake up periodically to detect potential preambles. This technique has been the basis for sender-initiated protocols.

X-MAC [17,18] are based on a similar approach. In X-MAC, nodes switch between active (20 ms) and inactive period (500 ms), but instead of using a long preamble, nodes send small preambles to inform the receiver. The maximum duration of the series of short preambles is one inactivity period (500 ms). Once the receiver wakes up and receives a short preamble, it replies by an acknowledgment to inform the transmitter of its availability to receive data. When a node having no packet to send wakes up and hears a preamble for another node, it immediately returns to sleep. When a node having packets to send wakes up and hears another preamble, it stops sending its own preamble and waits to receive the acknowledgment for the other transmission before attempting to send its own preamble again. In X-MAC, some source nodes remain active much longer than other nodes. This causes an inequity in energy consumption which reduces network lifetime. Moreover, X-MAC generally achieves a low end-to-end delay, but increases the risk of collisions due to the fact that nodes can interpret the duration between two preambles as a free channel.

In WiseMAC [19], preambles are used, but their length is reduced by allowing the sender to send data as soon as both nodes are active.

In [20], the authors proposed a distributed algorithm to control the sleep interval of nodes to achieve fairness of energy consumption in asynchronous duty-cycle WSNs. The mechanism can increase network lifetime, but has a significant impact on the delay.

In this paper, we decide not to use a sender-initiated approach, in order to avoid the overhead and energy consumption caused by preambles. Indeed, for very low duty-cycles, the average duration for a preamble is long.

Receiver-initiated Protocols. In RI-MAC [21], the receiver initiates the communication by sending a beacon to express its ability to receive data packets. RI-MAC reduces channel occupation (as it does not require nodes to send preambles), but introduces a wasted period as the sender has to wait for the reception of the beacon. The ABD protocol [22] adds a broadcast service to the RI-MAC protocol.

In PW-MAC [23], each node computes its awakening times according to a pseudo-random number generator rather than according to a fixed schedule. The drawback of PW-MAC is that sending beacons before frame transmissions generates overhead, and introduces a delay when listening to the channel.

In EM-MAC [24], nodes decide independently their wake-up time schedule and channel using a pseudo-random generator. EM-MAC allows the sender to wake up just before the beacon of the receiver. However, EM-MAC requires an initial neighbor discovery phase and each node needs to maintain information about all its neighbors.

HKMAC [25] uses an hybrid approach, where time is divided into random activation periods (similar as in RI-MAC) and scheduled activation periods (which requires synchronization).

The MAC protocol proposed in [26] is based on random wake-up times. Each node knows the duration of the cycle, denoted by C, and the duration of its activity within each cycle, denoted by A. Each node activates its radio module during A time units every C time units. The beginning of the activation within each cycle is chosen uniformly at random in $[0; C - A[$. When a node is active, it uses unslotted CSMA/CA to access the medium (as in the non beacon-enabled mode of IEEE 802.15.4 [6]). With this mechanism, nodes are not synchronized, and nodes do not make assumptions about the activity times of the others. Moreover, there is a non-null probability that any two neighbors share a common activity at each cycle. Figure 1 depicts an example of the activities of three neighbor nodes for this protocol: n_1, n_2 and n_3. We notice that the cycles of nodes are not synchronized. During the first cycle of n_1, nodes n_1 and n_2 share a common activity, during which they can communicate. However, for n_1 to communicate with n_3, both nodes have to wait until the middle of the third cycle of n_1.

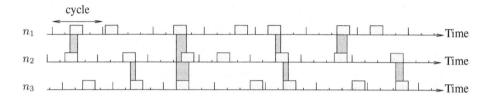

Fig. 1. Example of the activities of three neighbor nodes with the protocol of [26], with a duty-cycle of 25% (this long duty-cycle is chosen for clarity).

In this paper, we focus on a receiver-initiated protocol based on random node activities, as in [26]. Such protocols are generally more suitable to low duty-cycles of 1%.

3   Proposition of a MAC Protocol for Low Duty-Cycles

In this section, we describe our SLACK-MAC protocol and our methodology to choose its parameters.

3.1   SLACK-MAC Protocol

The main idea of SLACK-MAC is to maintain a history of times corresponding to successful communications with neighbors. In SLACK-MAC, nodes do not always choose their activation times uniformly at random. Instead, they have a high probability to choose times when successful communications occurred in the recent past. Figure 2 depicts an example of the activities of three neighbor nodes with SLACK-MAC: n_1, n_2 and n_3. Initially, all nodes choose their activation times uniformly at random. When a node chooses a time that yields to successful communications (reception or transmission of a frame), it memorizes it and the probability to choose this time increases, as can be seen towards the right of the figure.

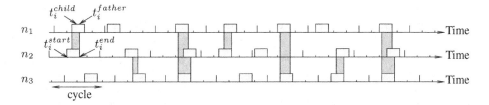

Fig. 2. Example of the activities of three neighbor nodes with the SLACK-MAC protocol, with a duty-cycle of 25% (again, this long duty-cycle is chosen for clarity).

SLACK-MAC requires each node to maintain two lists E (Emission) and R (Reception) that contain wake-up times in the cycle. Let us denote by t_i^{start} the start of activity in the current cycle i, and t_i^{end} is the end of activity time, as depicted on Figure 2. During this activity a node can send and receive one or several frames, and can add t_i^{start} in both lists, once or several times. Each node uses these two lists to determine its next wake-up time. A new time t_i^{start} is added to E when a node wakes up at time t_i^{start} and communicates with another node located closer to the sink at time t_i^{father}. Similarly, a new time t_i^{start} is added to R when a node wakes up in a given cycle and communicates with another node located further away from the sink at time t_i^{child}.

Figure 3 shows the evolution of lists E and R, at three different time steps. Step 1 shows the state of the lists when they are being filled (with one successful transmission and two successful receptions). When a list is full (see Step 2), the last entry is removed to add the newest entry to the front (using a first-in first-out mechanism, as shown on Step 3).

	E			R		
step 1	t_1^E		t_1^R	t_1^R		
step 2	t_2^E	t_1^E	t_3^R	t_2^R	t_1^R	t_1^R
step 3	t_1^E	t_2^E	t_2^R	t_3^R	t_2^R	t_1^R

Fig. 3. Example of the state of the E and R lists, at three different times.

More formally, the probability that a node selects its next wake-up time $t \in D$ (where D denotes all possible times) is given by the following formula:

$$Pr[X = t] = \frac{\mathbb{1}_{|R| \neq 0} \left(\frac{|R|_t}{|R|} \right) + \mathbb{1}_{|E| \neq 0} \left(\frac{|E|_t}{|E|} \right) + \frac{1}{|D|}}{\mathbb{1}_{|R| \neq 0} + \mathbb{1}_{|E| \neq 0} + 1},$$

where $|L|$ denotes the number of elements in list L, $|L|_t$ denotes the number of occurrences of time t in L, and $\mathbb{1}_P$ is the indicator function (it is equal to 1 when the predicate P is true and to 0 otherwise). Note that nodes consider that time is discrete (the granularity of time can be, for instance, 320 μs, as in IEEE 802.15.4, which results into 15,625 slots for a cycle of $C = 5$ seconds).

In Algorithm 1, we give a pseudo code of the behavior of a node when it wakes up. During this time, a node can receive and send some data. These two operations change the content of *SendQueue* and the two lists E and R. Before going back to sleep, a node uses these lists to determine its next wake-up time using the function Next-Wake-Up-Time presented in Algorithm 2, where random(x) draws an integer uniformly at random within $[0; x - 1]$, C denotes the duration of a cycle in time units, and A denotes the activity of a node in time units.

The function *Next-Wake-Up-Time* draws the next wake up time according to the content of the two lists and following the previous distribution. Note that initially, when both lists are empty, we have $Pr[X = t] = \frac{1}{|D|}$, meaning that the next wake-up time is chosen uniformly at random in D. If one of the two lists is empty, we select an element of the non empty list with a probability of $1/2$, and uniformly at random in D otherwise. If none of the list is empty, we select an element from list R with probability of 1/3, from list E with probability 1/3, and uniformly at random in D otherwise.

Moreover, each node has a packet queue of fixed size for packets that have to be sent, denoted *SendQueue*. If *SendQueue* is full and a node receives a new packet, the node ignores this last packet.

In order to optimize our protocol according to the state of *SendQueue*, each node adapts its selection strategy for its next wake-up time, according to the following rules:

- If *SendQueue* is empty ($state = 1$), a node has no packet to send, so it is useless to select times that are in the E list. The next wake-up time is chosen uniformly in R with probability $1/2$, and uniformly at random in D (*i.e.*, all possible times) otherwise.
- If *SendQueue* is full ($state = 2$), a node cannot accept any incoming packet, so it is useless to select times that are in the R list. The next wake-up time is chosen uniformly in E with probability $1/2$, and uniformly at random in D otherwise.
- In all the other cases ($state = 3$), a node selects its next wake-up time uniformly in E with probability of 1/3, uniformly in R with probability 1/3, and randomly in D otherwise.

3.2   Determination of the Size of SLACK-MAC Lists

In order to determine the size of both E and R lists, we need to specify the routing algorithm used in our experiments. We have taken a gradient-based routing protocol. Gradient-based routing protocols operate by estimating a distance, called the gradient, to the sink. When a node receives a frame to forward to the sink, the node sends the frame to any neighbor having a gradient smaller than its own gradient. The gradient is computed in the following way: initially, the sink has a gradient of 0; when a node has a gradient defined, it sends its gradient to its neighbors; when a node receives a gradient

---

Algorithm 1. Activity of a node.

Node n wake-up at time t_i^{start} for duration A time units in a cycle i of C time units.
while node n (at distance d) is active **do**
    if n has received a frame from n_r (at distance d_r) during cycle i **then**
        if $(d < d_r)$ and $(t_i^{start}$ has not yet been added) **then**
            add(n_r, t_i^S) to R
            add frame to *SendQueue*
        end if
    end if
    if n has sent a frame to n_s (at distance d_s) during cycle i **then**
        if t_i^{start} has not yet been added **then**
            add(n_s, t_i^{start}) to E
            remove frame from *SendQueue*
        end if
    end if
end while
if *SendQueue* is empty **then**
    $t \leftarrow$ Next-Wake-Up-Time(1);
else
    if *SendQueue* is full **then**
        $t \leftarrow$ Next-Wake-Up-Time(2);
    else
        $t \leftarrow$ Next-Wake-Up-Time(3);
    end if
end if
Schedule next activity at time t of the next cycle

---

from a neighbor, it updates its own gradient if it detects that this neighbor is closer to the sink than itself. The gradient is generally computed according to several parameters, including the hop count to the sink, link quality estimations, etc.

We first notice that for a routing protocol based on gradient and for a random topology with one sink (located at one corner of the area), a node is likely to have more neighbors further away from the sink than closer to the sink. We estimate that this ratio is about two, which means that the maximum size of R is set to be twice the maximum size of E. In order to determine the actual size of these lists, we perform 100 simulations over 10 random topologies (of average degree 8) for three different values of the traffic generation period P.

Figure 4 shows respectively the delivery ratio (left) and the end-to-end delay (right) as a function of the size of E, with $|R| = 2|E|$. We observe in these two figures that regardless of the period P, the best size is two for E and four for R when combining the two criteria. These parameters are used in the following. Note that a history of six entries is realistic for sensor nodes.

We also observed experimentally that on average, it takes about 12 cycles (60 seconds) for the nodes to fill E and about 50 cycles (250 seconds) for the nodes to fill R. This shows that the convergence of the lists is fast and negligible comparing to the life time of a node.

Algorithm 2. Next wake-up time in a cycle i.

```
Next-Wake-Up-Time(state);
if state=1 then
    indicator ← random(2);
    if indicator = 0 then
        position ← random(sizeOf(R));
        t ← R[position];
    else
        t ← random(C − A);
    end if
else
    if state=2 then
        indicator ← random(2);
        if indicator = 0 then
            position ← random(sizeOf(E));
            t ← E[position];
        else
            t ← random(C − A);
        end if
    else
        indicator ← random(3);
        if indicator = 0 then
            position ← random(sizeOf(E));
            t ← E[position];
        else
            if indicator = 1 then
                position ← random(sizeOf(R));
                t ← R[position];
            else
                t ← random(C − A);
            end if
        end if
    end if
end if
return t
```

4   Results

In order to evaluate the performance of SLACK-MAC, we conducted several simulations to compare SLACK-MAC with the protocol of [26] and with X-MAC [17] (as it is one of the most representative asynchronous MAC protocols). We also compared SLACK-MAC with the main MAC protocol with synchronized duty-cycle, which is the standard ZigBee [27]. ZigBee defines the upper layers of the network stack of a wireless personal area network, and assumes that the lower layers are compliant with IEEE 802.15.4. ZigBee uses either a tree-based routing protocol (when addresses are allocated hierarchically) or a protocol similar to AODV [28] (when addresses are allo-

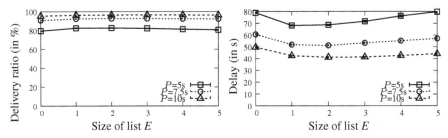

Fig. 4. Impact of the size of list E of SLACK-MAC on respectively the packet delivery ratio (left) and the end-to-end delay (right), with $|R| = 2|E|$ and a duty-cycle of 1%, where P is the traffic generation period.

cated randomly). In the following, we use ZigBee with the tree-based routing protocol as a comparison basis.

4.1 Simulation Parameters

Our simulations are performed using the network simulator NS-2 [29]. For all protocols, transmit power is set to 0 dBm, and the propagation model is the shadowing model with a path loss of 2.74. In our settings, 30 sources perform periodic measurements and route data (in a multi-hop manner) to a single sink located at one corner of the network. Nodes have a duty-cycle of 1% and the global cycle is 5 s (that is, nodes are active during A=50 ms every C=5 s), unless specified otherwise. For our simulations, we use 100 nodes randomly located on a size topology of 170 m x 170 m with a transmission range of 30 m, which yields a maximum number of hops of 7. All presented results are averaged over 100 repetitions per topology and each repetition lasts for 3600 seconds.

It should also be noted that apart from ZigBee [27] which incorporates a tree routing protocol, the same gradient-based routing protocol is used to route packets hop by hop towards the sink for all the other MAC protocols.

4.2 Simulation Results

Our objective being to provide a MAC protocol with a very low duty-cycle (1%), we initially show that the synchronous duty-cycle MAC protocols are not adapted to such low duty-cycles.

Figure 5 (left) shows the packet delivery ratio as a function of the traffic generation period for ZigBee, X-MAC [17], the protocol of [26] and SLACK-MAC. The traffic generation period ranges from 5 seconds (which corresponds to a high traffic generation for a duty-cycle of 1%) to 20 seconds (which corresponds to a relatively low traffic generation for such duty-cycle).

For the ZigBee protocol, the packet delivery ratio increases from about 25% to nearly 78%. This low packet delivery ratio with ZigBee is due to the fact that the low duty-cycle generates a strong contention, as nodes are all synchronized. This strong contention generates many collisions and causes overflows in nodes queues, causing a large

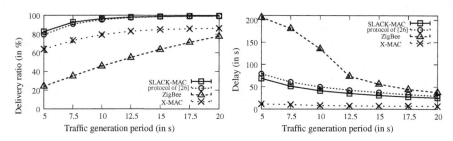

Fig. 5. The packets delivery ratio (left) and the end-to-end delay of data packets (right) as a function of the traffic generation period, for a duty-cycle of 1%, and for several protocols.

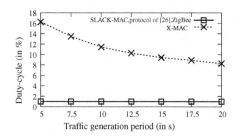

Fig. 6. Duty-cycle (which is an approximation of the consumed energy) as a function of the traffic generation period, for a duty-cycle of 1%, and for several protocols.

packet loss ratio. It is also important to note that these results do not take into account the cost of synchronization because we assume that all nodes are synchronized.

For the X-MAC protocol, the packet delivery ratio increases from about 64% to 86%. Although X-MAC does not set a fixed duty-cycle for each node, the delivery ratio is explained by the collisions due to the relatively high number of preambles, and by the fact that the sender has no knowledge of the successful reception of packets by the receiver.

For the protocol of [26], the packet delivery ratio increases from 79% to 99%. The packet delivery ratio is high: indeed, when nodes meets, they can benefit from this meeting time, as there are few simultaneously active nodes.

For the SLACK-MAC protocol, the packet delivery ratio increases from about 83% to 99%. Indeed, it takes advantage of a mechanism similar to the protocol of [26], and allows more common activities between nodes thanks to the history mechanism. SLACK-MAC also remains completely dynamic with a probability of 1/3 for nodes to choose a random mechanism. The results show that, in terms of packet delivery ratio, for traffic generation period from 5 seconds to 20 seconds, SLACK-MAC provides a gain over X-MAC of 29.61% for a period of 5 seconds and of 15.10% for a period of 20 seconds, a gain over ZigBee of 241.26% for a period of 5 seconds and of 27.70% for a period of 20 seconds, and a gain over the protocol of [26] of 3.98% for a period of 5 seconds and the same delivery ratio for a period of 20 seconds.

Figure 5 (right) shows the average delay of data packets as a function of the traffic generation period (from 5 seconds to 20 seconds) for ZigBee, X-MAC, the protocol of [26] and SLACK-MAC. The delay of X-MAC is very low (from 6 seconds to 11 seconds) compared to the other protocols, because of its large duty-cycle relative to other protocols (see figure 6). We note that SLACK-MAC provides a lower end-to-end delay (going from 25 seconds to 68 seconds) than ZigBee (from 37 seconds to 205 seconds) and the protocol of [26] (from about 29 seconds to 79 seconds). SLACK-MAC provides a gain over ZigBee in terms of end to end delay of 66.61% for a period of 5 seconds and of 32.37% for a period of 20 seconds, and a gain over the protocol of [26] of 12.90% for a period of 5 seconds and of 13.87% for a period of 20 seconds. This significant gain of more than 12% compared with the literature comes at a very small cost of an history of only six entries.

Figure 6 shows the duty-cycle in percent for each protocol. For ZigBee, the protocol of [26] and SLACK-MAC, the duty-cycle is set to 1% and is fixed. For X-MAC, the duty-cycle of node actually depends on the communication opportunities, as nodes having frames to send remain active until they can send their frames. Thus, X-MAC yields large duty-cycles, and consumes more energy than the other protocols.

5   Conclusion

In this paper, we proposed the SLACK-MAC protocol for WSNs with low duty-cycles of 1%. Initially, nodes in SLACK-MAC activate their radio module randomly and independently, and build a history of successful communications. The history is used to determine the next activation times, which results into a self-adaptive behavior. We show that SLACK-MAC reaches a good behavior with a limited history size of only six entries. Only few activity cycles are needed to fill the memory lists. Then, we compare SLACK-MAC with existing protocols in terms of frame loss, end-to-end delay and consumed energy. We show that our low-cost protocol is able to significantly improve the performance of existing protocols. As future work, we aim to see if using an history can be applied to other existing probabilistic MAC protocols.

Acknowledgments. This research was partially supported by the "Digital Trust" Chair from the University of Auvergne Foundation.

References

1. Geoffrey, W., Jeff, J., Mario, R., Jonathan, L., Matt, W.: Monitoring volcanic eruptions with a wireless sensor network. In: European Workshop on Wireless Sensor Networks, (EWSN 2005) (2005)
2. Robert, S., Alan, M., Joseph, P., John, A., David, C.: An analysis of a large scale habitat monitoring application. In: ACM Sensys, pp. 214–226 (2004)
3. Hart, J., Martinez, K.: Environmental sensor networks: A revolution in the Earth system science? Earth Science Reviews 78(3), 177–191 (2006)
4. Nagayamaa, T., Ushitab, M., Fujinoa, Y.: Suspension bridge vibration measurement using multihop wireless sensor networks. In: East Asia-Pacific Conference on Structural Engineering and Construction (EASEC), pp. 761–768. Elsevier (2011)

5. Altisen, K., Devismes, S., Jamet, R., Lafourcade, P.: SR3: Secure resilient reputation-based routing. In: IEEE International Conference on Distributed Computing in Sensor Systems, DCOSS 2013, Cambridge, MA, USA, May 20–23, pp. 258–265. IEEE (2013). http://doi.ieeecomputersociety.org/10.1109/DCOSS.2013.33

6. IEEE 802.15, Part 15.4: Wireless medium access control (MAC) and physical layer (PHY) specifications for low-rate wireless personal area networks (WPANs). ANSI/IEEE, Standard 802.15.4 R2006 (2006)

7. Lu, G., Krishnamachari, B., Raghavendra, C.: An adaptive energy-efficient and low-latency MAC for tree-based data gathering in sensor networks. In: Wireless Communications and Mobile Computing, vol. 7, pp. 863–875, September 2007

8. Sun, Y., Du, S., Gurewitz, O., Johnson, D.B.: DW-MAC: A low latency, energy efficient demand-wakeup MAC protocol for wireless sensor networks. In: ACM MobiHoc (2008)

9. Choi, L., Lee, S.H., Jun, J.A.: SPEED-MAC: Speedy and energy efficient data delivery MAC protocol for real-time sensor network applications. In: Proceeding of the International Conference on Communications (ICC), pp. 1–6, May 2010

10. Wen-Zhan, S., Renjie, H., Behrooz, S., Richard, L.: Treemac: localized TDMA MAC protocol for real-time high-data-rate sensor networks. In: Pervasive and Mobile Computing, pp. 750–765, December 7, 2009

11. Ozlem, D.I., Lodewijk, V.H., Pierre, J., Paul, H.: MC-LMAC: A multi-channel MAC protocol for wireless sensor networks. In: Ad Hoc Networks, vol. 9. Elsevier (2011)

12. Zhao, Y.Z., Miao, C.Y., Ma, M.: An energy-efficient self-adaptive duty cycle MAC protocol for traffic-dynamic wireless sensor networks. In: Wireless Personal Communications, pp. 1287–1315 (2012)

13. Hoon, O., Trung-Dinh, H.: A demand-based slot assignment algorithm for energy-aware reliable data transmission in wireless sensor networks. In: Wireless Networks (2012)

14. Deng, X., Yang, Y.: Cluster communication synchronization in delay-sensitive wireless sensor networks. In: IEEE International Conference on Distributed Computing in Sensor Systems, pp. 36–43 (2013)

15. Ganeriwal, S., Tsigkogiannis, I., Shim, H., Tsiatsis, V., Srivastava, M.B., Ganesan, D.: Estimating clock uncertainty for efficient duty-cycling in sensor networks. IEEE/ACM Transactions on Networking (2009)

16. Polastre, J., Hill, J., Culler, D.: Versatile low power media access for wireless sensor networks. In: ACM Sensys, November 2004

17. Buettner, M., Gary, Y., Anderson, V.E., Han, R.: X-MAC: A short preamble MAC protocol for duty-cycled wireless sensor networks. In: ACM Sensys, November 2006

18. Tom, P., Gertjan, H., Maarten, B., Koen, L.: The MAC framework: redefining MAC protocols for wireless sensor networks. In: Wireless Networks, pp. 2013–2029 (2010)

19. El-Hoiydi, A., Decotignie, J.-D.: WiseMAC: An ultra low power MAC protocol for multi-hop wireless sensor networks. In: Nikoletseas, S.E., Rolim, J.D.P. (eds.) ALGOSENSORS 2004. LNCS, vol. 3121, pp. 18–31. Springer, Heidelberg (2004)

20. Li, Z., Li, M., Lui, Y.: Towards energy-fairness in asynchronous duty-cycling sensor networks. ACM Transactions on Sensor Networks (TOSN) 10, April 2014

21. Sun, Y., Gurewitz, O., Johnson, D.B.: RI-MAC: a receiver-initiated asynchronous duty cycle MAC protocol for dynamic traffic loads in wireless sensor networks. In: ACM Sensys (2008)

22. Sun, Y., Gurewitz, O., Du, S., Tang, L., Johnson, D.B.: ADB: an efficient multihop broadcast protocol based on asynchronous duty-cycling in wireless sensor networks. In: ACM Sensys, pp. 43–56 (2009)

23. Tang, L., Sun, Y., Gurewitz, O., Johnson, D.B.: PW-MAC: An energy-efficient predictive-wakeup MAC protocol for wireless sensor networks. In: INFOCOM, pp. 1305–1313 (2011)

24. Tang, L., Sun, Y., Gurewitz, O., Du, S., Johnson, D.B.: EM-MAC: A dynamic multichannel energy-efficient MAC protocol for wireless sensor networks, p. 23. ACM (2011)

25. Tang, H., Sun, C., Liu, Y., Fan, B.: Low-latency asynchronous duty-cycle MAC protocol for burst traffic in wireless sensor networks. In: IWCMC 2013, pp. 412–417, July 2013
26. Aby, A.T., Guitton, A., Misson, M.: Asynchronous blind MAC protocol for wireless sensor networks. In: IWCMC (International Wireless Communications and Mobile Computing Conference) (2014)
27. ZigBee, ZigBee Specification, ZigBee Standards Organization, Standard ZigBee 053474r17, January 2008
28. Perkins, C., Belding-Royer, E., Das, S.: Ad hoc on-demand distance vector (AODV) routing. IETF Request For Comments 3561, July 2003
29. Network simulator 2 (2002). http://www.isi.edu.nsnam/ns

High Adaptive MAC Protocol for Dense RFID reader-to-reader Networks

Ibrahim Amadou[1,2] and Nathalie Mitton[1]

[1] Inria Lille - Nord Europe - France,
`firstname.lastname@inria.fr`,
[2] LAMIH, University of Valenciennes, France
`firstname.lastname@univ-valenciennes.fr`

Abstract. This paper proposes a *high adaptive contention-based medium access control (HAMAC)* protocol that considerably reduces RFID readers collision problems in a large-scale dynamic RFID system. HAMAC is based only on realistic assumptions that can be experimented and does not require any additional components on RFID reader in order to improve the performance in terms of throughput, fairness and coverage. The central idea of the HAMAC is for the RFID reader to use a WSN-like CSMA approach and to set its initial backoff counter to the maximum value that allows the system to mitigate collision. Then, according to the network congestion on physical channels the reader tries to dynamically control its contention window by *linear decreasing* on selected physical channel or *multiplicative decreasing* after scanning all available physical channels. Extensive simulations are proposed to highlight the performance of HAMAC compared to literature's work where both readers and tags are mobile. Simulation results show the effectiveness and robustness of the proposed anti-collision protocol in terms of network throughput, fairness and coverage.

Keywords: RFID systems, Medium Access Control (MAC), Network protocol design, Anti-collision protocol, Capacity, Fairness.

1 Introduction

Most radio frequency identification applications, such as supply markets, localization and objects tracking, activity monitoring and access control, etc., use passive RFID tags, which communicate with the RFID reader by modulating its reflection coefficient (backward link) to incoming modulated RF signal from the reader (forward link). However, unlike the traditional radio communication systems, in such systems, the RF signal does not provide reciprocity between forward and backward links because the reflected RF signal from a tag is inversely proportional to the fourth power of the distance between reader and tag [11]. This link unbalance requires in above large-scale applications of RFID systems to deploy a large number of RFID readers allowing the coverage of the interested environment. A direct consequence of this feature deployment is the operation within the closest proximity of several tens or hundreds of readers in

© Institute for Computer Sciences, Social Informatics and Telecommunications Engineering 2015
N. Mitton et al. (Eds.): AdHocNets 2015, LNICST 155, pp. 82–93, 2015.
DOI: 10.1007/978-3-319-25067-0_7

order to overcome the shortcoming of the backward communication distance. However, due to readers close proximity, when nearby readers simultaneously try to communicate with tags located within their *interrogation range*, serious interference problems may occur on tags. This is mainly due to the overlapping of readers' fields. Such interferences may cause signal collisions that lead to the reading throughput barrier and degrade the system performance. Furthermore, when mobility is also considered in RFID systems because it extends coverage, facilitates inventory or stock and avoids installation and maintenance costs, the performance drops significantly due to both the interference and classical *hidden node* problems that can frequently appear.

In the literature, collision problems can be broadly classified into two categories. The first category, called *tag-to-tag* collision [9] occurs when multiple tags try to respond simultaneously to a reader *query*. This category is considered to be solved and is part of patents developed by EPCglobal standard [1]. While the second category, called *reader-to-reader collision* (RRC) and *multiple reader-to-tag collision* (RTC), obtained few attention because previous applications of RFID systems considered only a reader with several tags, the design of an efficient reader anti-collision protocol has emerged as the most interesting research issues in recent years.

The state-of-the-art protocols can be broadly classified as CSMA-based [2–4] and activity scheduling based [5, 6, 8] through time division, frequency or by putting together both approaches. The former approach is considered as an efficient and more adaptive approach in large-scale RFID reader networks because it is *full-distributed* algorithm and it does need neither synchronization nor additional resource (e.g. server) like in the latter approach. However, the existing protocols still suffer from traditional *backoff scheme* in dense RFID networks as it is recently observed in NFRA [6] and GDRA [5]. To the best of our knowledge, the design of an efficient anti-collision protocol with an efficient backoff algorithm is still missing and this is the focus of our paper.

This paper presents *High Adaptive MAC (HAMAC)* a distributed CSMA-based anti-collision protocol. HAMAC adapts the reader behavior according to the network congestion on multichannel dense RFID networks. It operates by dynamically controlling the reader contention window through *linear decreasing scheme* on selected physical channel or *multiplicative decreasing scheme* after scanning all available physical channels. To cope with the collision problem brought by mobility, HAMAC borrows the idea of *control channel* from [3]. HAMAC improves the performance such as throughput, fairness behavior during channel access in large-scale RFID system.

The rest of this paper is organized as follows. Section 2 formally defines our objective, the collision problem in RFID system and introduces the system model. Section 3 presents our new anti-collision protocol. In Section 4, we show simulation results to validate the accuracy of our model under various RFID environment scenarios and according to several criteria. Finally, Section 5 concludes by discussing future research direction.

2   Preliminaries

In this section, we formally define the collision problem in RFID systems, our objectives and introduce the underlying modeling assumptions.

2.1   Problem Statement

Single Radio Channel. In passive RFID, tags have no energy embedded. They are activated only when they pass through the electromagnetic field of a reader. When a wave bounces on a tag, the reader can read data stored in the tag [7]. However, when a tag enters an interference area, reader electromagnetic fields will overlap, transmitted signals will collide thus, tags will be unable to answer readers queries. This is called reader collision. The tag then becomes unresponsive and according to the kind of tags, may not be detected until it leaves all readers fields (and not just the interference area). It will be responsive again once it enters an area where there is no active field. So, on Figure 1a, if $R1$ and $R2$ are activated at the same time, $tag1$ will not be read. This is called *multiple Reader-to-Tag Collision (RTC)* and can occur only if the distance between operating readers is lower than $2 \times d_{RT}$ (e.g. d_{RT} is *reader-to-tag reading* range). It can be avoided by making them to operate onto different time-slots. Note that all tags are not impacted but only the ones in overlapping areas. For instance, $tag2$ and $tag3$ will still be successfully read by readers $R2$ and $R1$ respectively. However, in practice this does not hold true. Because, even when it has no overlapping areas and the distance is higher than $2 \times d_{RT}$, but less than or equal to the interference range (i.e. d_{RR}), if they operate at the same time, collison can occur at readers side. It is called *Reader-to-Reader Collision (RRC)* and can occur when $tag2$ (respectively $tag3$) answer interferes with the $R1$ (respectively $R2$) query. It is illustrated by the Figure 1b and can be avoided by using different channel frequencies or time-slots or by combining together both.

Multichannel Radio Network. In a multichannel network scheme, readers could use different channels to read the tags but still this does not prevent all collisions [2]. To better illustrate it, let's consider Figure 1c. On this figure, dotted lines represent the communication links between readers, small circles display the reader's reading range, dotted circles show the interference range of adjacent channels and big circles illustrate the reader's interference range. Readers $R1$ and $R2$ can communicate in a wireless adhoc manner and they are in communication range of each other, i.e. $d_{R1R2} < d_{RR}$ where d_{R1R2} is the Euclidean distance between $R1$ and $R2$.

In a multichannel RFID network, if two readers use the same frequency to read tags, whatever the distance between them, tags laying on the overlapping area of their fields will not be read. (On Figure 1c-1d, $tag1$, $tag2$ and $tag3$ will not be read if $R1$ and $R1$ use the same frequency at the same time). But, if two readers use different reading channels, even if they are active at the same time, tags laying in the overlapping area of their fields will be successfully read if and only the distance between the readers is larger than $3.3 \times d_{RT}$. For instance, on Figure 1c, even if $R1$ and $R2$ use different frequencies to interrogate tags, if they are activated at the same time, they will still collide since they are too close to each other. But, if $R1$ and $R2$ use different channels, as illustrated by Figure 1d, their tags will be successfully read.

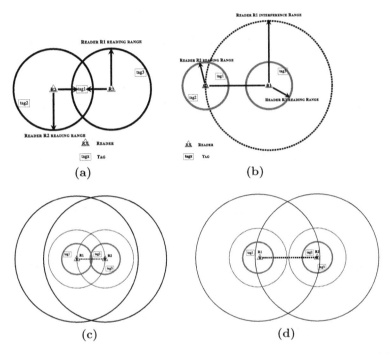

Fig. 1. (a) Multiple Reader-to-Tag Collision, (b) Reader-to-Reader Collision, (c) Multichannel Reader-to-Reader interference, (d) Multichannel Reader Reading

HAMAC will address both RTC and RRC in a multichannel environment, taking advantage of all inherent physical properties and optimizing the system performances.

2.2 System Model and Assumptions

We consider a large-scale mobile RFID system with multiple readers and homogeneous local density of RFID tags within the interrogation area. We assume that both readers and tags are mobile according to random mobility model. Readers' communication range is assumed to be the same. We assume that readers have two wireless interfaces. Similar to ETSI EN 302 208-1 regulation [4], in this paper, we assume the use of multichannel network scheme. Thus, we assume the use of f_{max} data channels on the first radio interface. According to this regulation, we assume that a reader has output power of 2 Watt Effective Radiated Power (ERP). This limits the *reader-to-tags* read range (d_{RT}) to a maximum distance of 10 meters while *reader-to-reader* interference range (d_{RR}) may reach 1000 meters [12]. Since mobility is considered in this paper, we assume that the second radio interface is used by all readers to send a *control channel*. To save energy, we assume that it is switched on only during the *reader-to-tags* reading process. This interface, which operates on a different channel, is used only during *reader-to-tags* communication. It consists in sending periodically an advertisement messages up to $3.3 \times d_{RT}$ as defined in [2]. Our aim is to cope with the *multiple reader-to-tag collision (RTC)*, from tag point of view, when closest readers are operating on different data channels. Since the advertisement channel is shared by all operating readers, they are able to detect their transmissions and thus, to re-schedule quickly their activities in order to minimize a collision impact. Therefore, in order to limit the occurrence of adjacent channel interference and to avoid undecodable radio frequency signals inside tags, the distance between two closest readers must be at least $3.3 \times d_{RT}$ further away.

2.3   Motivations and Objective

Motivations and State of the Art
The issue of reader collision problem has been extensively studied in the context of RFID system [2–6, 8], where the main objective was to maximize network throughput while trying to mitigate MAC-level interference. These approaches can be broadly classified as CSMA-based [2–4] and activity scheduling [5, 6, 8] through time division (TDMA), frequency division (FDMA) or by putting together both approaches. To achieve this objective, the former approach is considered a more suitable solution and more adaptive approach for large-scale RFID networks because it is full-distributed algorithm and scalable, it does need neither synchronization nor additional resource such as centralized server which can address the synchronization problem or the use of bistatic antenna [5] in order to detect collision, in the latter approach. Although some activity scheduling approaches are also based on distributed TDMA algorithm [8], these protocols are based on an unrealistic radio channel assumption when collision appears. They basically assume that a reader is able to detect a collision, so that readers can randomly select different slots during the next round. Note that in this category, communication is organized in groups of timeslots called rounds. As a consequence, the latency of tags' coverage gradually increases. To the best of our knowledge, GDRA [5] is the only one that overcomes this unrealistic assumption by using a bistatic antenna. It is proposed to be compliant with the EPCglobal standard and ETSI EN 302 208-1 regulation and to minimize the reader collision by using SIFT [10] probability distribution function to choose the timeslot. However, as we have previously shown in [13], the use of the geometric distribution only does not totally eliminate collisions. Moreover, by reducing the contention window size at the minimum value (e.g. 32) order to minimize the delay, GDRA performs poorly in terms of collision. In contrast to minimizing

this parameter, the achieved throughput also decreases due to the contention latency. So, there is a tradeoff in such conditions.

Even if the former approach [2–4] has been proposed in order to cope with the activity scheduling protocols weakness, however, all these protocols still suffer from traditional *backoff scheme* when the number of readers increases in the system. Because the maximum contention window size is set to a time, which is proportional to twice the time to read a tag in the worse case scenario [4]. In the existing CSMA-based approach, how to set the backoff algorithm during channel access in order to make them efficient, however, is far less investigated. They use an arbitrary value without any discussion about its impact on the performance. Moreover, to improve the read tags size, [2] proposed to use a *forwarding mechanism* between readers. Thus, is not acceptable in real RFID system and can increase the design complexity. By inspiring from MANET CSMA-based protocols, that have already investigated this problem and have proved their efficiency, we have adapted and characterized them in RFID system in [13]. Our aim was to mitigate both reader-to-reader collision (RRC) and multiple reader-to-tags collision (RTC) by using together a multichannel mechanism and efficient backoff algorithm. Thus, according to these observations, we plan to propose, in this paper, a new CSMA-based protocol, that outperforms most of existing protocols such as GDRA [5]. It should perform efficiently regardless of the radio frequency (RF) resource because RF spectrum is a scarce and expensive resource that needs to be managed carefully.

Objective

Our objective is to propose an efficient, fair and scalable full-distributed CSMA-based protocol, called *high adaptive medium access control (HAMAC)*, in large-scale mobile RFID system. HAMAC takes advantages of the CSMA approach together with the multichannel characteristics. To the best of our knowledge, HAMAC is the first one to cope with the fact that multichannel use does not prevent from all collisions and takes advantage of the different properties and features.

3 Design of HAMAC Protocol

3.1 Overview of HAMAC

With respect to the problem statement, in order to optimize the reading throughput, HAMAC is split into two parts that are detailed in this section. The idea is to first select a channel which is not used by neighboring readers in order to limit the number of collisions. This is the purpose of the first algorithm, HAMAC-channel. Then, once a channel is selected, HAMAC aims to prevent from colliding with close readers which can collide even if they use a different channel. This is the purpose of the second algorithm HAMAC-reading. Table 1 lists the notations used in the description of HAMAC protocol.

In CSMA-based protocol, every reader contends for its own medium access opportunity independently. We therefore describe below how a reader can gain

Table 1. Notations Used in HAMAC's algorithms

Symbols	Notations
r_x	Reader x
f^{adv}	Advertisement channel frequency
f_x^d	Data channel frequency of reader x
f_x^u	The set of occupied channel frequency during carry sensing (CS) of reader x
CW_x	Backoff counter value of reader x
CW_x^r	The remaining backoff counter value of the reader x
CW_{max}	The maximum backoff counter value
R_{adv}	Advertisement message transmission range
d_{RT}	Tags reading range
d_{RR}	Reader communication range

the data channel access in its vicinity. The basic idea operation of HAMAC can be subdivided in two parts.

3.2   Algorithm 1 - HAMAC-channel

Before beginning tags reading process, the reader first sets the initial parameters to default value (e.g. $W_{max} = 1024$), randomly selects its data channel frequency among the available channel lists $[1 : f_{max}]$ and its backoff counter over an interval $[0 : 1023]$ and sets the occupied channel frequency to an empty set (lines $1-6$). Then, it begins to listen the selected data channel by decreasing its backoff counter each timeslot (e.g. $500\mu s$). Two actions can occur:

- In the best case, the selected data channel remains *idle* during the listen process and the reader decreases each timeslot its backoff counter until it reaches zero (lines 9-10). Then, algorithm 2 is called in order to process the second part of the HAMAC operation (lines 23).
- The selected data channel is busy, this means that the condition of line 9 is *false*. In such case, the reader checks if its occupied channel frequency list was reached its maximum value (line 12). If this condition of line 12 is satisfied, the reader adds this frequency identifier in the list of occupied channel frequency and randomly selects a new channel frequency, which it is not in the occupied channel frequency list, and goes back to the line 8 to continue the listen process on the new selected channel (lines 11-16). Otherwise, the condition of line 12 is not satisfied. The reader reaches its maximum occupied channel frequency value, saves its backoff counter in its remaining backoff counter and divides by two its maximum backoff counter (lines 17-18).

Then, the reader checks if the minimum backoff counter value is reached (line 19). If this condition is false, the reader jumps to the process of line 4 and repeats the same process again until it gains the channel by jumping to algorithm 2 or it loses by reaching the minimum backoff counter. For both conditions, line 19 is false and the reader lost by reaching the minimum backoff counter, it jumps to line 1 and repeats all the process of channel access until the channel becomes idle.

Algorithm 1. High Adaptive MAC Anti-Collision Protocol operating for the reader r_i

---

1: **Set** reader r_i's **state** to IDLE
2: $CW_{max} \leftarrow 1024$
3: $CW_i^r \leftarrow 1024$
4: $CW_i \leftarrow MIN\{CW_i^r, random(0, CW_{max})\}$
5: $f_i^d \leftarrow (int)random(1, f_{max})$
6: $f_i^u \leftarrow \emptyset$
7: **Data Channel Access Process:**
8: **while** $CW_i \neq 0$ **do**
9:     **if** $(CS(f_i^d) == IDLE)$ **then**
10:         $CW_i \leftarrow CW_i - 1$
11:     **else**
12:         **while** $| f_i^u | \neq f_{max}$ **do**
13:             **Add** f_i^d to f_i^u
14:             **while** $(f_i^d = (int)random(1, f_{max})) \in f_i^u$ **do**
15:                 $f_i^d = (int)random(1, f_{max}))$
16:             go to 8
17:         $CW_i^r \leftarrow CW_i$
18:         $CW_{max} \leftarrow \frac{CW_{max}}{2}$
19:         **if** $(CW_{max} > 32)$ **then**
20:             go to 4
21:         **else**
22:             go to 1
23: CALL *Read tags subroutine*(f_i^d)

3.3 Algorithm 2 HAMAC-Reading

By calling algorithm 2 subroutine, this means that the reader have successfully gained its data channel frequency. Here, it first switches on the second radio interface, initializes its transmission power value so that the maximum transmission range is $3.3 \times d_{RT}$ [2], sets the new backoff counter to 20 timeslots that corresponds to twice the advertisement message period and begins to listen on the advertisement channel frequency (lines 1-8). Two actions can occur:

- In the best case, the reader finishes its backoff counter on advertisement channel and sends its first advertisement message in order to avoid the nearest readers to try gaining the channel, schedules periodically the advertisement message transmission with $5ms$ as period and begins the tags reading process. The tags reading process depends on its tags' neighborhood size (lines 7-9 and lines 12-14).

- Otherwise, the channel is occupied by a nearest reader in its local environment, the reader jumps to line 4 and repeats the same process until the channel becomes idle.

Algorithm 2. Read tags subroutine(f_i^d)

1: **Switch on the advertisement radio channel interface**
2: **Set** f^{adv}'s transmission power to a value so that its communication range $R_{adv} \longleftarrow 3.3 \times d_{RT}$
3: $CW_i^r \leftarrow 20$ ▷ Set the backoff counter twice
4: tag reading period
5: **Advertisement Channel Access Process**
6: **while** $CW_i \neq 0$ **do**
7:     **if** $(\text{CS}(f_i^{adv}) == \text{IDLE})$ **then**
8:         $CW_i \longleftarrow CW_i - 1$
9:     **else**
10:         go to 3   ▷ Repeat this process until the selected channel becomes free
11: Send Advertisement message up to $3.3 \times d_{RT}$
12: Scheduler a periodic Advertisement Transmission each $5ms$
13: **Read tags subroutine on data channel on** f_i^d

---

4   Performance Evaluation

In order to highlight the benefit brought by the proposed protocol, we implemented *HAMAC* and *GDRA* [5] on WSNet [1], an event-driven simulator and fairly evaluate their performance under various network scenarios. For GDRA, the protocol specification and parameter settings follow the recommendation of [5]. We consider a dense and mobile RFID system where both readers and tags are randomly deployed with uniform distribution on a 1000×1000 square network. We use the *random waypoint model* as mobility model, where V_{max}^{reader} and V_{max}^{tag} are respectively reader and tag's speeds. V_{max}^{reader} is twice the tag's speed, which is $10km/h$. Readers and tags's pause time are respectively set to $2s$ and $10s$, because in the most RFID system, tags mobility is very rare, while reader can be moved more frequently in order to deal with uncovered area. We assume that the time necessary for reading one tag is about $5ms$ and $460ms$ is the maximum time that reader can spend to read tags in its reading range. Each simulation run lasts for 500 seconds, and each data point is an average of 50 simulation runs. Table 2 sums up all parameters.

---

[1] WSNet:http://wsnet.gforge.inria.fr/

Table 2. Simulation models parameters

HAMAC Parameters		GDRA [5] Parameters	
Parameters	Value	Parameters	Value
f_{max}	4	AC Packet	2.83 ms
Advertisement packet	34 m	Beacon Packet	0.3 ms
Trans. range (R_{adv})		Contention Window Size	32
Timeslot size (T_{slot})	$500\mu s$	Timeslot size (T_{slot})	5ms

4.1 Results

The section presents the simulation results. It first introduces the performance evaluation of HAMAC and GDRA in regardless the number of tags deployed in the network. Our aim is to show how efficient is the proposed protocol compared to GDRA according to some traditionnal performance evaluation metrics. In this scenario, 100 to 500 readers are deployed. We then present the reading performance metrics' results where 100 to 400 readers and 100 tags are deployed. The throughputs for HAMAC and GDRA [5] are depicted in Figure (2a) for different network density. We defined the throughput as the ratio of the average number of successful queries to read tags per reader over the simulation duration. The higher system throughput, the more efficient protocol. As the results

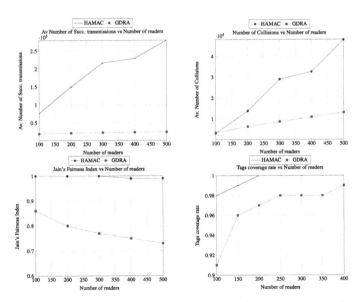

Fig. 2. Performance of HAMAC and GDRA protocols. (2a) Throughput, (2b) Number of collisions, (2c) Jain's Fairness Index and (2d) Number of covered tags vs The number of readers

shown, HAMAC has a throughput that is nearly independent of the number of readers with HAMAC achieving much better performance than GDRA [5] protocol. Moreover, as the density increases, the throughput of HAMAC gradually increases, while GDRA presents a performance which slightly increases by 3%. The gap observed in this work can be mainly explained by the use of a high adaptive maximum backoff algorithm combined with the beaconing mechanism, which is used to cope with the mobility impact and interference inside tag when nearest readers operate on adjacent channel. Fig. (2b) shows the number of collisions based on the number of readers. Whatever the network density, the results show that GDRA outperforms HAMAC. However, as we have previously observed with the throughput, HAMAC has twelve times more throughput than GDRA. Thus, by basing our analysis only on this amount of successful queries to read tags sent by of HAMAC, we can intuitively conclude that HAMAC outperforms GDRA. Fig. (2c) exhibits the Jain's fairness Index based on the number of readers in the system. This index allows to show how fair is the access to the transmission medium among readers. Because HAMAC uses an adaptive algorithm for accessing the channel, which tries to dynamically control its contention window, by *linear decreasing* on selected physical channel or *multiplicative decreasing* after scanning all available physical channels, according to the network congestion on channels, it presents a powerful results in term of fairness compared to GDRA which uses an unfair SIFT distribution as it is already shown in [10,13]. HAMAC has a gain that is 25% greater than GDRA's gain. Fig. (2d) illustrates the average number of covered tags according to the number of readers in the system. The high performances observed with HAMAC is obviously confirmed by these results. It displays growing performance that reach 100% of covered tags when the number of reader reaches 200. While GDRA presents a performance that is 98% slightly more.

5   Discussion and Conclusions

This paper presents *high adaptive MAC* (HAMAC), a distributed CSMA-based MAC protocol for mitigating reader collision problems in dense RFID systems. HAMAC is a simple and effective approach that outperforms the state-of-art proposals regarding to the main performance criterias such as the throughput, the fairness and the reading performance such as the percentage of successful reading tags. Unlike the existing approaches, HAMAC incurs no extra cost in terms of additional resources or unrealistic assumptions, and is compliant with the EPCglobal and ETSI EN 302 208 standards. Therefore, HAMAC takes advantage of the multichannel characteristics by maximizing the network throughput and mitigating a part of happened collision. HAMAC adapts the reader behavior according to the network congestion on multichannels dense RFID network. It operates by dynamically controlling the reader contention window through *linear decreasing scheme* on selected physical channel or *multiplicative decreasing scheme* after scanning all available physical channels. To cope with the collision problem brought by mobility during the reading process, HAMAC periodically sends an *advertisement message* over the *control channel*. Our extensive simulations on WSNet highlights significant performance gain of HAMAC over GDRA [5], which is presented as the most powerful reader-to-reader anti-collision protocol.

The next steps of this work will include its performance evaluation in real RFID testbed in order to really confirm the simulations performance in terms of the throughput, fairness, collision mitigating efficiency and reading performance.

Acknowledgments. This work is partially supported by a grant from CPER Nord-Pas-de-Calais/FEDER Campus Intelligence Ambiante.

References

1. EPCglobal Standard specification. EPC TM radio-frequency identity protocols class-1 generation-2 UHF RFID protocol for communications at 860 Mhz - 960 Mhz version 1.2.0 (2007)
2. Yu, J., Lee, W.: GENTLE: Reducing reader collision in mobile RFID networks. In: The 4th Intern. Conf. on MSN (2008)
3. Birari, S.M., Iyer, S.: PULSE: A MAC protocol for RFID networks. In: Enokido, T., Yan, L., Xiao, B., Kim, D.Y., Dai, Y.-S., Yang, L.T. (eds.) EUC Workshops 2005. LNCS, vol. 3823, pp. 1036–1046. Springer, Heidelberg (2005)
4. ETSI EN 302 208-1 Version 1.4.1 2011. www.etsi.org
5. Bueno-Delgado, M.V., Ferrero, R., Gandino, F., Pavon-Marino, P., Rebaudengo, M.: A Geometric Distribution Reader Anti-Collision Protocol for RFID Dense Reader Environments. IEEE Trans. Automa. Science 10(2), 296–306 (2013)
6. Eom, J.-B., Yim, S.-B., Lee, T.-J.: An Efficient Reader Anticollision Algorithm in Dense RFID Networks With Mobile RFID Readers. Trans. Ind. Electron. 56(7), 2326–2336 (2009)
7. Finkenzeller, K.: RFID Handbook: Fundamentals and Applications in Contactless Smart Cards and Identification, chapter 3. John Wiley & Sons (2003)
8. Gandino, F., Ferrero, R., Montrucchio, B., Rebaudengo, M.: DCNS: an Adaptable High Throughput RFID Reader-to-Reader Anti-collision Protocol. IEEE Trans. Parall. Distr. Syst. 99, 1045–9219 (2012)
9. Simplot-Ryl, D., Stojmenovic, I., Micic, A., Nayak, A.: A hybrid randomized protocol for RFID tag identification. Sensor Review 26(2), 147–154 (2006)
10. Jamieson, K., Balakrishnan, H., Tay, Y.C.: Sift: A MAC protocol for event-driven wireless sensor networks. In: Römer, K., Karl, H., Mattern, F. (eds.) EWSN 2006. LNCS, vol. 3868, pp. 260–275. Springer, Heidelberg (2006)
11. Kim, D.-Y., Yoon, H.-G., Jang, B.-J., Yook, J.-G.: Interference analysis of UHF RFID systems. Progress in Electromagnetics Research B 4, 115–126 (2008)
12. Leong, K.S., Leng Ng, M., Cole, P.H.: The reader collision problem in RFID systems. In: Proc. IEEE MAPE (2005)
13. Amadou, I., Mbacké, A.A., Mitton, N.: How to improve CSMA-based MAC protocol for dense RFID reader-to-reader networks? In: Guo, S., Lloret, J., Manzoni, P., Ruehrup, S. (eds.) ADHOC-NOW 2014. LNCS, vol. 8487, pp. 183–196. Springer, Heidelberg (2014)

A Probabilistic Interest Forwarding Protocol for Named Data Delay Tolerant Networks

Paulo Duarte, Joaquim Macedo, Antonio Duarte Costa,
Maria João Nicolau, and Alexandre Santos

Centro ALGORITMI, Universidade do Minho, Portugal
{a58655@alunos,macedo@di,costa@di,joao@dsi,alex@di}.uminho.pt

Abstract. Delay Tolerant Networks (DTN) were designed to allow delayed communications in mobile wireless scenarios where direct end-to-end connectivity is not possible. Nodes store and carry packets, deciding whether to forward them or not on each opportunistic contact they eventually establish in the near future. Recently, Named Data Networking (NDN) have emerged as a completely new paradigm for future networks. Instead of being treated as source or destination identifiers, nodes are viewed as consumers that express interests on information or producers that provide information. Current research is carried on the combination of these two concepts, by applying data-centric approach in DTN scenarios. In this paper, a new routing protocol called PIFP (Probabilistic Interest Forwarding Protocol) is proposed, that explores the frequency of opportunistic contacts, not between the nodes themselves, but between the nodes and the information, in order to compute a delivery probability for interest and data packets in a Named Data Delay Tolerant network (ND-DTN) scenario. The protocol design and a prototype implementation for The ONE Simulator are both described. Simulation results show that PIFP presents significant improvements in terms of interest satisfaction, average delay and total cost, when compared to other ND-DTN approaches recently proposed.

1 Introduction

Delay Tolerant Networks (DTN) [3] emerged to deal with connectivity disruption in many scenarios, for instance interplanetary communications [1], military ad-hoc networks, remote places with no communication infrastructures or even in urban scenarios where portable devices carried by humans can communicate between them spontaneously. At a given time, a node may not have a path to a destination node, either because obstacles obstructed the communication or due to nodes mobility. The opportunity to a new contact may be expected (as in space orbits or public transportations) or unknown (as in human movements). All nodes must behave as routers, storing the packets and waiting for a chance to forward them to another node, either the destination node or a good intermediary candidate. For that reason, this model of communication is sometimes called by store-carry-and-forward in opposition to traditional store-and-forward model used in direct end-to-end communications.

The most challenging problem in DTN is how to route packets [13]. An epidemic approach may be used, forwarding packets on every opportunistic contact, with good

© Institute for Computer Sciences, Social Informatics and Telecommunications Engineering 2015
N. Mitton et al. (Eds.): AdHocNets 2015, LNICST 155, pp. 94–107, 2015.
DOI: 10.1007/978-3-319-25067-0_8

results in terms of delivery probability but high global network overhead. Other approaches include direct delivery, where a packet is delivered directly by the source to destination. Probabilistic approaches, based on contact history statistics, have also been experimented. One example is PROPHET (Probabilistic Routing Protocol using History of Encounters and Transitivity) [6] that computes a delivery probability $DP = P(a,b)$ for every node a and every destination b. Nodes with higher delivery probability to a destination are better forwarders. At each opportunistic contact, the two nodes exchange between them the DP vectors, and update their own information. Then, based on the final values of DP vector, the forwarding decision is taken. PROPHET provides great improvements in packet delivery ratios when compared to epidemic protocol.

Named Data Networking (NDN) [12] is a new architecture designed to meet current and future needs of the Internet. NDN shifts communication paradigm from host-centric to data-centric. This new paradigm differs from the current Internet in some respects. First, all contents are identified following a naming scheme based on URIs. Second, the communication is driven by the consumer. When a user needs data, it shows interest in it by sending an interest packet. When an interest packet reaches a node that has the desired content, a data packet is sent back. Third, storing packets on the network facilitates content delivery. NDN provides native support for mobility since there is no association between the identification and the location of information. The main components of each network node in this architecture are Forwarding Information Base (FIB), Pending Interest Table (PIT), and Content Store (CS) as shown in Figure 1.

NDN and DTN architectures have been developed for different purposes. DTN architecture is dependent on a model based on communication entities, unlike NDN architecture that focuses on data, enabling storage and reuse of data on the network. Despite of different purposes, these architectures have some similarities: flexible routing, data transport preventing loops and network packet storage. The last item is used by DTN for persistence and interruption tolerance and by NDNs to reduce latency, interruption tolerance, increase reliability and achieve higher performance.

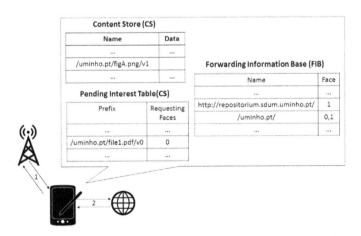

Fig. 1. NDN Architecture based on [9]

In this paper we explore new data-centric forwarding strategies for delay tolerant network scenarios. The proposed protocol, called PIFP (Probabilistic Interest Forwarding Protocol) is based on delivery probabilities computed based on statistics updated on node contacts and is inspired on a similar approach followed by PROPHET. The rest of the paper is structured as follows. Section 2 presents brief overview of relevant related work. Section 3 discusses protocol design issues in detail. Section 4 details the implementation efforts in *The ONE Simulator* [5]. Section 5 presents and discusses the results obtained in simulation. Finally the conclusions and future work in Section 6

2   Related Work

Recently, several proposals have emerged with the aim of exploring the potential of combining the concepts of NDN and DTN architectures to deal with the existing problems in DTN networks.

NAIF (Neighborhood-Aware Interest Forwarding) [11] is a routing protocol that uses named data adapted to MANETs. This approach emerges as an improvement to the original NDNF protocol [4], also based on named data. Unlike NDNF, which broadcasts interests, NAIF nodes cooperatively propagate interest packets from consumer to data sources based on forwarding statistics. A relay node decides to broadcast or drop interest packets based on data packet transmission statistics in its neighborhood.

CEDO (Content-Centric Dissemination Algorithm) [2] is an algorithm for dissemination of content in delay tolerant networks. The aim is to maximize the delivery rate in a distributed environment, where contents that can be ordered and stored have different degrees of popularity. By defining a *delivery-rate utility per content*, this protocol make appropriate decisions on scheduling and content management.

The STCR (Social-Tie based Content Retrieval) [7] is an algorithm that allows retrieval of content in Named Data Delay Tolerant Networks. Over time, nodes store information that will be used later to make forwarding decisions. Using K-mean clustering algorithm, a hierarchical graph is computed based on social ties between nodes. When there is no direct contact with the producer of the content, each node transmits the interest packet only to a node belonging to a higher hierarchy set, with higher social level.

3   PIFP Protocol Design

In this Section, we describe PIFP protocol, whose goal is to increase the number of messages delivered in a named-data network where the nodes are able to store, carry and forward messages in order to deal with frequent connection failures and long periods of time without connectivity, typical in high mobility networks.

3.1   Overview

The approach presented in this paper aims to identify the most advantageous intermediate node to forward an interest packet and it is based on the following main principles:

- The nodes presents mobility patterns and based on these patterns it is possible to predict new encounters between nodes and their content;
- A higher frequency of contact with a specific content indicates that there is a strong likelihood of a new contact with that content;
- Forwarding interests and contents based on names and not on addresses enables better strategies to data storage and reuse.

Inspired on PROPHET, PIFP uses frequency and freshness to evaluate if nodes have a strong relationship with a specific content, but in PIFP, information about the contacts between a node and a specific content is used, instead of the contacts between nodes. This is because PIFP is focused on information and not on hosts. It is assumed that if a node lies often with a content, it is very likely that it will meet again with that content in the near future.

The frequency represents how many times one node meet with one specific content. The freshness reflects how much this information is updated. These two parameters are combined in one metric, called Delivery Predictability (*DP*), which is maintained for each interest in the FIB of a node. So, every node maintains a set of Delivery Predictabilities (*DP*) on the FIB, that are updated on each encounter. The Delivery Predictability $DP(a,c)$, indicates the probability of node a to encounter again the content c.

When a node detects another node in the neighborhood, a connection is established (encounter) and the node records the timestamp of the event. After that, it uses the decay Equation 1 where $\gamma = 0.98$ is the aging constant, and κ is the number of time units (seconds) that have elapsed since the last time the metric was aged. This equation is applied to all content *DP* values that exist in the FIB of the node. *DP* value is affected due to its age. It will decrease over time.

$$DP(a,C_i) = DP(a,C_i)_{old} \times \gamma^\kappa \qquad (1)$$

After this, two types of information are exchanged between the nodes: FIB routing information and cached data summary. Then Equation 2 is used to update the *DP* value of each content within cached data summary of the other node. The idea is to increase $DP(a,C_i)$ whenever the node a meets C_i. In the first contact with the content, $DP(a,C_i)_{old}$ is 0. The variable α is a scaling factor that sets the rate at which the Delivery Predictability increases in encounters.

$$DP(a,C_i) = DP(a,C_i)_{old} + [1 - DP(a,C_i)_{old}] \times \alpha \qquad (2)$$

Through information that is exchanged by FIBs, the predictability of each node to find the contents can be updated. To do so, we can use the PROPHET transitivity property witch was adapted to handle contents. The original rule of transitivity used by PROPHET says that if a node a frequently encounters node b, and node b frequently encounters node c, then node b probably is a good node to forward packets from a destined for node c. To deal with the data-centric paradigm, this rule was rewritten in another way: in a connection between a pair of nodes a and b, if b is often in contact with content C_i, then node b will probably be a good node to forward interests belonging to node a for content C_i.

In Equation 3 we can see the result of the rewritten rule, where $DP(a,C_i)$ is the predictability of a finding C_i and $DP(b,C_i)$ is the predictability of b finding C_i. β is a scale factor that adjusts the weight of the transitive property. If β is defined as zero, the transitive property has no effect and Delivery Predictability is based only in the direct encounters with the contents. High values for β, increases the impact of the transitive property in the likelihood of delivery. In the implementation of PIFP the value set for α variable was 0.75, and value set for β was 0.25. Thus, the property of transitivity has a smaller impact when compared to the use of direct encounters with the contents. Nodes with greater delivery predictability will be those that were in direct contact with the contents.

$$DP(a, C_i) = DP(a, C_i)_{old} + [1 - DP(a, C_i)_{old}] \times DP(b, C_i) \times \beta \qquad (3)$$

The main goal of using Delivery Predictability metric is to reduce the number of interest messages sent and to improve the message delivery ratio. This is accomplished because interest messages will only be transmitted to the nodes with higher delivery predictability for that content.

3.2   Information Exchange

As mentioned earlier, each node maintains a CS and FIB table. Data packets passing through the node are temporarily kept in the CS. FIB maps a content identifier with the predictability of an encounter with the same content. During the contact period, the nodes announces its cached content name digest and a summary of its routing table with the corresponding probabilities.

Pseudocode 1. Convergence Process

 1: **for all** connections to another node **do**
 2:     apply decay equation (1) $[DP(a, C_i) = DP(a, C_i)_{old} \times \gamma^{\kappa}]$ to own DP sets
 3:     **for all** cached-content digest received from connected node b **do**
 4:         **if** there is NO match with local CS **then**
 5:             apply equation (2) $[DP(a, C_i) = DP(a, C_i)_{old} + [1 - DP(a, C_i)_{old}] \times \alpha]$
 6:             update the result into FIB
 7:     **for all** routing digests received from connected node b **do**
 8:         check my local CS and content digest from other node
 9:         **if** there is NO match with local CS **then**
10:             apply equation (3) $[DP(a, C_i) = DP(a, C_i)_{old} + [1 - DP(a, C_i)_{old}] \times DP(b, C_i) \times \beta]$
11:             update the result into FIB

At each encounter, DP values are updated as shown in Pseudocode 1. When a node receives a summary of content that the other node has cached (direct contact with data), the corresponding DP values are increased by using the Equation 2. When a node receives the routing digest from another node (transitive contact), it will also increase the DP values by applying Equation 3, but only to contents not stored in the two nodes. The calculated values are saved in FIB table for further forwarding of messages.

The process of convergence is very slow due to the long delays caused by DTNs. Over time the nodes will exchange routing information and eventually, the node will have a high knowledge of contents on the network.

3.3   Forwarding Strategy

As described above, the communication is driven by the consumers showing interest in content, i.e., when a node wants to receive data it shows interest on this data by sending one message of interest. The forwarding of interests messages is achieved based on the probability of other node to meet the content. Each node carries interest packets and forward them to a node with a higher Delivery Predictability (*DP*) for that content than itself.

Despite the existing delay in the convergence process, the nodes will have an extended knowledge about the existing contents on the network, which tends to increase the number of extra interest messages sent over the network. To reduce this number, the last *DP* for which the interest was sent is recorded in the PIT ($LastDP(C_i)$). Thus, the interest is sent only if the $DP(C_i)$ of the other node is higher than the $LastDP(C_i)$.

Pseudocode 2. Processing pending interest messages

1: **for all** connected node b **do**
2:      **for all** pending interest message in node a PIT **do**
3:          **if** $DP(b,C_i) > DP(a,C_i) \wedge DP(b,C_i) > LastDP(C_i)$ **then**
4:              add interest message in C_i to the outgoing list O
5:      **if** outgoing list O is not empty **then**
6:          order list by predictability value
7:          update *LastDP* and sends messages to the other node

---

The strategy of sending out interests showed in Pseudocode 2 is not applied when the other node has cached content for the respective interests. When a node receives the summary of data cached, it checks whether there are data that can satisfy the pending interests. If so, the respective messages of interest are sent.

Whenever a node receives an interest packet, it checks the CS table for contents corresponding to this interest. In case of content matching in the CS, the content is delivered to the other node. Otherwise, the unsatisfied interest is stored in PIT, but only if node has knowledge of the content (routing entry in FIB). Only one entry is created on the PIT for the same interest. The identifier of the node that sent the interest is also stored.

Pseudocode 3. Processing incoming interest message

1: **for all** interest packet on C_i received **do**
2:      check my local CS
3:      **if** there is a match **then**
4:          send the content message to the other node
5:      **else**
6:          check my local FIB
7:          **if** there is a match **then**
8:              add interests to the PIT

PIT also stores information about the validity of its inputs, which are discarded after expired. A Time-To-Live (TTL) is configured in interest packet and decreases over time. A routing cycle will causes the TTL to reach zero, removing the PIT entry. To relax the validity of entries in the PIT, when an existing interest packet is received, the TTL is checked and the validity of the input in the PIT is updated, by incrementing the difference between the TTL of the arrived interest packet and the current TTL of the PIT entry.

After the interest reaches the content producer, a content message is created and sent back trying to reach the consumer. Over time, interest messages are forwarded and "crumbs" are left on the network for subsequent forwarding the content message to consumers. Multiple paths are created, increasing the likelihood of reaching the consumers.

Finally, when a content packet reaches a node, the PIT table is checked for interests corresponding to it, as shown in Pseudo-code 4. If correspondence does not exist in PIT, data is simply discarded. To ensure free storage space, a life time to the contents stored in the CS is defined. In this way, the older contents are eliminated leading to contents that were requested most recently.

Pseudocode 4. PIFP: Processing incoming content message

```
1:  for all incoming content message C_i received do
2:      check my local CS and my buffer
3:      if there is a match then
4:          discard the content C_i
5:      else
6:          check my local PIT
7:          if there is a match then
8:              store the content C_i
9:              if isSubscriber() then
10:                  set satisfied interest
11:          else
12:              discard content C_i
```

Assuming the nodes have storage space available they could store the contents even if there were no correspondence in PIT. This approach is exploited by creating a variant of PIFP, called *PIFP-Proactive*, with proactive transmission and storage. This mechanism may improve performance in delivering the contents, but will increase the network load. In this variant, the mechanism for content distribution has been modified, by removing the restriction of transferring data for the same node which has received the interest. It was also removed the verification of valid PIT entries to enable the creation of new entries in CS. Thus, any content received by the node can be stored unless there is no storage space as shown in pseudo-code 5. This approach provides a proactive content delivery, spreading several replicas of the message content with the goal of reaching the node that requested the message content.

Pseudocode 5. PIPF-Proactive: Processing incoming content message

```
 1: for all incoming contente message of C_i received do
 2:     check my local CS and my buffer
 3:     if there is a match then
 4:         discard the content C_i
 5:     else
 6:         check my local PIT
 7:         if there is a match then
 8:             store the content C_i
 9:             if isSubscriber() then
10:                 set satisfied interest
11:             else if (there is enough space in my CS) then
12:                 store the content C_i
```

4 Implementation

PIFP was implemented on a specially modified version of *The ONE* (Opportunistic Network Environment simulator [5], v1.5.1 RC2), called ICONE (Information Centric ONE [8], v1.0).

The ONE is a well known DTN simulator, written in Java, originally designed for accessing the performance of DTN protocols. The approach followed was to provide only a simplified model of the lower layers (physical and logical), giving more importance to applications, routing protocols and good mobility models, either synthetic ones or based on real life traces. Settings can be adjusted to create distinct scenarios, changing the frequency, duration and other properties of opportunistic node encounters.

However, The ONE supports only a node-to-node communication model, with source and destination addresses, and has no support for the NDN paradigm. The first step was therefore to extend and modify it, in order to implement a simplified NDN model.

4.1 ICONE Overview

Figure 2 shows the architecture of ICONE with the new and modified components. Messages have to carry information names and nodes must incorporate the three basic components of NDN architecture: CS, PIT, and FIB. Forwarding decisions are based on content name matching (best match) in FIB. *NDNRouter* is a major class in this architecture. It extends *ActiveRouter* object in order to incorporate CS, PIT and FIB storage components. All specific routing strategies already implemented (*PIPF*, *PIPFProactive* and *STCR*) are subclasses of *ActiveRouter*, inheriting all basic operations on CS, PIT and FIB structures.

Entries in data structures are stored by name. Names are strings of variable and unbound length. In order to allow faster searches and also an efficient usage of memory, Counting Bloom Filters [9] were used to implement PIT, FIB and CS structures. A bloom filter consists of a bit vector of length m, initialized with all bits set to zero. Whenever a new element is added, multiple hash functions are used to compute k hash positions. The correspondent bits in those positions are set to 1. The exact same k bits

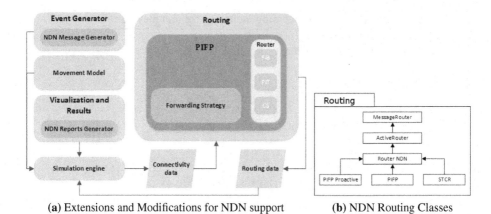

(a) Extensions and Modifications for NDN support   (b) NDN Routing Classes

Fig. 2. ICONE Framework

are verified on a element lookup operation. If they are all set to 1, there is a match with limited probability of being a "false positive". Otherwise, there is no match, with zero probability of "false negatives".

4.2 ICONE Components

A new *NDNMessage* was defined with a common set of fields. Instead of the usual "to" and "from" fields, useless in NDN networks, a *NDNMessage* contains the *ContentName*, *MessageType* and *TTL*. All messages have a finite TTL and are discarded when that TTL expires. Two types of messages were defined: *Interest* and *Data*. Consumers express their "interest" on a specific content by creating a message with type *Interest*, entering the name of content into *ContentName* field and sending it to the network. When an *Interest* message reaches a node with the content in the CS (either a producer or a caching node) a reply message of type *Data* is sent back.

Message Generator. In this paradigm, all communications are driven by consumer through the transmission of interest packets. Distinct application scenarios can therefore be created by the way consumers generate interests on data. A message generator module was created in order to generate events. Each event corresponds to the generation of an interest message by a given node. All events are generated at once, according to a set of input parameters, and stored in a trace file. During simulation, the trace file is loaded and events added to the scheduler on the right node.

Current implementation tries to mimic realistic web browsing sessions, based on the study reported in [10]. All important features were identified and are preserved by the message generator, like the number of requests per session, time between sessions and request size. In addition, data message events are also generated when a producer or intermediate caching node receives an interest whose name matches an entry. The size of data can be configured between a minimum and a maximum.

Content Store. Producers are initialized with a set of contents. The CS is populated with the contents. When an interest arrives, CS is checked to see if there is a match.

Network Faces. Unlike static networks, within a mobile ad-hoc wireless network there is no concept of face. In ICONE, the IDs of node are used as a Face. When a packet of interest arrives, the associated incoming face is the ID of the requesting node.

NDN Reports. Due to the change of paradigm, a few new reports were implemented. A set of metrics can be obtained during simulation, including the number of interest packets generated, the number of interest packets sent, the number of satisfied interests, the number of data packets sent, the number of satisfied interest in the local node, the delay and message size.

5   Performance Evaluation

PIFP was experimentally evaluated using ICONE and compared *PIFP-Proactive* and *SCTR*. *PIFP-Proactive* is a variant of *PIFP* described in previous section (see pseudocode 5). STCR was originally designed for delay-tolerant MANETS. It builds a social hierarchy and groups nodes together in clusters using the k-mean algorithm. *SCTR* was also implemented from scratch on ICONE.

To evaluate PIFP, the following metrics were used: *HitRate* (number of interests satisfied on the node and by the network), *AverageDelay* (average delay time, measured from the generation of the interest packet up to the reception of content that satisfies it), and *TotalCost* (total number of interest packets and data packets in the network).

5.1   Simulation Scenario

The proposed solution was evaluated using two different scenarios. Table 1 details the parameters for both scenarios. These two scenarios were selected in order to evaluate the performance of PIFP in dense and sparse networks. As in PROPHET, the PIFP may have a higher rate of delivery in denser networks. The convergence of the names is expected to be faster. In a sparse scenario, due to lack of connectivity, the interest rate is expected to be lower and with higher message delivery delays.

In the first scenario, a more dense opportunistic network is created, with a total of 98 nodes. Nodes consist of two groups of pedestrians (one with thirty two elements and the other with thirty), a group of cars (thirty two elements) and two groups of trains (with two trains each). Nodes move according to the map of Helsinki, Finland. Pedestrian group move according to the Shortest Path Map-Based model. Cars are forced to follow only on the roads using the same movement pattern of pedestrians. Trains use the Routed Map-Based Movement Model. In the second scenario, the total number of nodes was reduced to 49, in order to create a sparser network.

The *MessageGenerator* module was used to create a trace file modeling several user web sessions. Given a simulation time, the generator produces a number of sessions distributed along the entire time of the simulation. Each session has a number of requests. A request in this paradigm represents an interest message. When the simulation starts, the events are loaded from a file. A different message set was generated for each scenario, according to the simulation time and the number of nodes. The module is parameterized with the number of nodes in the network and the simulation time. The larger the value of these parameters, the greater the number of generated interests.

Table 1. Simulation Parameters

Parameter	Value
Simulation Time	86400s
Deployment field	4500m×3400m
Node speed	Pedestrian: 0.5 to 1.5 m/s Cars: 2.7 to 13.9 m/s Trams: 10 to 30 m/s
Request lifetime	8 hours
Radio	Bluetooth
Transmission range	Pedestrians and Cars: 10m Trams and Special Pedestrians: 1km
Transmission rate	Simple Interface: 250kbps High Speed Interface: 10Mbps
Storage capacity	Consumers: 50MB Producers: 100MB

5.2   Experimental Results

Figures 3 and 4 show the results obtained by the three different strategies (*PIFP*, *PIFP-Proactive* and *SCTR*) in the two simulation scenarios (dense and sparse).

Number of Interests Satisfied. Regarding the *HitRate*, represented in Figure 3a (dense scenario) and Figure 4a (sparse scenario), graphs show that the number of satisfied interests increases with the number of nodes in the network. Since there are more nodes

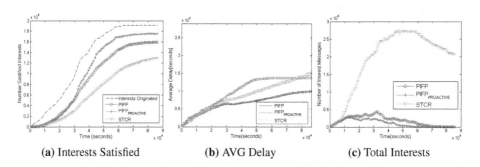

(a) Interests Satisfied   (b) AVG Delay   (c) Total Interests

Fig. 3. Results for Scenario 1 (dense)

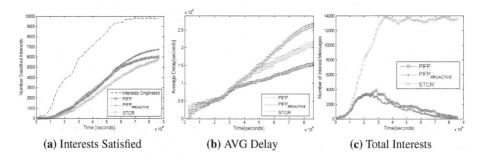

(a) Interests Satisfied   (b) AVG Delay   (c) Total Interests

Fig. 4. Results for Scenario 2 (sparse)

in the network, there is a greater number of distributed caches. Intermediate nodes, that have contents, become also content servers.

Comparing the three approaches, one can see that the *PIFP-Proactive* scheme has the highest number of satisfied interests in both scenarios. Its proactive delivery of contents creates more opportunities to reach the consumers. Proactive PIFP achieved 92% satisfaction of interests on Scenario 1 (dense). Furthermore, the PIFP overcomes STCR. The interest satisfaction rate for STCR protocol is about 70% while for PIFP is approximately 83%. In Scenario 2 (sparse), the schemes PIFP, STCR and *PIFP-Proactive* had similar behavior. The number of satisfied interests was related.

Figure 5a shows the number of interests satisfied locally by the node or by the network. When a node generates an interest, the CS is checked to see if there is any correspondence. If so, then the interest is locally satisfied. The PIFP presents a higher number of satisfied interests in the network than locally. In Proactive solution approximately 60% of interests are satisfied locally. PIFP and STCR satisfy respectively about 31% and 45% of interest in the node.

Average Delay. Figure 3b and Figure 4b illustrate the average delay over time for the three protocols. Only delays for interests satisfied with data received from the network are presented. Interests satisfied in the node itself are not included.

Once an interest packet arrives to a producer or intermediate node in procession of the content, a data message is sent back to the consumer. In the case of *PIFP-Proactive* the data is sent to any node with available cache space. In case of PIFP data is sent to nodes that have the interest in the PIT. Finally, in the case of STCR, the data is only sent to nodes with a stronger social relationship with the consumer.

Apparently, the lower average delay time should occur for the strategy that gets more data paths to the consumer, which is *PIFP-Proactive*. However, the network flood with the data sent using this strategy, limits the data storage for subsequent interests. This reason makes the average waiting time for *PIFP-Proactive* greater than the PIFP. PIFP, in turn, obtains more paths than the STCR. The amount of data in the network for the different strategies can be seen in Figure 5b.

At the beginning of simulation, the sending of interest packet by an STCR node is faster since it is made to nodes with greater centrality. Unlike STCR, PIFP sends only interest packet to a node with knowledge of the associated content. Due to the slow convergence of routing tables at beginning of simulation, many contents may be unknown. This justify the better results of STCR at beginning of simulation.

In Figure 4b(Scenario 2), the behavior was similar for all approaches. The delay was increased when compared with Figure 3b (scenario 1). This is due to the fact that the network is not as dense as in Scenario 1. The number of available paths decreases and this had an impact in the delivery of contents.

Total Cost. Regarding *TotalCost*, the number of interests in the network was evaluated in both scenarios and also the number of data packets in scenario 1.

As shown in Figure 3c and Figure 4c, STCR has an higher number of interests in the network, when compared with the remaining protocols. STCR initially transmits the interests to nodes with highest centrality and from different clusters. When the producer

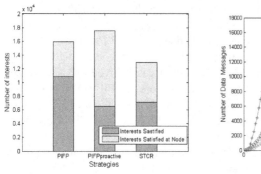
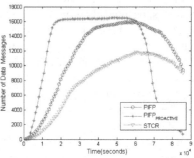

(a) Network vs Node Satisfaction   **(b)** Total number of data packets (scenario 1)

Fig. 5. Other results

is known the interest is sent to him using social relationships. Apparently, this approach makes more interest replicas than the one used by PIFP, which sends the interests only to nodes with higher predictability to reach the content. Furthermore, PIFP discards interest messages when the interest is satisfied or has a TTL expired. STCR does not discard the interest message when the TTL expires, and it is sent epidemically, which increases the number of replicas in the network.

Figure 5b presents the total number of data packets for Scenario 1 (dense). As described before, *PIFP-Proactive* sends data packets whenever the neighbors nodes have free space in cache. So this strategy has the higher number of data packets in the network. PIFP sends the data packet to all nodes with the interest in the PIT. STCR send the data packet to nodes with higher social relationship with the consumer.

6   Conclusions

In this paper, a new routing protocol called PIFP (Probabilistic Interest Forwarding Protocol) is presented. PIFP uses a probabilistic approach to forward interest in a Named Data Delay Tolerant Newtork. PIFP is inspired on PROPHET, a well known protocol for Delay Tolerant Networks. Like PROPHET, PIFP computes a delivery probability based on the history of encounters. But while PROPHET records the frequency of encounters between the node and the other nodes, PIFP records the frequency of encounters between the node and the data contents. It is therefore adapted to the named data networking paradigm. A proactive variant of PIFP protocol is also described. The main difference is that proactive version stores data packets, proactively, in all forwarding nodes that have enough free space in the cache memory. The goal is to increase data availability and reduce the delivery time to the consumer, at the expense of available storage space, and without extra communication overhead.

The performance of the new protocols was evaluated in comparison with STCR, an existing NDN forwarding mechanism for MANETs. STCR is based on social relations between devices, while PIFP constructs relationships between the devices and the contents. The three protocols were implemented in a modified version of ONE, called ICONE. ICONE results from extending and modifying ONE in order to support the named data paradigm. For the two simulated scenarios (dense and sparse), results obtained show that the proposed PIFP protocols present better values in terms of the number of interest satisfied, the average delay and total number of interest packets in network. STCR obtains better values on the total number of data packets transmitted in the network. More extensive evaluation, in distinct scenarios, is however required.

As future work, we plan to use this named data based protocol in scenarios with selfish nodes. Knowing in advance the interests of a given node may reduce the uncertainty about his behavior when processing a given packet.

Acknowledgments. This work has been supported by FCT – Fundação para Ciência e Tecnologia, in the scope of the project: UID/CEC/00319/2013.

References

1. Burleigh, S., Hooke, A., Torgerson, L., Fall, K., Cerf, V., Durst, B., Scott, K., Weiss, H.: Delay-tolerant networking: An approach to interplanetary internet. IEEE Commun. Magazine 41(6), 128–136 (2003)
2. De Meneses Neves Ramos Dos Santos, F., Ertl, B., Barakat, C., Spyropoulos, T., Turletti, T.: CEDO: content-centric dissemination slgorithm for delay-tolerant networks. In: Proceedings of ACM/IEEE MSWiM 2013, pp. 377–386. ACM, November 2013
3. Fall, K.: A delay tolerant network architecture for challenged internets. In: Proceedings of SIGCOMM 2003, p. 27. ACM Press (2003)
4. Jacobson, V., Smetters, D.K., Thornton, J.D., Plass, M., Briggs, N., Braynard, R.: Networking named content. Communications of the ACM 55(1), 117 (2012)
5. Keränen, A., Ott, J., Kärkkäinen, T.: The ONE simulator for DTN protocol evaluation. In: Proceedings of SIMUTools 2009. ICST, New York, NY, USA, p. 55 (2009)
6. Lindgren, A., Doria, A., Schelén, O.: Probabilistic routing in intermittently connected networks. ACM SIGMOBILE Mobile Comput. and Commun. Review 7(3), 19 (2003)
7. Lu, Y., Li, X., Yu, Y.T., Gerla, M.: Information-centric delay-tolerant mobile ad-hoc networks. In: Proceedings of IEEE INFOCOM Workshops 2014, pp. 428–433. IEEE (2014)
8. Macedo, J., Costa, A., Nicolau, M.J., Santos, A.: Icone (information centric one) documentation, March 2015. http://marco.uminho.pt/projects/ICONE/
9. Quan, W., Xu, C., Guan, J., Zhang, H., Grieco, L.A.: Scalable name lookup with adaptive prefix bloom filter for named data networking. IEEE Commun. Letters 18(1), 102–105 (2014)
10. Schneider, F., Agarwal, S., Alpcan, T., Feldmann, A.: The new web: characterizing AJAX traffic. In: Claypool, M., Uhlig, S. (eds.) PAM 2008. LNCS, vol. 4979, pp. 31–40. Springer, Heidelberg (2008)
11. Yu, Y.T., Dilmaghani, R.B., Calo, S., Sanadidi, M.Y., Gerla, M.: Interest propagation in named data manets. In: Proceedings of ICNC 2013, pp. 1118–1122. IEEE, January 2013
12. Zhang, L., Afanasyev, A., Burke, J., Jacobson, V., Claffy, K., Crowley, P., Papadopoulos, C., Wang, L., Zhang, B.: Named Data Networking. ACM SIGCOMM Comput. Commun. Review 44(3), 66–73 (2014)
13. Zhang, Z.: Routing in intermittently connected mobile ad hoc networks and delay tolerant networks: overview and challenges. IEEE Commun. Surveys & Tutorials 8(1), 24–37 (2006)

Mobility in Networks

TAG: Trajectory Aware Geographical Routing in Cognitive Radio Ad Hoc Networks with UAV Nodes

Mehdi Harounabadi, André Puschmann, Oleksandr Artemenko, and Andreas Mitschele-Thiel

Integrated Communication Systems Group,
Ilmenau University of Technology, Ilmenau, Germany
{mehdi.harounabadi,andre.puschmann,
oleksandr.artemenko,mitsch}@tu-ilmenau.de

Abstract. Routing real-time packets in Cognitive Radio Ad Hoc Networks (CRAHNs) with mobile nodes is a challenging task. Mobile SUs can move into PU regions where the radio spectrum may not be accessible due to PU activity. In this case, real-time packets may be delivered to their destinations beyond their latency constraints. Unmanned Aerial Vehicles (UAVs) are mobile wireless ad hoc nodes that plan for their trajectory at any given time. In this paper, a Trajectory Aware Geographical (TAG) routing for CRAHNs with UAV nodes is proposed. TAG employs the trajectory information of UAVs and avoids selecting a UAV as a next hop if the UAV will fly inside a PU region or close to it. This strategy protects real-time packets from experiencing a long delay due to the PU activity. Our simulation results show that TAG effectively decreases the average end-to-end delay compared to Greedy geographical routing in the considered scenario.

Keywords: routing, ad hoc networks, cognitive radio, UAV, real-time.

1 Introduction

A Cognitive Radio Ad Hoc Network (CRAHN) is one example of applying cognitive radio capabilities to wireless ad hoc nodes. It consists of two types of nodes with different priorities for spectrum access. Primary Users (PUs) are licensed users and have higher priority to access the radio spectrum. On the other hand, Secondary Users (SUs) are unlicensed users and have lower priority in a CRAHN. SUs may access the licensed band opportunistically without making any harmful interference to PUs. They need to have the information about the activity and the coverage area of PUs to access the spectrum dynamically. This information can be obtained by an SU through sensing or querying a geolocation database. The geolocation database provides a radio resource map [1] for SUs to use for dynamic spectrum access. Database-assisted spectrum access has been applied in some IEEE standards such as IEEE 802.22 [2] and the recently proposed IEEE 802.11af (White-Fi) [3].

© Institute for Computer Sciences, Social Informatics and Telecommunications Engineering 2015
N. Mitton et al. (Eds.): AdHocNets 2015, LNICST 155, pp. 111–122, 2015.
DOI: 10.1007/978-3-319-25067-0_9

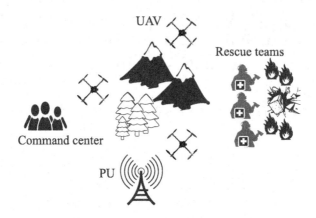

Fig. 1. A CRAHN in a disaster scenario

There are several applications for CRAHNs such as military and disaster scenarios. CRAHNs are appropriate candidates to be applied in disaster scenarios. Nodes in a CRAHN work autonomously and their dynamic spectrum access capability may increase their available radio resources in addition to the unlicensed band. In this paper, we consider the network to consist of flying Unmanned Aerial Vehicles (UAVs) in the air and a number of mobile ad hoc nodes on the ground. Figure 1 illustrates our assumption for a CRAHN in a disaster scenario.

UAVs in CRAHNs are highly mobile nodes that could be employed in a network for various missions. The missions of the UAVs in a disaster scenario are:

- Scanning disastrous area: UAVs scan a disaster area to localize wireless devices on the ground. Moreover, UAVs can construct a map of the area to be used by rescuers.
- Message ferrying: A UAV can act as a ferry in Delay Tolerant Networks (DTNs) when the network is partitioned and has a disconnected topology. In this case, a UAV flies between the location of the ground nodes which are source and destination of packets and carries the delay tolerant packets [4].
- Relaying: In multi-hop communication, UAVs can act as a relay in routing. UAVs can also be placed optimally in the air to improve the performance of the network [5].

Based on the various missions of a UAV in the network, the UAV has different mobility models for different missions. Paparazzi mobility model has been proposed in [6] for a group of UAVs. In a group of UAVs, each UAV must plan for its trajectory at any given time. It should inform its entire neighborhood about the planned trajectory. This should be done periodically by all UAVs to avoid any physical collision between them.

In our proposed routing protocol, UAVs act as relays in a CRAHN. They relay packets between ground nodes but this is not their only mission in the CRAHN.

For example, a UAV node is scanning the area or doing message ferrying while a ground node is using this UAV opportunistically to relay real-time packets.

Generally, routing in ad hoc networks can be categorized into two main classes: topology based and location based (geographical).

Topology based routing is based on the topological information of ad hoc nodes. Such a global information should be collected in one node and then an end-to-end route can be established. AODV, DSR and OLSR are some examples of topology based routing protocols in ad hoc networks [7]. These routing protocols are vulnerable to the dynamics of the network and produce large amount of overhead for route maintenance in case of frequent link breaks. Initial attempts for routing in CRAHNs were modifications on the topology based protocols like [8]. CRAHNs with UAV nodes are highly mobile and link availability is uncertain in this type of network. Therefore, adoption of the topology based protocols is not an appropriate solution.

Geographical routing is another class of routing in ad hoc networks that is based on geographical location of ad hoc nodes. It is assumed that each node obtains its position using Global Positioning System (GPS) or any other localization method. All the nodes inform their neighbors about their current position using periodic, small size beacon packets. Besides, the destination position is provided by a location service in the network. Having the position of all neighbors and the destination, a node in each hop selects the closest neighbor to the destination as the next hop to forward a packet.

The distributed decision making (hop by hop) in geographical routing makes it an appropriate candidate for CRAHNs. In case of a link break, the route maintenance can be done with less overhead in geographical routing comparing with topology based routing. However, each link break effects on packet routing latency in the network. Therefore, the routing protocols must avoid unstable links in real-time packets routing.

In a CRAHN, a mobile SU like a UAV can move inside a PU region or too close to it where the transmission of the UAV may make interference for PU receivers. In this situation, the UAV is not allowed to transmit while the PU is active. Therefore, link breaks may be more frequent when the UAV flies inside a PU region or too close to it. When a link between two nodes in a route breaks, existing packets in the buffer of the transmitter node should wait for a new link to be established. This delay may not be tolerable for real-time packets.

In this paper, a Trajectory Aware Geographical (TAG) routing protocol is proposed. In TAG, each UAV informs all its neighbors about its future position based on its planned trajectory. Knowing the future position of all neighbors, a UAV forwards a real-time packet greedily if the closet neighbor to the destination is far from PU regions. On the other hand, TAG avoids greedy forwarding if the closest UAV to the destination will fly inside a PU region or too close to it in the future.

The remainder of this paper is as follows: Section 2 surveys the state-of the art for routing protocols in CRAHNs and some of the related works in UAV ad hoc networks. Section 3 describes the network model that is assumed in this paper.

TAG routing is described in Section 4. Section 5 is the performance evaluation of the proposed routing protocol and discussion. In the last section, we conclude the paper and propose the future works.

2   Related Work

In this section, we survey some of the existing geographical routing protocols in ad hoc networks and CRAHNs.

GPSR [9] is one of the first and most cited works among geographical routing protocols in ad hoc networks. In GPSR, the main metric to choose a next hop (next forwarder of a packet) is the distance to the destination. SEARCH [10] is an early work that has adopted geographical routing for CRAHNs. It uses RREQ and RREP, like AODV, to establish an end-to-end route from the source to the destination. The difference between AODV and SEARCH is that the latter does not flood the RREQ packets in the network and forwards them in a greedy manner using the geographical position of neighbor nodes. RREQ is sent in all available channels between nodes. Nodes that are located inside a PU region do not participate in the route establishment. Destination collects all the RREQ packets which have been passed through different routes and selects optimal combination of paths and channels. The main drawback of SEARCH is inherited from the topology based protocols that is the need for rerouting in case of link breaks. LAUNCH [11] is another geographical routing in CRAHNs. It uses control packets to establish a link between two nodes. In LAUNCH, a source node sends RREQ to all neighbors which are closer to the destination and waits for their RREP. Its metrics to select a node as a next hop are the distance to the destination and stability of the link regarding to the probability of PU appearance and the channel switching time. It produces high overhead for link establishment in each hop which can degrade the throughput of the network with frequent link breaks. OCR [12] is a geographical opportunistic routing in CRAHNs that considers distance, link throughput and link reliability. It applies a heuristic algorithm to find the optimized combination of next hop and channel. It repeats this algorithm for each packet. The drawback of OCR is waiting time for each packet to find an idle channel to send the request to its neighbors. TIGHT [13] is another geographical routing in CRAHNs. Authors of this work assume that each SU senses the environment and finds the location of PUs and their coverage area. SUs share this information with their neighbors. An SU selects the closest neighbor to the destination, if this neighbor is not affected by a PU. In the case, in which the greedy forwarding fails due to the closeness to a PU region, TIGHT selects next hop such that to traverse the perimeter of PU regions. It finds the shortest path to the destination without selecting nodes that are located inside a PU region. This strategy is an alternative for greedy routing and based on the current position of the nodes.

None of the mentioned works consider movement of nodes toward PU regions in CRAHNs. They select next hop based on the current position of the nodes.

Mobility of the nodes is an influencing metric on performance of a routing protocol that has been neglected in many existing works.

UAVs in a CRAHN have a planned trajectory to do their mission in a network. Based on our knowledge these mobility information have never been used in decision making of existing routing protocols. There are several works to predict next position of nodes based on the history, velocity and direction of movement but they are based on the probability and proposed for mobile nodes with unknown trajectory of mobility. Authors in [14] and [15] proposed prediction based routing in UAV ad hoc networks. They do not consider the planned trajectory of the UAVs to find the future position of a UAV. Using the planned trajectory of a UAV can provide more accurate estimation about the future position of a UAV than prediction based methods. The main contribution of this paper is to use the knowledge of the planned trajectory of UAVs in CRAHNs to route real-time packets with strict delay constraints.

3   Network Model for Disaster Scenario

In a disaster scenario as assumed in this paper, the network infrastructure has been damaged by a natural disaster like an earthquake and all nodes should work in ad hoc mode. There are some ad hoc nodes on the ground to do the rescue operations and management of these operations. Figure 1 shows rescue teams and a command center that are ad hoc nodes on the ground. There is a need for packet exchange between ad hoc nodes on the ground but the distances between these nodes are bigger than the radio transmission range. Moreover, some natural barriers avoid placing any vehicular communication node on the ground for relaying. In such a scenario, we assume that there is a group of UAVs in the air.

We also assume that UAVs plan their trajectory based on their missions. Before any movement, a UAV must inform its entire neighborhood about its flying trajectory. This should be done periodically by all UAVs to avoid any physical collision between them. We will use trajectory information in our TAG routing protocol.

Moreover, it is assumed that all the nodes are SUs (UAVs or ground nodes) and access the spectrum using a geolocation database. The geolocation database is located in each SU and provides the location of PUs and their coverage area in the network. In each geographical location, an SU queries the database using its geographical position to find out if it is allowed to use the spectrum or not.

Considering the mobility of UAVs, we classify the states of a UAV in a CRAHN regarding to its distance to the PU region.

- Far from a PU region: UAV is located far from a PU coverage area. It can receive and transmit without making any interference to the PU receivers.
- Close to a PU region: UAV is outside a PU region but its transmission range has an overlap with the PU coverage area. In this case, the UAV can receive from other UAVs (or SUs) but it is not allowed to transmit when the PU is

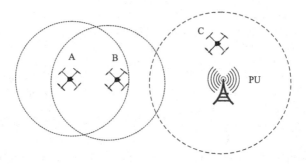

Fig. 2. States of a UAV in a CRAHN

active. The UAV may cause interference to PU receivers which are inside the PU coverage area.

– Inside a PU region: UAV is inside a PU coverage area. It is not allowed to transmit when the PU is active and may not receive from other UAVs (or SUs) due to the strong interference of the PU transmissions.

Figure 2 demonstrates UAV A, B and C together with their transmission ranges and the mentioned states for a UAV in a CRAHN. UAV_A is "Far from a PU region" and can receive from UAV_B or others. Besides, it can always transmit to UAV_B. UAV_B is "Close to a PU region". It can receive from UAV_A but it is not allowed to transmit when the PU is active. UAV_C is "Inside a PU region" and cannot transmit or receive during PU transmissions.

In our network model, we assume that the PU is highly active and when a node is inside the PU region or close to the PU region it is not allowed to transmit. In the next section, we propose our trajectory aware routing using the mobility information of the UAVs and their states in a CRAHN.

4 TAG: Trajectory Aware Geographical Routing

In a disaster scenario, different types of traffic may be forwarded between ground nodes or UAVs. The data belongs to different applications with specific requirements. One of the most common requirements of the applications is delay constraint. Considering the mobility model of a UAV and its states (mentioned in Section 3), it cannot access the radio spectrum during its flying time when it is located "inside a PU region" or "close to a PU region". Depending on the closeness of a UAV to a PU region, packets inside the buffer of the UAV may experience some queuing delays. According to the strict delay constraints for real-time traffic, a UAV node with a planned trajectory that is inside or too close to a PU region should not be participating in real-time packets routing. Greedy geographical routing protocols consider distance as the main metric for the next hop selection without paying attention to the state of a UAV and its mobility. With using distance metric for the next hop selection, real-time packets may be received by a destination beyond their delay constraints.

In our proposed Trajectory Aware Geographical (TAG) routing, the next state of UAVs is considered using their planned trajectory to avoid long queuing delay in the buffer of UAVs for real-time packets. TAG uses periodic beacon packets in each neighborhood to collect local information. In TAG, a beacon has one additional field for the next position of a UAV. A beacon in TAG routing contains current location (l_t) of the node at the time of current beacon time (t) and its next location (l_{t+1}) at the time of next beacon time $(t + 1)$. The next location of a UAV can be estimated from the its planned trajectory. Having the current and the next location of all neighbors, a source UAV queries the geolocation database to find the next state of a candidate (neighbor) UAV. If the next state of a candidate UAV is "inside a PU region" or "close to a PU region", it is not a good candidate to be selected as next hop to forward a real-time packet, even if the UAV is the closest neighbor to the destination. TAG uses Algorithm 1 in each hop to select the next hop for a real-time packet.

Algorithm 1. TAG routing

1: **procedure** NEXT HOP SELECTION
2:     **for** n **neighbors do**
3:         $State(n) \leftarrow 1$
4:         **if** $l(t + 1) = insidePU || closetoPU$ **then**
5:             $State(n) \leftarrow 0$
6:         **if** $State(n) = 1$ **then**
7:             $f(n) \leftarrow \frac{1}{D_n}$.
8:         **else**
9:             $f(n) \leftarrow 0$.
10: Next hop $= argmax\, f(n)$.

$State(n)$ is a variable that reveals the next state of the UAV_n in a CRAHN. If the next state of candidate n is "inside a PU region" or "close to a PU region", then $State(n)$ is 0. When the next state of UAV_n is "far from a PU region", the value for $State(n)$ is 1. $f(n)$ is the utility function for each candidate neighbor n and D_n is the distance of UAV_n to the destination.

TAG behaves greedily and selects the closest neighbor to the destination if the next state of a neighbor UAV is "far from a PU region". On the other hand, it avoids a UAV that will fly close or inside a PU region. This strategy protects real-time packets from experiencing a long delay due to the PU regions.

5   Performance Evaluation

In this section, we evaluate the performance of the proposed TAG routing algorithm. To do this, we modeled a CRAHN in OMNeT++. The model is based on the disaster scenario depicted in Figure 1. We compare TAG with a geographical routing protocol that only uses the distance to destination as the metric for next hop selection. The distance based geographical routing will be called Greedy routing in this paper.

In our model, source and the destination are stationary nodes on the ground, such as a command center and a rescue team. The distance between source and destination is about 1500 meter. The radio transmission range of each node is approximately 250 meter. The source node generates constant bit rate traffic destined to a specific destination. The intermediate nodes, i.e., the UAVs, are mobile following a mobility model proposed in [6]. The speed of a UAV is randomly selected at the beginning of each simulation run and stays constant till the end of simulation. UAVs act as relays between the source and the destination for our TAG routing. The PU is stationary and permanently active. The source and the destination nodes are out of the PU region. However, the state of a UAV may change during a flight, according to one of the three states that were described in Section 3. In order to determine the location and coverage area of the PU, we assume to have access to a geolocation database. Table 1 lists the assumptions of our simulation model.

Table 1. Simulation assumptions

Parameters	Value
Number of channels	1
Data rate	2 Mbps
Simulation time	200 s
Packet length	128 bytes
UAVs speed	0-20 mps
Number of SUs	10
Number of PUs	1

Figure 3 compares the average end-to-end delay for packet routing from the command center (source) to a rescue team (destination) as a function of offered load. The average end-to-end delay of the proposed TAG routing is compared with Greedy routing at different load levels.

Note that the average end-to-end delay differs significantly at lower rates. This is because TAG exploits its knowledge about the next state of a UAV before selecting it as a next hop. In other words, it avoids UAVs as a potential next hop which are close to or inside a PU region. On the other hand, Greedy routing does not consider the next state of a UAV during the selection of the next hop. Therefore, packets that reach such a UAV must wait inside the buffer till it flies out of the PU region.

In our model, we assumed a permanently active PU which is the worst case for SUs. However, even having low activity PUs, forwarding packets to a UAV that will be located inside or close to a PU region causes higher packet delay. TAG avoids such UAVs as a next hop. With increasing offered load, there is a drastic increase in average delay. This is because beyond this point, i.e., the saturation point, packets start to queue up at source node. After the saturation

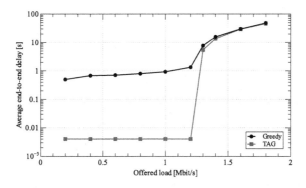

Fig. 3. Average end-to-end delay as a function of offered load

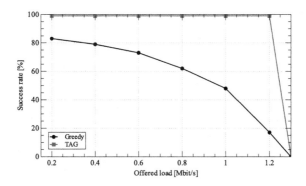

Fig. 4. Percentage of packets that meet the delay constraint as a function of offered load

point, however, the difference between both approaches diminishes and TAG asymptotically approaches Greedy routing.

Averaging the end-to-end delay of all packets cannot clearly illustrate the delay of each individual packet. For real-time applications, however, the maximum delay of each individual packet is of paramount importance. Therefore, in the second experiment, we defined a latency constraint of 10 milliseconds for all packets and calculated the percentage of packets that met this constraint.

Figure 4 depicts the success rate for TAG and Greedy routing at different levels of offered load. In TAG, all packets can meet the defined constraint at low packet rates before the saturation point of the network. On the contrary, Greedy routing can meet the delay constraint for 60 to 80 % of packets at low traffic loads. The reason for the unsuccessful packets at low packet generation rates is again the queuing delay in the UAVs that fly too close or inside a PU region. In Greedy routing, the queuing delay goes beyond the defined constraint for the real-time packets. After the saturation point, at which also the source starts to queue packets, the success rate drops down to less than 1 % of packets and both approaches have approximately similar success rates. Table 2 shows the maximum delay that occurs for real-time packets in TAG and Greedy routing.

Table 2. Maximum end-to-end delay comparison (in seconds)

Offered load (Mbit/s)	TAG	Greedy
0.8	0.005	5.8
1	0.005	7.35
1.2	0.005	9.27
1.4	24.38	38.75
1.6	81.89	99.7

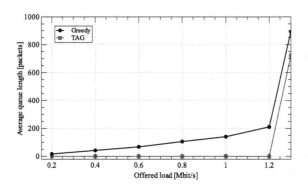

Fig. 5. Average queue length vs. packet generation rate for TAG and Greedy routing

As you can see in the table, the maximum delay in Greedy routing is far beyond the constraint for real-time packets having low packet generation rates. This delay reflects mostly the effect of queuing delay in intermediate UAVs that fly through PU regions.

Figure 5 illustrates the average queue length in the network for both routing protocols. Before the saturation point, the average queue length is approximately zero in TAG because it avoids PU regions. Therefore, in TAG we have no packet queuing due to PU activity. On the other hand, in Greedy routing, there are number of queued packets in low packet generation rates before the saturation point. The average queue length increases rapidly with increasing offered load. Note that we assumed an unlimited buffer in the nodes. However, with a limited buffer, there will always be packet drops in Greedy routing.

In our implementation of TAG and Greedy routing, we defined the beacon validity time equal to two beacon intervals. In other words, if a source node does not receive any beacon from any neighbor, it will not consider this node as the next hop. This is an indirect message from a node to its neighbors that the node has moved to a PU region or close to it and cannot send the beacon. This seems to be beneficial for Greedy routing to stop selecting a node which is inside or close to a PU region after two beacon intervals. Therefore, shorter beacon intervals can improve the performance of Greedy routing.

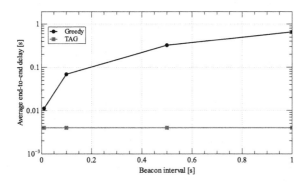

Fig. 6. Average packet delay vs. beacon interval for TAG and Greedy routing

In another experiment, we measured the average packet delay for different beacon intervals, but kept the offered load constant. Figure 6 shows the average packet delay for different beacon intervals in TAG and Greedy routing. For the short packet intervals, the difference between TAG and Greedy routing is less compared to longer beacon intervals. TAG always achieves better average delay because it does not wait for two beacon intervals to know that the neighbor is inside or close to a PU region. TAG recognizes the mobility of a neighbor UAV toward a PU region from its planned trajectory. Moreover, the cost for decreasing the average delay in Greedy routing is increasing the overhead of more beacon generation in the network. In TAG routing, a UAV adds its next geographical location to the beacon and sends it to its neighbors. Therefore, the beacon size in TAG is bigger than Greedy geographical routings. However, the amount of additional overhead in TAG is restricted to two numeric values for the coordinates of the next location of a UAV. The size of this extra overhead in our implementation is 128 bit, i.e., 64 bit for both longitude and latitude. This amount of overhead is the cost for the TAG routing improvements.

6   Conclusion

UAVs are autonomous flying wireless nodes that can be employed in disaster scenarios. They may have various missions in the network and their flying trajectory is usually according to their mission. At any given time they have a planned trajectory and follow it. In this paper, a geographical routing protocol was proposed that employs UAVs trajectory information to avoid routes inside or close to PU region. TAG routing improves average end-to-end delay, maximum delay, and success rate for real-time packets in the network comparing with Greedy geographical routing. UAV is one of the applications for TAG routing. It can be applied to other types of wireless ad hoc networks that consist of nodes with defined trajectories. One of the potential applications for TAG could be Vehicular Ad hoc NETworks (VANETs) with driver-less cars that have been proposed recently. Employing TAG in VANETs with autonomous vehicles is one of our future works.

References

1. Zhao, Y., Gaeddert, J., Bae, K.K., Reed, J.H.: Radio environment map enabled situation-aware cognitive radio learning algorithms. In: SDR Forum Technical Conference (2006)
2. Cordeiro, C., Challapali, K., Birru, D., Sai Shankar, N.: IEEE 802.22: the first worldwide wireless standard based on cognitive radios. In: First IEEE International Symposium on New Frontiers in Dynamic Spectrum Access Networks(DySPAN), pp. 328–337 (2005)
3. Flores, A.B., Guerra, R.E., Knightly, E.W., Ecclesine, P., Pandey, S.: IEEE 802.11 af: A Standard for TV White Space Spectrum Sharing. IEEE Communications Magazine 51(10), 92–100 (2013)
4. Simon, T., Mitschele-Thiel, A.: A self-organized message ferrying algorithm. In: 14th International Symposium and Workshops on a World of Wireless, Mobile and Multimedia Networks (WoWMoM), pp. 1–6 (2013)
5. Rubin, I., Zhang, R.: Placement of UAVs as communication relays aiding mobile Ad hoc wireless networks. In: Military Communications Conference (MILCOM), pp. 1–7 (2007)
6. Bouachir, O., Abrassart, A., Garcia, F., Larrieu, N.: A mobility model for UAV Ad hoc network. In: International Conference on Unmanned Aircraft Systems (ICUAS), pp. 383–388 (2014)
7. Rajaraman, R.: Topology Control and Routing in Ad Hoc Networks: A Survey. SIGACT News 33(2), 60–73 (2002)
8. Cacciapuoti, A.S., Calcagno, C., Caleffi, M., Paura, L.: CAODV: Routing in mobile Ad-hoc cognitive radio networks. In: Wireless Days (WD), pp. 1–5 (2010)
9. Karp, B., Kung, H.-T.: GPSR: Greedy perimeter stateless routing for wireless networks. In: Proceedings of the 6th Annual International Conference on Mobile Computing and Networking, pp. 243–254 (2000)
10. Chowdhury, K.R., Felice, M.: SEARCH: A Routing Protocol for Mobile Cognitive Radio Ad-hoc Networks. Journal of Computer Communications 32(18), 1983–1997 (2009)
11. Habak, K., Abdelatif, M., Hagrass, H., Rizc, K., Youssef, M.: A Location-aided routing protocol for cognitive radio networks. In: International Conference on Computing, Networking and Communications (ICNC), pp. 729–733 (2013)
12. Liu, Y., Cai, L.X., Shen, X.: Spectrum-aware Opportunistic Routing in Multi-hop Cognitive Radio Networks. IEEE Journal on Selected Areas in Communications 30(10), 1958–1968 (2012)
13. Jin, X., Zhang, R., Sun, J., Zhang, Y.: TIGHT: A Geographic Routing Protocol for Cognitive Radio Mobile Ad Hoc Networks. IEEE Transactions on Wireless Communications 3, 4670–4681 (2014)
14. Rosati, S., Kruzelecki, K., Traynard, L.: Speed-aware routing for UAV Ad-hoc networks. In: IEEE Globecom Workshops, pp. 1367–1373 (2013)
15. Lin, L., Sun, Q., Wang, S., Yang, F.: A geographic mobility prediction routing protocol for Ad hoc UAV network. In: IEEE Globecom Workshops, pp. 1597–1602 (2012)

Evaluation of Different Static Trajectories for the Localization of Users in a Mixed Indoor-Outdoor Scenario Using a Real Unmanned Aerial Vehicle

Oleksandr Artemenko, Alina Rubina, Tobias Simon,
and Andreas Mitschele-Thiel

Integrated Communication Systems Group, Technische Universität Ilmenau,
98693 Ilmenau, Germany
{Oleksandr.Artemenko,Alina.Rubina,Tobias.Simon,Mitsch}@tu-ilmenau.de

Abstract. This paper focuses on the experimental exploration of static trajectories applied for the localization of wireless nodes using unmanned aerial vehicles. Furthermore, a unique scenario is investigated that includes both indoor and outdoor areas. While moving around a building, an unmanned aerial vehicle localizes wireless nodes that are positioned inside that building.

First, a classification of up-to-date static trajectories is provided. Later on, an adaptation of several state-of-the-art static trajectories is presented. The latter include the so called Triangle and Circle trajectories which are investigated in real-world experiments using a single unmanned aerial vehicle serving as a mobile anchor. The experimental data is used to validate the trajectories. Experimental results show that Triangle is better suited for our unique indoor-outdoor scenario.

Keywords: Localization, Static trajectories, Mobile beacon, Disaster, Unmanned aerial vehicle, Experiment.

1 Introduction

Location information can be used for many purposes including rescue, coverage, routing, navigation and target tracking [6]. Localization in Wireless Networks (WNs) is a very challenging task and can be implemented in many different ways. A straightforward approach would be to use the Global Positioning System (GPS). However, equipping every node with a GPS-receiver is not practical because of high cost, limited precision and high power consumption. Moreover, GPS fails in indoor environments or under the ground [17]. Another approach named Mobility-Assisted Localization (MAL) uses only one or a few mobile anchor nodes that are equipped with a GPS module. Generally, an *anchor* represents a reference data set collected during the localization [14]. The main idea of MAL is to use a mobile anchor which traverses the network and periodically

© Institute for Computer Sciences, Social Informatics and Telecommunications Engineering 2015
N. Mitton et al. (Eds.): AdHocNets 2015, LNICST 155, pp. 123–133, 2015.
DOI: 10.1007/978-3-319-25067-0_10

receives beacon messages coming from unknown nodes. A beacon is a short message, containing information specified by the used standard, e.g. IEEE 802.11x standard family.

Recently, considerable attention has been paid to the problem of *anchor placement* – methods to design a trajectory for a mobile anchor. It has been proven in the literature that a well-planned mobile anchor trajectory increases the speed and accuracy of the localization [14].

A very challenging scenario is considered – a disaster relief. Suppose, an unmanned aerial vehicle (UAV) is flying over an urban area, which suffers from a disaster. The purpose of a UAV is to localize 'survived' devices, enabled with Wi-Fi module. The obtained information will help to accelerate the rescue process of people who are stuck inside a building. Here, we consider the IEEE 802.11x standard family for the communication among nodes. In the literature, numerous trajectories have been proposed for steering a UAV. However, none of them fits to our scenario. Let us take a closer look at the scenario.

We consider a mixture of indoor and outdoor areas. We assume multiple wireless nodes, e.g. personal mobile devices like smartphones, tablets or notebooks, that are placed in an indoor area, e.g. a building of the university campus, and a UAV that can move outside this building. The mobile devices are periodically transmitting beacons (for this, the so called ad hoc mode is being applied). After collecting these beacons, the UAV will estimate the distance from its current location to the emitters and after some time will be able to calculate their positions. What is the challenge here?

The list of open issues includes, among many others, an accurate sensing strategy, distance calculation techniques, reference data selection approaches, and efficient trajectory planing algorithms. The latter will be in focus of this work. Moreover, in this paper, we present the results for the experimental evaluations of the trajectories that are represented by an adaptation of several state-of-the-art approaches.

The rest of the paper is organized as follows. In Section 2, a classification of the anchor placement algorithms will be given. Section 3 introduces an adaptation of the selected trajectories. Then, Section 4 describes our experiment setup. Section 5 presents an extensive analysis of the obtained results according to different metrics. In Section 6, conclusions are given.

2   Related Work in Anchor Placement

Current classifications of anchor placement algorithms found in [20,10,21] lack some of the most recently developed static trajectories. Moreover, a separation into two-dimensional (2D) and three-dimensional (3D) algorithms is missing. As a consequence, Fig. 1 presents the classification of the most important approaches.

In this regard, all anchor placement algorithms can be roughly divided into random and planned. The latter can be further subdivided into static and dynamic. Next, we present the details of every category.

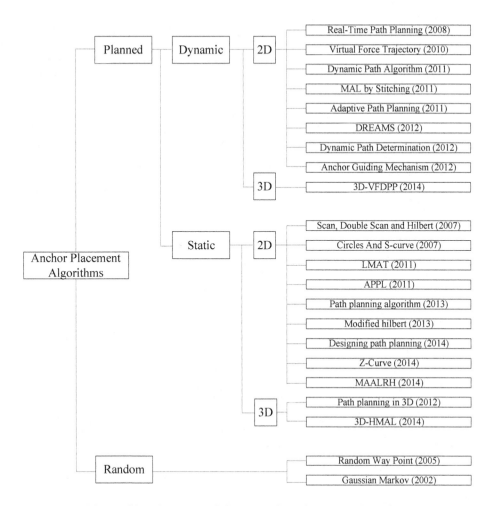

Fig. 1. Classification of different anchor placement algorithms

Random/Probabilistic Trajectories. If a trajectory does not follow a certain pattern or is based on a probabilistic scheme, we can classify it as random. Algorithms based on Random Way Point and Gauss-Markov Mobility models are the most common examples here [4]. These approaches are simple in their execution and provide non-uniform and unpredictable coverage of the area. If there is no information about the explore area random trajectories can be the best choice. Otherwise, according to [19], planned trajectories result in higher localization accuracy in comparison to random movements.

Dynamic Trajectories. With a little more information about the area (e.g., distribution of nodes, size of the area, nodes density), dynamic trajectories can be applied. These trajectories are not fully planned in advance. Instead, they are adapted based on the obtained information while the anchor is in motion. One of the drawbacks of those algorithms is the message overhead between the mobile anchor and unknown nodes. Furthermore, it is not possible to predict the moving time of the anchor as well as the path distance in advance. Under the time restrictions, as for example in disaster scenarios, it can be unsafe to apply such trajectories. Nevertheless, the literature on dynamic trajectories shows a variety of approaches as in [13,16,5].

Static Trajectories. One of the first examples of static trajectories is proposed by Koutsonikolas et al. in [15]. Three trajectories have been developed, particularly – SCAN, DOUBLE SCAN and HILBERT. CIRCLES and S-CURVES were proposed in [11] and were designed to reduce the collinearity problem of SCAN and DOUBLE SCAN.

A so-called LMAT (**L**ocalization with a **M**obile **A**nchor node based on **T**rilateration in Wireless Sensor Networks) trajectory was proposed in [12]. It was proven that if a trajectory consists of equilateral triangles, it ensures the best node coverage and leads to the increased degree of the non-collinearity [12]. LMAT has demonstrated an average localization error of up to 0.7 m in the deployment area of 100×100 m^2. This trajectory indeed shows good performance and was already experimentally validated in an outdoor scenario in [1].

Benkhelifa et al. proposed three new modifications – SQUARES, ARCHIMEDEAN SPIRAL and WAVES in [3]. Farmani et al. in [9] defined a Modified-Hilbert approach. It is an improved version of the Hilbert trajectory. Another algorithm based on the *hexagonal* pattern was proposed by Kaushik et al. in [18]. The Z-curve was introduced by Rezazadeh et al. in [21]. The main element of the trajectory is build using the shape of the letter Z. Based on the simulation results, the Z-curve just slightly outperforms the LMAT and HILBERT trajectories. Here, a log-normal signal propagation model was included in the performed simulations. One further algorithm is proposed in [10] – MAALRH (**M**obile **A**nchor **A**ssisted localization algorithm based on **R**egular **H**exagon).

All approaches, mentioned above, have been designed to explore a simple outdoor scenario. They do not take into account any obstacles like buildings that must be avoided. One such algorithm has been proposed by Chia-Ho et al. in [19]. It ensures the location estimation of all unknown nodes and reduces the localization error. For this, a new position estimation algorithm based on the chord method is used along with the adopted SCAN trajectory. The designed trajectory can be also applied in case of obstacles. The size of obstacles is considered to be 10×30 m^2 or 30×10 m^2. However, the algorithm does not consider the exploration of obstacles and only implements a strategy to avoid them.

The same disadvantage is present in novel 3D path planning algorithms from recent research works. Here, such trajectories like five 3D curves, Layered-Scan, Layered-Curve, Triple-Scan, Triple-Curve and 3D-Hilbert can be mentioned [7].

In summary, static trajectories like LMAT, Z-curve, HILBERT and MAALRH have demonstrated the best performance in terms of the localization accuracy, length, difficulty and non-collinearity. Nevertheless, these trajectories fail in our considered scenario, because they are not suited for areas which include buildings. Z-curve and Improved Scan while considering obstacles present simple

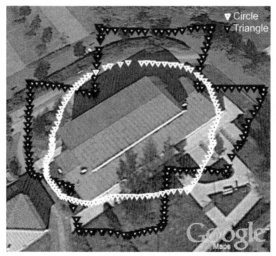

(a) The top view of the building with the positions of the UAV obtained experimentally (© Google Maps ™).

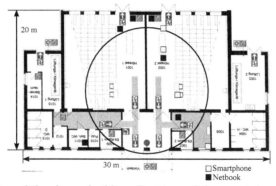

(b) The floor-plan of the chosen building. Positions of the smartphones and netbooks are marked accordingly.

Fig. 2. The working area of the experiment

obstacle avoidance strategy. None of the present trajectories consider the unknown nodes to be located inside buildings. The unknown nodes are always assumed to be located randomly in a region of interest. As a consequence, new building-aware trajectories are required.

3   Design of New Trajectories

It is a well-known fact that a trajectory consisting of equilateral triangles leads to a better localization accuracy [12]. The triangular shape ensures at least three non-collinear anchors to every unknown node. The LMAT trajectory, being one

Table 1. Weather and experiment setup

Parameter	Value/Name
Air temperature	$7\,^{\circ}C$
Humidity	75, %
Speed of wind	5, m/s
Air pressure	1008, mb
Building size	30×20 m^2
Number of unknown nodes	10
Experiment repetitions	6
Number of trajectories	2
Data Acquisition Algorithm	RSS
Anchor Selection technique	SS
Distance Calculation	$d = 10^{\frac{P_{r_0} - P_r + W}{10\alpha}}$
Position Calculation Algorithm	Multilateration, Centroid, Min-Max

Table 2. Technical parameters of the UAV

Technical Characteristic	Model or Parameter
Processor	600MHz Cortex A8
RAM	256MB
Gyroscope/Acceleration	MPU6050
Magnetic Field Sensor	HMC5883L
GPS Receiver	UBLOX6
Barometric Pressure Sensor	MS5611
Ultrasonic Sensor	MaxSonar I2CXL
Operating System	Gentoo Linux
Flight and Measurement Software	PenguPilot (github.com/PenguPilot)

of the most efficient approaches presented in the literature, follows the triangular pattern. In this regard, an isosceles triangle was chosen as a pattern for the first trajectory called *Triangle*.

The next trajectory, called *Circle*, follows a circular shape which is another popular pattern used in the literature to design a path for a mobile anchor. Circle represents a path that is simple and short.

Both trajectories can be observed in Fig. 2(a) that shows positions of a UAV which was flying around a building in our experiments. Next, the experiment setup and the detailed analysis of the results are presented.

4   Experiment Setup

The experiment was conducted at the Ilmenau University of Technology in Germany. One of the campus buildings, named Leonardo da Vinci Bau, was chosen for the experiment. The size of the building was 30×20 m^2. The experiment

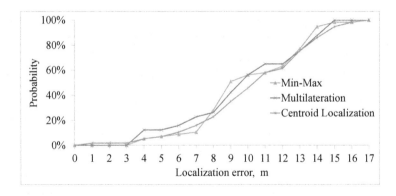

Fig. 3. Localization error CDF. Performance of different position estimation techniques.

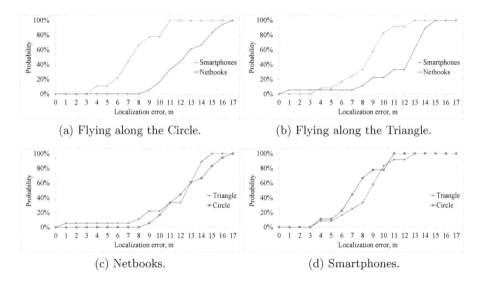

(a) Flying along the Circle.

(b) Flying along the Triangle.

(c) Netbooks.

(d) Smartphones.

Fig. 4. Difference in localizing smartphones and netbooks

setup and the weather conditions at the time of the experiment are summarized in Table 1.

During the experiment, a UAV, represented by a quadrocopter with the parameters shown in Table 2, was flying around the building along the two chosen trajectories and receiving beacons once per second from unknown wireless nodes that were placed inside the building. For every beacon, a received signal strength (RSS) estimate has been obtained and stored along with the corresponding GPS position of the UAV representing an anchor. The GPS-position itself was Kalman-filtered, using acceleration and attitude data from a CHR-6DM attitude and heading reference system. The accuracy of the GPS module has been evaluated. For that, we kept the UAV in 15 different positions around the building for 3 minutes measuring a new GPS estimate every second. The average error for the GPS positioning was less than 0.9 m with a standard deviation of less than 0.5 m. Since the error introduced by the GPS positioning was much smaller that the error of the distance estimation, we consider GPS to be a ground truth for our experiments. To calculate the distance between the UAV and a corresponding wireless node, the received signal strength (RSS) method has been used along with a log-distance path loss model from [8]. This model considers wireless communication among nodes in a mixed outdoor-indoor environment. The model predicts a received signal strength $P_r(d)$ at a distance d as follows:

$$P_r(d) = P_r(d_0) - 10\alpha \log_{10}(d/d_0) + X_\sigma - W \ [dBm], \tag{1}$$

where $P_r(d_0)$ is a signal strength at the reference distance d_0; α is the path loss exponent; and W is the wall attenuation factor. In [8], the following values have been proposed: $P_r(d_0) = -40$ dBm, $\alpha = 3.32$, $W = 4.8$ dBm.

The building along with the trajectories can be seen in Fig. 2(a). Inside the building, 10 unknown nodes were randomly located. A floor plan of the building as well as the positions of the unknown nodes can be observed in Fig. 2(b).

In the performed experiment, five netbooks ASUS Eee PC Seashell series and five smartphones Samsung Galaxy S were used. Netbooks were equipped with Wi-Fi IEEE 802.11 b/g modules, running in an ad hoc mode. Smartphones were launched in Wi-Fi IEEE 802.11 access point mode. The UAV was operated manually and experiment was repeated six times – three times for every trajectory. The average speed of the UAV, while moving along Circle and Triangle, was 0.8 m/s and 1.2 m/s accordingly. In one of the experiments, speed of the UAV was increased to 4.4 m/s, while moving along the Triangle. All results are presented in the form of a cumulative distribution function (CDF).

5   Results Analysis

To obtain the accuracy of the localization, an average localization error was calculated. As follows, different metrics will be used to evaluate the performance of both trajectories.

The Type of the Position Calculation Method: Fig. 3 shows the localization error CDF for the three different position calculation methods – classical Centroid localization, Multilateration and Min-Max from [2]. All methods demonstrate a similar behavior. In case of small errors (less than 3 m), Centroid Localization demonstrates the best performance. In the range of average and big errors, Multilateration is the best. This is due to the fact that the multilateration minimizes the mean square distance error of the reference points to the unknown target position. Min-Max demonstrates quite an unstable behavior. Since Centroid Localization has demonstrated the highest probability of small errors, we used this method for the further analysis.

The Type of the Device to Be Localized: The performance of smartphones and netbooks was also compared. The key observation is, that smartphones are localized better than netbooks as shown in Fig. 4(a) and Fig. 4(b). Here, the

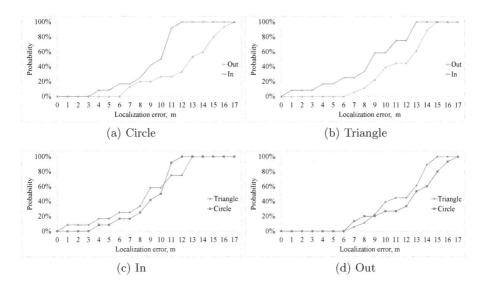

Fig. 5. Performance of the nodes, located closer to the center (In) or to the edges (Out) of the building in case of the Triangle and Circle

difference between smartphones and netbooks reaches up to 60% in the case of the Circle and Triangle. It can be explained as follows: Smartphones usually produce weaker RSS readings at the receiver with a smaller standard deviation as compared to the netbooks. As a consequence, when applying a signal model, a smaller uncertainty factor is reached. In addition, we have investigated whether there is a relation between trajectories and a device type. Fig. 4(c) and Fig. 4(d) show the performance of netbooks and smartphones in the case of two different trajectories. It can be observed that the Triangle is better suited for the localization of netbooks and smartphones tend to be localized better when using Circle trajectory. The last can be explained as follows: Smartphones were located mostly in the right plane of the building. As a result, the strongest RSS readings were produced at this side. Since, the Circle trajectory approached building closer than the Triangle, this could have resulted in a higher localization precision for the smartphones.

Positions of Nodes: Here, the relation between a node's position and a localization accuracy was investigated. We have related the position of a node to the center of the building. To determine which nodes were located closer or farther from the center, a circle was drawn. Radius of the circle was equal to the half of the buildings width. As a result, six nodes were located outside of the circle and four of them inside, as shown in Fig. 2(b). The obtained results are seen in Fig. 5(a) and Fig. 5(b). Nodes, located closer to the center of the building are localized better, than the nodes located closer to the walls of the building. This was the case for both of the trajectories. It can be explained as follows. Nodes which were inside the circle produced more uniform RSS readings from all four sides of the building, this resulted in a better performance of the position estimation techniques. As opposite, nodes outside the circle had strong RSS readings only on one side of the building. As a result, this led to a poorer localization.

In overall, the Triangle trajectory demonstrated a better performance for all the nodes.

6   Conclusion

In this paper, location estimation strategies have been explored in a unique indoor-outdoor scenario. We showed that the current research does not provide us with the building-aware static trajectories. As a result, two modifications of the state-of-the-art trajectories were introduced – Triangle and Circle. We can conclude that the Triangle performs better than Circle in terms of the localization error. The Triangle trajectory has achieved an average error of about 9 m, while Circle demonstrated only 11 m. Different metrics have been applied for the analysis of the experimentally obtained data. The main observations are:

- Three different position estimation algorithms were applied. The Centroid localization algorithm performed best in case of small localization errors.
- The obtained results indicate that smartphones are localized better than netbooks. This could have resulted due to a weaker RSS readings with a smaller standard deviation than that of the netbooks.
- Nodes, located closer to the center of the building are localized better, than the nodes located closer to the walls of the building. Nodes which were inside the circle produced more uniform RSS readings from all four sides of the building. As a consequence, this resulted in a better performance of the position estimation techniques.

References

1. Artemenko, O., Rubina, A., Golokolenko, O., Simon, T., Römisch, J., Mitschele-Thiel, A.: Validation and evaluation of the chosen path planning algorithm for localization of nodes using an unmanned aerial vehicle in disaster scenarios. In: Mitton, N., Papavassiliou, S., Kantarci, M.E., Gallais, A. (eds.) ADHOCNETS 2014, LNICST, vol. 140, pp. 192–203. Springer, Heidelberg (2014)
2. Artemenko, O., Simon, T., Mitschele-Thiel, A., Schulz, D., Ta, M.R.S.: Comparison of anchor selection algorithms for improvement of position estimation during the wi-fi localization process in disaster scenario. In: The 37th IEEE Conference on Local Computer Networks (LCN), October 2012
3. Benkhelifa, I., Moussaoui, S.: Appl: Anchor path planning based localization for wireless sensor networks. In: The 4th International Conference on Communications, Computers and Applications (MIC-CCA 2011), pp. 48–53. Mosharaka for Researches and Studies (2011)
4. Camp, T., Boleng, J., Davies, V.: A survey of mobility models for ad hoc network research. Wireless Communications and Mobile Computing 2(5), 483–502 (2002)
5. Chang, C.-Y., Chang, C.-Y., Lin, C.-Y.: Anchor-guiding mechanism for beacon-assisted localization in wireless sensor networks. IEEE Sensors Journal 12(5), 1098–1111 (2012)

6. Cheng, L., Wu, C., Zhang, Y., Wu, H., Li, M., Maple, C.: A survey of localization in wireless sensor network. In: IJDSN (2012)
7. Cui, H., Wang, Y., Lv, J.: Path planning of mobile anchor in three-dimensional wireless sensor networks for localization. J. Inf. Comput. Sci. 9, 2203–2210 (2012)
8. Faria, D.B.: Modeling Signal Attenuation in IEEE 802.11 Wireless LANs - Vol. 1. Technical Report TR-KP06-0118, Kiwi Project, Stanford University, January 2006
9. Farmani, M., Moradi, H., Dehghan, S.M.M., Asadpour, M.: The modified hilbert path for mobile-beacon-based localization in wireless sensor networks. Transactions of the Institute of Measurement and Control (2013)
10. Han, G., Zhang, C., Lloret, J., Shu, L., Rodrigues, J.J.: A mobile anchor assisted localization algorithm based on regular hexagon in wireless sensor networks. The Scientific World Journal 13 (2014)
11. Huang, R., Zaruba, G.V.: Static path planning for mobile beacons to localize sensor networks. In: PerCom Workshops, pp. 323–330. IEEE Computer Society (2007)
12. Jiang, J., Han, G., Xu, H., Shu, L., Guizani, M.: Lmat: Localization with a mobile anchor node based on trilateration in wireless sensor networks. In: GLOBECOM, pp. 1–6. IEEE (2011)
13. Kim, K., Jung, B., Lee, W., Du, D.-Z.: Adaptive path planning for randomly deployed wireless sensor networks. J. Inf. Sci. Eng. 27(3), 1091–1106 (2011)
14. Koubaa, A., Khelil, A.: Mobility-assisted localization techniques in wireless sensor networks: Issues, challenges and approaches. In: Koubâa, A., Khelil, A. (eds.) Cooperative Robots and Sensor Networks 2014. SCI, vol. 554, pp. 43–64. Springer, Heidelberg (2014)
15. Koutsonikolas, D., Das, S.M., Hu, Y.C.: Path planning of mobile landmarks for localization in wireless sensor networks. Computer Communications 30(13), 2577–2592 (2007)
16. Li, X., Mitton, N., Simplot-Ryl, I., Simplot-Ryl, D.: Dynamic beacon mobility scheduling for sensor localization. IEEE Transactions on Parallel and Distributed Systems 23(8), 1439–1452 (2012)
17. Mesmoudi, A., Feham, M., Labraoui, N.: Wireless sensor networks localization algorithms: a comprehensive survey. CoRR, abs/1312.4082 (2013)
18. Mondal, K., Karmakar, A., Mandal, P.S.: Designing path planning algorithms for mobile anchor towards range-free localization. CoRR, abs/1409.0085 (2014)
19. Ou, C.-H., He, W.-L.: Path planning algorithm for mobile anchor-based localization in wireless sensor networks. IEEE Sensors Journal 13(2), 466–475 (2013)
20. Rezazadeh, J., Moradi, M., Ismail, A., Dutkiewicz, E.: Impact of static trajectories on localization in wireless sensor networks. Wireless Networks, 1–19 (2014)
21. Rezazadeh, J., Moradi, M., Ismail, A., Dutkiewicz, E.: Superior path planning mechanism for mobile beacon-assisted localization in wireless sensor networks. IEEE Sensors Journal 14(9), 3052–3064 (2014)

A Novel Predictive Link Quality Metric for Mobile Ad-Hoc Networks in Urban Contexts

Sebastien Bindel[1]*, Serge Chaumette[1], and Benoit Hilt[2]

[1] LaBRI, University of Bordeaux, Talence, France
[2] MIPS, University of Haute Alsace, Colmar, France

Abstract. In Mobile Ad hoc networks (MANETs), advanced routing metrics use Link Quality Estimators (LQE) for making routing decisions. To be efficient and in a strong interaction with the physical layer transmission conditions, the accuracy and the reactivity of LQE used by metrics are crucial for maintaining connectivity. Current LQE estimates the link quality into a single value. This method limits the accuracy of the estimators, especially in highly volatile environments such as VANETs in urban environments. In this paper we propose multi-estimators LQE approach that provides both a better link quality and a link behavior assessment. These novel estimators deal with LQE requirements, reactivity, stability and accuracy to become a reliable LQE. We evaluate they reactivity and accuracy with realistic physical layer and mobility patterns and also found their forecasting properties.

Keywords: F-ETX, forecasting, routing, link quality.

1 Introduction

Link quality estimation is one of the main concerns for applications running in Mobile Ad-Hoc Networks (MANET), Vehicular (VANET) and emerging Unmanned System networks. In such networks, the radio signal is affected by several phenomena including shadowing, fading and Doppler effect which degrade its quality. Resulting perturbations contribute to undermine current algorithms, that impact applications performances. For instance, routing protocols often rely on link quality estimations to select reliable links and maintain efficient network operation. Link quality estimation also plays a significant role in topology discovery mechanisms to build a neighborhood knowledge. However the lossy and the dynamic behavior of the links makes this task non trivial.

In the past, several research papers have been focused on the design of link quality estimators and have tackled some received wisdoms. Firstly, empirical studies have shown the absence of correlation between the link quality and the distance between nodes [1]. Secondly, the transitional phase of link quality is often longer than expected and characterized by a significant level of unreliability and asymmetry [16]. Thirdly, the correlation between the Packet Reception Ratio (PRR) and the physical information (i.e. RSSI, SNR and LQI) is not easily

* This research was supported by a DGA-MRIS scholarship

deductible while these indicators have a limited efficiency to assess the link quality [1] [17] [13]. It is therefore important to take into account these observations
to design effective metrics.

Fast ETX (F-ETX) is a novel metric [3] that uses dynamic windows size to
sense the link and overcomes intrinsic limitations of static window size and empirical filters such as EWMA. As a result, F-ETX performs better than current
ETX based metrics. Even if the metric reacts quickly to persistent changes, transient fluctuations also affects the estimation. F-ETX features make it reactive
but instable in some situations. We observed in our experimentations that F-
ETX provides additional information about link features not yet characterized.
This paper completes [3] by providing an extended version of F-ETX combining
additional companion-metrics to give a multi faced assessment in order to make
the metric stable, reactive and accurate. Additionally, it shows the companion-
metrics ability to provide reliable predictions of link quality.

The remainder of this paper is divided into five parts. Section 2 reviews current
techniques to estimate the quality of a link. Section 3 gives the F-ETX technical
background. Section 4 presents the design of the predictive companion-metrics.
Section 5 shows a comparative evaluation of our estimators with other metrics.
Section 6 concludes this paper and opens up new perspectives.

2   Related Work

Effective link measurement is a fundamental building block in wireless networks
and especially if the propagation channel is subject to important variations. This
section summarizes current wireless link quality estimation techniques and point
out the main challenges of this hot topic.

2.1   Logical Information as Link Quality Metrics

Traditional metrics in wired networks, (i.e. hop count) fail to give an estimation
on the paths reliability in wireless networks. De Couto et al. have suggested the
Expected Transmission Count (ETX) metric [6], which combines forward and
backward packet reception to compute a packet delivery success probability.
Draves et al [7] have experimented four type of metrics (ETX, hop count, Per-
hop Round Trip Time and Per-hop Packet Pair Delay) through a test bed placed
in an indoor environment. They observed that ETX performs better than the
others but in a mobility case, the performance of the hop count metric exceeds
the ETX metric. Due to fixed size window based estimation, we showed [3] a
short window size leads to a reactive estimation, while a larger window size
reduces its agility. The Required Number of Packet (RNP) metric suggested by
Cerpa et al [5] performs at MAC layer and counts the average number of packet
retransmissions required to deliver it successfully. They observed the temporal
properties of low power wireless links and described the usefulness of such a
metric to measure the link quality compared to reception rate (RR). Unlike the
RR information, RNP metric takes into account the underlying distribution of

losses because the link quality is characterized in both directions. However, this metric requires an ARQ (Automatic Repeat-Request) mechanism to retransmit lost packets in order to determine the number of retransmission required to achieve a successful reception. Woo et al [15] designed a routing protocol based on the channel snopping an introduced an agile filter called Window Mean with EWMA (WMEWMA) as an empirical estimator technique [14]. Authors have shown its performance, over the others filters based on the Exponential Weighted Moving Average (EWMA).

2.2 Physical Informations as Link Quality Metrics

Other metrics, which perform at the PHY layer provide an immediate quality information about the wireless channel. This type of metric has the advantage to be implemented without any additional costs and provides a valuable snapshot of the link state. Such metrics are relied on three kinds of information provided by the PHY layer: the Received Signal Strength Indicator (RSSI), the Signal to Noise Ratio (SNR) and the Link Quality Indicator (LQI). Current works try to establish a correlation between PHY parameters and the PRR but none of them found a satisfactory solution. Zhao et al. [17] showed the difficulty to make a good estimation of the link quality based on RSSI values. Even if a high signal strength can be associated to a high packet reception, the reverse relationship is not true. The use of the SNR was often proposed to overcome RSSI based indicators limitations. However, experimental evaluations have shown that the correlation between the SNR and the PRR is not directly deductible. This is due to the hardware sensitivity and the environmental effects, especially for intermediate link quality [1]. In addition, Boano et al. [4] have shown the limitation of SNR based indicators to differentiate the possible states of a wireless link (transitional and bad), excepted for good links (result confirmed by [13]). The last hardware based metric called LQI has been proposed for the 802.15.4 standard but it can only be exploited on specific radio chips. Even if LQI presents a certain correlation (better than the RSS and closer to the SNR) with the PRR [10], it does not provide a relevant estimation for intermediate link quality [13].

A recent generation of link quality estimators based on the packet decoding process has been proposed. The first one deals with the DSSS decoding error analysis [9] [12] to assess the link quality. The second one proposed by Gabteni et al. [8] uses the OFDM decoding process in order to make an interesting link state indicator which predict future link disruptions. Unfortunately, these estimators are only available on specific radio chips for the first one and only tested in simulations for the second one.

2.3 Metrics with Multi-estimators

An interesting novel approach supports that the link assessment can be made with multi-estimators to have a multi-faced vision of the link in order to compute a scored quality link estimation. Baccour et al. [2] designed an hybrid metric based on logical and physical information to provide multi-estimators that assess the packet delivery ratio, the link asymmetry level, the link stability and the channel quality. These estimators are aggregated into a single metric following a fuzzy logic method. The Holistic Packet Statistic (HoPS) metric suggested by Renner et al. [11] incorporates four estimators; namely short-term, long-term, absolute deviation and trend estimation; computed with the EWMA filter. However an intrinsic problem of the use of this filter limits the agility of estimators. It also has the disadvantage to require a large amount of traffic to train the estimators and consequently increases the detection time of link state changes.

3   F-ETX Metric

The use of a static window size and filters based on EWMA limit the agility of link quality estimators. The F-ETX metric [3] overcomes these limitations by monitoring the link with a dynamic window size. Two windows are maintained, one to estimate the PRR and the second one for the ARR (Acknowledgment Reception Ratio) estimation, respectively represented by d_f and d_r ratios. Theses windows are also managed by two algorithms; one dealing with their reductions to increase the reactivity of the metric and another one takes care about their growth in order to increase the accuracy and the stability of the metric.

3.1   Reactivity Improvement – Window Size Reduction

As reactivity is the major concern for link quality metrics, F-ETX uses an algorithm that ensures both a fresh and an accurate estimation. Each ratio (i.e. d_f and d_r) computation uses a binary filter based on the Weighted Moving Average (WMA). It keeps the newest correctly received packet information and penalizes the target ratio according to the current number of lost packets. Let $x_1 \ldots, x_n$ the values representing the current states of reception maintained by a window W at the time n. The associated binary weight, w, represents the reception state of the x data packet and fixed at 0 for lost and 1 for a good reception. Let α be the number of packets marked as lost in the window and $|W_n|$ the window size at the time n. If a loss is detected, the new window size is determined as follows:

$$|W_n| = \frac{|W_{n-1}|}{2^\alpha} \tag{1}$$

Th reception probability is computed by:

$$probability = \frac{w^n x_n + w^{n-1} x_{n-1} + \ldots + w^1 x_1}{|W_n|} \tag{2}$$

As shown in [3], in case of successive packet losses, the algorithm enables an exponential (2^α) decrease of the window size that leads to a rapid link state detection.

3.2 Accuracy and Stability Improvement – Growth of the Window

To adapt the link quality assessment according to the link stability, a dedicated algorithm manages the growth of the window size after its reduction. This guarantees a proper estimation of the link quality adjusted to the link stability. When a packet loss occurs, the algorithm saves the current window size, called in the rest of this paper the threshold, T_h. For each new packet marked as received, the window size is incremented. From the moment the window size reaches the threshold, each new received packet increments a dedicated counter C_n. Then, the window (W) is increased or shifted (the window is shifted left) under the following conditions.

$$W \begin{cases} Increased\ if & W_n \geqslant T_h \wedge C_n \geqslant \frac{W_n}{2} \\ Shifted & else \end{cases} \tag{3}$$

After each increase, the counter C_n is reset. This approach limits the speed of the window size according to the loss occurrence and adjusts the accuracy of the estimation according to the link stability.

3.3 Discussion

F-ETX appears as reactive and accurate, but reacts also to transient losses. This makes the metric instable and does not meet requirements to be a suitable LQE. As a matter of fact, reactivity and stability are at odds, a single metric cannot be both reactive and stable. However additional information can be extracted from the metric to assess different link features. This information is fully exploited to provide companion metrics about the link quality trend, the link stability and an indicator about the potential switch from a bidirectional to an unidirectional link. The goals of these companions metrics is to offset the weakness of the link quality assessment and provide additional information on the link states to predict local links features.

4   Companion Estimators of F-ETX

The F-ETX metric only deals with a single estimation while the algorithm assesses other link features that could be suitable both for local link evaluation and end-to-end path exploration required by routing protocols as example. We argue that a multi-faced representation of the link provides detail information about its state and helps the routing process to select the best suitable link. These estimators are described next.

Link quality : This estimator is based on the link quality performed by the F-ETX metric. It uses the forward d_f and the backward d_r ratios, which represent the probability of a packet to be delivered to a neighbor and the probability of its ACK packet to be successfully received back.

$$\chi^{LQ} = \frac{1}{(1 - d_f)(1 - d_r)} \tag{4}$$

Link quality trend : This indicator tracks the course of the link quality by computing the variation between the current χ_t^{LQ} and the previous estimation χ_{t-1}^{LQ}. To provide a long term estimation the result is averaged with an EWMA.

$$\Delta_t^{LQ} = \chi_t^{LQ} - \chi_{t-1}^{LQ}$$
$$\chi_t^{Trend} = \beta \cdot \Delta_t^{LQ} + (1 - \beta) \cdot \chi_{t-1}^{Trend} \tag{5}$$

The coefficient β influences the sensitivity of the filter. Choosing a small β value is advisable to achieve a long term estimation. Note that two successives χ^{LQ} set to 0 indicate a long-term disruption and resets the link quality trend estimator.

Link stability estimation : We observed that a fine analysis of the d_f and d_r maintained windows content provides a link stability information. Let a binary state $[0, 1]$ that represents the reception state of an excepted packet in a window. We note W_{max} the maximum window size, W_n the current window size and the W_i the ith element in the window. The windows maintained to compute the d_f and d_r probabilities are respectively noted W^{d_f} and W^{d_r}. The link stability indicator is computed with an EWMA filter tacking into account the absolute Ξ and the relative stability ξ.

$$\Xi = \frac{\sum_{i=1}^{W_n^{d_f}} W_i^{d_f} + \sum_{i=1}^{W_n^{d_r}} W_i^{d_r}}{2W_{max}}$$
$$\xi = \frac{\sum_{i=1}^{W_n^{d_f}} W_i^{d_f} + \sum_{i=1}^{W_n^{d_r}} W_i^{d_r}}{W_n^{d_f} + W_n^{d_r}} \tag{6}$$
$$\chi_t^{Stab} = \Xi_t \cdot \gamma + (1 - \gamma) \cdot \xi_t$$

The absolute estimation (Ξ) computed from the maximum window size (fixed value) represents the absolute level of stability of the link. The relative estimation (ξ) computed from the current window size (dynamic value) represents the relative stability. This third estimation gives the level of the link stability according to the current window size. This information is useful, since, for a same absolute value, the relative link estimation gives an additional assessment taking into account losses which took place recently. Both absolute and relative information are suitable to characterize the link stability, hence we advise a γ value fixed at 0.5.

Unidirectional link level : This last estimator deals with the detection of bidirectional links becoming unidirectional. Current approaches like F-LQE with the ASL estimator, track the difference between the uplink and downlink reception rates. Such a method becomes inefficient if the link has a short life time or experiment an high level of packets losses. In this case, windows are not sufficient trained to give a trustworthy estimation. Our method overcomes this limitation by measuring the variation of the up and downlink reception ratios. This makes it independent of the window size and does not require any training period. Let W be a window and W_n^t its size at time t. The variations of the reception ratio provided by the window W at time t is noted Δ_t^{Win}. The indicator is given by:

$$\Delta_t^{Win} = \sum_{i=1}^{W_n^t} W_i - \sum_{i=1}^{W_n^{t-1}} W_i$$

$$\chi_t^{ULL} = \chi_{t-1}^{ULL} \cdot \lambda + (1 - \lambda) \cdot \varphi(\Delta_t^{d_f}, \Delta_t^{d_r}) \tag{7}$$

$$with\ \varphi(x, y) = \begin{cases} -1 & x < 0 \wedge y > 0 \\ 1 & x > 0 \wedge y < 0 \\ 0 & else \end{cases}$$

To give a tendency we advise a λ value fixed at an high value. When this indicator becomes negative, a link may become unidirectional (e.g. nodes with different transmit power level) .

5   Evaluation

This evaluation compares the performances and the robustness of F-ETX and companion metrics to current scored metrics, namely F-LQE and HOPS. Tests were run in an urban environment with both realistic propagation and mobility into the NS-3 simulator. Simulations ran 30 mobile nodes in a $500m \times 500m$ area with realistic urban Manhattan 4×4 grid based mobility. Nodes have different relative speeds in $[0:30]$ m/s. The realistic wireless channel was setup with a ThreeLogDistanceLossModel for modeling shadowing (Exp0: 2.5, Exp1: 5, Exp2: 10, D0: 1m , D1: 75m, D2: 114m). Fading effect was setup with a RicianPropagationLossModel with a LineOfSightPower fixed at 1. Communications performed with 802.11g at 6Mbp/s. Link quality metrics are measured at the receiver side by monitoring probe packets. Details can be found in [3]. Parameters of LQEs have been set according to [2] for F-LQE and [11] for HoPS.

For F-LQE [2] the parameter of the WMEWMA filter used to determine the packet delivery ratio is set to 0.6. An history based of 30 PRR is used to compute the link stability and the link quality estimations. Until to reach this threshold, the minimal required history is set to 5 PRR. HoPS [11] uses EWMA filters to compute short- and long-term link quality estimations and their deviation. Coefficients are respectively set to 0.9 and 0.997 and its initializes short- and long-term estimations at 50% for new links. For F-ETX, parameters λ, β and γ are respectively set to 0.9 , 0.1 and 0.5. To evaluate both the agility of the metrics to track fluctuations of the link quality and the accuracy/robustness of the metrics, we achieved temporal and statistical evaluations.

5.1   Temporal Behavior

The reliability of metrics were tested under two scenarios; a fast and a slow crossing cases involving two nodes. In the first one, the relative speed is 50 m/s and the communication time is 5s while in the second one, they are respectively 3 m/s and 24s.

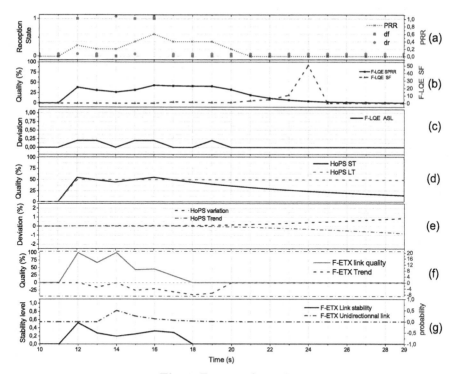

Fig. 1. Fast speed crossing

Fast Speed Scenario. According to the distribution of the d_r and d_f in the figure 1(a) the link lifetime is very short (5s between 12s and 17s, while important stochastic losses can be observed resulting from a significant fading (Rayleigh) effect). The PRR computed over an history of 5 packets declares the link disrupted at 21s, but in fact the disruption occurs at 17s, in addition a single d_f and d_r reading is not sufficient to determine the link state. For instance, at 13s on a single reading the link could be considered as disrupted, whereas it was a transitory loss (the link remains up until 17s).

About the F-LQE, figure 1(b) shows the smoothed PRR (SPRR) evaluating the link quality and the link stability estimation (SF). Below, the figure 1(c) shows the unidirectionality level of a link estimator (ASL). The SPRR follows the corresponding PRR (fig 1) trace with a smoothing trend, but the estimator is clearly not enough reactive and detect the disruption too late. This result from the EWMA filter that gives more important stability than reactivity to the estimator. The SF estimator also suffers from a lag to indicate a decrease of the stability from 22s, while the link is disrupted, because it is based on an history of five packets to compute the stability estimation. About the ASL indicator, the variation of d_r and d_f distribution introduces light fluctuations indicating a low probability to have asymmetric link.

Regarding estimators from HoPS (fig 1(d) and (e)) it is observed the slow convergence time of the short-term estimation, while a link is disrupted, the

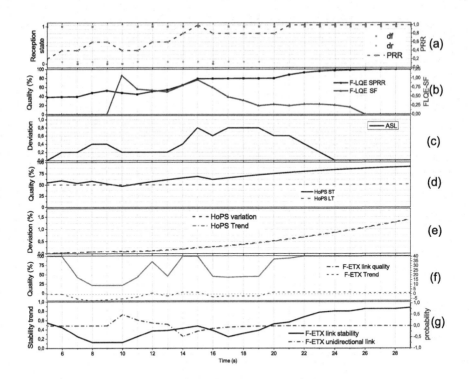

Fig. 2. Slow speed crossing

estimator declares the link quality as not disrupted. But the long-term estimator indicates a correct trend of decrease. Consequently, the EWMA filter is well used for long-term estimation but not suitable for short-term estimation which too smooth estimations. In the same manner, the link quality trend and the variation indicators are affected by the long reactivity of the short estimation and react too slowly when a disruption occurs.

The estimators of F-ETX are shown figure 1(f) and (g). In contrast with LQE, F-ETX is more reactive than the others and declares the link disrupted earlier (at 18s). The trend estimation indicates a degradation of the link quality via consecutive negative values. This is confirmed by the link stability estimator indicating a low level of stability and a decrease. About the unidirectional indicator, its gives a false positive value (at 14s) indicated that the link can be unidirectional in the opposite direction.

Slow Speed Scenario. The distribution of d_r and d_f and the PRR indicate a progressive increase of the link quality, fig 2(a).

Concerning F-LQE, the SPRR (fig 2(b)) progressively increases and confirms this tendency. The stability is correctly estimated by the SF estimator, indicating a decrease of the stability at the beginning of the communication and a progressively increase for the rest of the simulation. About the ASL, stochastic

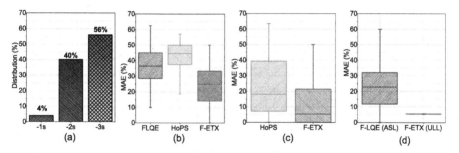

Fig. 3. Statistical analysis

losses disturb the estimator (fig 2(c)), that indicates the possibility of the link to be unidirectional.

About HoPs the short-term link quality estimators also indicates an improvement of the link quality and is confirmed by the long-term indicator that progressively increases (fig 2(d)). We note that the HoPS ST increases faster than HoPS LT. But the HoPS trend and variation (fig 2(e)) take the same course indicating an increase of the link stability and a variation between HoPs ST and LT.

Regarding F-ETX (fig 2(f) and (g)) the link quality estimation also increases, this is confirmed by the trend estimators indicating a decrease at the beginning, but progressively indicates an improvement of the link quality. The same observation can be pointed out on the link stability indicator. Unlike the ASL indicator the link unidirectionality level estimator of F-ETX varies a little and reflects the constant bidirectional property of the link.

5.2 Statistical Evaluation

While previous evaluations give a detail about the strength and weakness of LQEs, this evaluation is extended with statistical analysis from all links of the simulation. Over 470 links have been analysed where 1800 packets have been exchanged.

Previously we have observed that the link quality estimator of F-ETX is more reactive than F-LQE and HoPs. In this statistical study we are focus on how this estimator can anticipate disruption compared to the PRR solution based on an history of 5 packets . Figure 3 (a) shows that F-ETX is clearly the best solution by anticipated disruption before the PRR solution. Because based on the dynamic window size the metric is more reactive and track very well link states changes. In addition, F-ETX assess both link direction unlike a PRR solution that only evaluates downlink.

The rest of the statistical analysis is made with the Mean Absolute Error (MAE) that measures the magnitude of the predicted estimation and the current outcome. A low score indicates a good prediction while a bigger value indicates a greater error between the prediction and the current value. Tracking link stability is an essential feature to detect and differentiate transient and persistent link. We have compared Fig 3 (b) the variation of the value given by these estimators to the current variation observed from the delivery and forward ratios. F-ETX estimator gives the lowest MAE compared to the other. Because HoPS indicator only tracks the variation between the HoPs ST and LT estimations, that not really related with the link stability and about F-LQE, the estimation is based on a PRR history that produce a lag generating consecutive error predictions.

The link quality trend is a complementary information that determines the current course of the link quality. Fig 3 (c) shows the link quality trend of HoPs and F-ETX. We observe the better ability of our estimator to give the tendency of the link quality compared to HoPS. Even if each of them is based on the link quality estimator and both are computed with an EWMA filter. Their abilities to track the link quality course depends on the ability of link quality estimator, as HoPS-ST suffers from lag with the use EWMA filter impacting the HoPS-LT. On the other hand, the link quality estimator from F-ETX is react but instable. That is why with the use of EWMA the estimation is stabilized given a better long-term estimation than the HoPS-LT overestimating the tendency.

Figure 3 (d) shows the unidirectional link estimator of the F-LQE and F-ETX. During the simulation, any effective unidirectional link are present. ASL estimation only made a single reading on the reception ratio of the up and downlink often different when highly propagation disturbances are present. Our indicator adopts another strategy based on the variation between the up and downlink, this results that our estimation is more robust to disturbance and give more suitable information about the potential of a bidirectional link to become unidirectional.

6   Conclusion

In this paper we presented novel companion-metrics of our recently proposed F-EXT metric [3]. Each of them evaluates a specific link feature; (i) the link quality, (ii) its trend, (iii) its stability and (iv) the detection of unidirectional links. They do not require a training period and are computed efficiently by the use of dynamic sized windows and moving average filters. These four metrics have then be compared to popular propositions of LQEs from the literature (e.g. F-LQE and Hops). Comparisons took two forms. First showed the capacity of the metrics to track accurately link disruption and link upcoming in two nodes crossing scenarios (e.g. a fast 50m/s and an slow 3m/s one). They also highlighted prediction capabilities of the metrics. The second evaluation confirmed this prediction capability through a statistical analysis that show how F-ETX and its companion-metrics overcomes other LQE when dealing with link disruption forecasting. The capability to detect a wireless link that switches from bidirectional to unidirectional was also tested. To test the robustness of the new metrics, simulations ran realistic channel propagation models and realistic urban mobility. This work shows two important elements relating to link quality monitoring; to track efficiently a link expecting volatile channel propagation conditions, the use of dynamic sized windows overcomes the classical methods, a metric associated to companion-metrics allows a better assessment of channel properties and is therefore more suitable for usage into higher levels.

This is precisely the aim of our future works. We plan to test the F-ETX and companion-metrics in other contexts such as building environments to confirm the suitability of our approach. We will also integrate the F-ETX and companion-metrics into routing protocols to test their efficiency in multi-hop path setup.

References

1. Baccour, N., Koubâa, A., Mottola, L., Zúñiga, M.: all: Radio link quality estimation in wireless sensor networks: A survey. In: ACM TOSN (2012)
2. Baccour, N., Koubâa, A., Youssef, H., Ben Jamâa, M., do Rosário, D., Alves, M., Becker, L.B.: F-LQE: A fuzzy link quality estimator for wireless sensor networks. In: Silva, J.S., Krishnamachari, B., Boavida, F. (eds.) EWSN 2010. LNCS, vol. 5970, pp. 240–255. Springer, Heidelberg (2010)
3. Bindel, S., Chaumette, S., Hilt, B.: F-ETX: An enhancement of ETX metric for wireless mobile networks. In: Kassab, M., Berbineau, M., Vinel, A., Jonsson, M., Garcia, F., Soler, J. (eds.) Nets4Cars/Nets4Trains/Nets4Aircraft 2015. LNCS, vol. 9066, pp. 35–46. Springer, Heidelberg (2015)
4. Boano, C.A., Zúñiga, M.A., Voigt, T., Willig, A., Romer, K.: The triangle metric: Fast link quality estimation for mobile wireless sensor networks. In: IEEE ICCCN (2010)
5. Cerpa, A., Wrong, J.L., Potkonjak, M., Estrin, D.: Temporal properties of low power wireless links: modeling and implications on multi-hop routing. In: ACM MobiHoc (2005)
6. Couto, D.S.J.D., Aguayo, D., Bicket, J., Morris, R.: A high-throughput path metric for multi-hop wireless routing. In: ACM MobiCom (2003)
7. Draves, R., Padhye, J., Zill, B.: Comparison of routing metrics for static multi-hop wireless networks. In: ACM SIGCOMM (2004)
8. Gabteni, H., Hilt, B., Drouhin, F., Ledy, J., Basset, M., Lorenz, P.: A novel predictive link state indicator for ad-hoc networks. In: IEEE Globecom (2014)
9. Heinzer, P., Lenders, V., Legendre, F.: Fast and accurate packet delivery estimation based on DSSS chip errors. In: IEEE INFOCOM (2012)
10. Liu, T., Cerpa, A.: Data-driven link quality prediction using link features. In: ACM TOSN (2014)
11. Renner, C., Ernst, S., Weyer, C., Turau, V.: Prediction accuracy of link-quality estimators. In: ACM EWSN (2011)
12. Spuhler, M., Lenders, V., Giustiniano, D.: BLITZ: Wireless link quality estimation in the dark. In: Demeester, P., Moerman, I., Terzis, A. (eds.) EWSN 2013. LNCS, vol. 7772, pp. 99–114. Springer, Heidelberg (2013)
13. Srinivasan, K., Kannan, D., Tavakoli, A., Philip, L.: An empirical study of low-power wireless. In: ACM TOSN (2010)
14. Woo, A., Culler, D.: Evaluation of efficient link reliability estimators for low-power wireless networks. Tech. Rep. UCB/CSD-03-1270, EECS Department, University of California, Berkeley (2003)
15. Woo, A., Tong, T., Culler, D.: Taming the underlying challenges of reliable multi-hop routing in sensor networks. In: ACM Senys (2003)
16. Zamalloa, M.Z., Krishnamachari, B.: An analysis of unreliability and asymmetry in low-power wireless links. In: ACM TOSN (2007)
17. Zhao, J., Govindann, R.: Understanding packet delivery performance in dense wireless sensor networks. In: ACM Sensys (2003)

Associative Search Network for RSSI-Based Target Localization in Unknown Environments

V. Loscrí[1], S. Guzzo Bonifacio[1], N. Mitton[1], and S. Fiorenza[2]

[1] Inria Lille - Nord Europe, France
[2] University of Calabria, Italy

Abstract. Received Signal Strength Indicator (RSSI) is commonly considered and is very popular for target localization applications, since it does not require extra-circuitry and is always available on current devices. Unfortunately, target localizations based on RSSI are affected with many issues, above all in indoor environments. In this paper, we focus on the pervasive localization of target objects in an unknown environment. In order to accomplish the localization task, we implement an Associative Search Network (ASN) on the robots and we deploy a real test-bed to evaluate the effectiveness of the ASN for target localization. The ASN is based on the computation of weights, to "dictate" the correct direction of movement, closer to the target. Results show that RSSI through an ASN is effective to localize a target, since there is an implicit mechanism of correction, deriving from the learning ASN approach.

Keywords: ASN, Target Localization, RSSI, robots, experimentation.

1 Introduction

In the recent years, research communities have focused and considered pervasive target localization [1] and cooperative target localization. Target localization can be also envisaged as a sub-problem of coverage of specific areas, where events of interest occur [17], and where the correct and timely localization is mandatory. Among all the parameters that a wireless device (e.g. a robot) can measure, the Received Signal Strength Indicator (RSSI) is one of the most popular considered for target localization [14] [15], above all in the context of Wireless Sensor Networks. Its popularity is due to different factors, such as it is always available between communicating devices, and it does not require extra-circuitry that would result in higher costs and energy consumption. Furthermore, the availability of the RSSI measure on all the devices, makes possible the implementation of a localization technique for heterogeneous nodes. This latter feature increases the potential scalability of this kind of approach, as envisaged in [16].

In this paper, we propose to exploit the RSSI parameter to localize a target in an unknown environment. The localization technique is based on an Associative Search Network (ASN) [2] and is performed in indoor environments. The network we implement on top of our robots is Hopfield-inspired [6] and we will show that it shares, with this type of system, the capability to converge towards stable

© Institute for Computer Sciences, Social Informatics and Telecommunications Engineering 2015
N. Mitton et al. (Eds.): AdHocNets 2015, LNICST 155, pp. 146–157, 2015.
DOI: 10.1007/978-3-319-25067-0_12

states. By providing our robots with learning capabilities, we make RSSI a viable solution for target localization. One of the main premises related with the system developed, is that the computation of the weights for the direction decisions, is performed without any external oracle. This feature comes down to provide our devices with the possibility to dynamically adapt the weights without the intervention of an external central unit. In practice, the resulting system will be totally distributed and evolutionary by dynamically adapting its behavior to the external conditions. As a proof of concept of the proposed approach, we developed the whole ASN on Arduino-based mobile robots. These robotic platforms have been built from scratch and are totally reprogrammable. The brain of the robot is a mini-pc.Even if the robots are also able to communicate with each others, in this context, we have only used the communication paradigm to assign the task (i.e. the identity of the target to be localized). The Arduino module is mainly used to "transfer" the movement commands to the four wheels and to implement all the components related to the movement. In summary, the main contributions of the paper are as follows:

- a new Received Signal Strength (RSSI)-based Associative Search Network (ASN) for target localization;
- an evaluation though ASN implementation on real hardware (Arduino robots).

The rest of the paper is organized as follows. Section 3 browses the literature for the three macro topics tackled in this paper : *a*) Target Localization, *b*) Associative Search Networks and *c*) RSSI use in localization processes. In Section 4, we state the Associative Search Network problem (ASN) for target localization. Section 5 details our contribution. Section 6 describes the scenario considered for evaluation purpose and the test-bed deployment. Section 7 gives the main features of the ASN implementation on robots. Finally, Section 8 concludes this work and explores future research paths.

2   The Associative Search Network Problem

In this section, we introduce the ASN Problem. We start by considering an ASN that can be defined as a system where there is no outside process that suggests the correct association between a pattern with a key. Instead, for each key, the associative system searches for the pattern that minimizes a reinforcement signal (i.e. a payoff). The system is able to store, by the mean of an associative memory, the results of reinforcement feedback coming from the environment. In the ASN, is not considered at all the presence of a "oracle", that has to provide the pattern to be stored. This feature makes this system similar to an Hopfield-network [6]. Another important feature is that it does not require an a priori knowledge about the best associations. ASN combines two learning methods that are usually considered separately: *(i)* a pattern recognition mechanism to respond to each key with the appropriate output pattern and *(ii)* a stochastic automaton method to maximize a reinforcement signal or payoff [18] [19]. If we consider that the ASN interacts with an environment E, at each time unit

t, E provides a context vector $X(t) = (x_1(t), x_2(t), ..., x_n(t))$, where $x_i(t)$ is a positive real number and n is the number of inputs. E will also provide a payoff or reinforcement learning $z(t)$. The ASN produces an output pattern $y(t) = (y_1(t), ...y_m(t))$, where m is the number of outputs, where each $y_i(t) \in \{0,1\}$ and is received by E. In practice, the vector $X(t)$ is to provide information about the environment to the ASN. Different contexts may require different actions from the ASN. As an example, we can consider a mobile device that is required to reach a specific target. The context is represented by an estimation of the distance. After a movement, a different context will require a different action, that could correspond to a request of changing direction (this is a different action required). The reinforcement signal is intended as a kind of evaluation of how much an action is appropriate in a certain context. A more appropriate formulation of the problem could be: let us assume that $X(t)$ belongs to a finite set $X = (X^1, ..., X^k)$ of context vectors and let also assume that to each $X^\alpha \in X$ corresponds a payoff or reinforcement function Z^α. If E always evaluates an output vector in one time step and if $X(t) = X^\alpha$, then $Z(t+1) = Z^\alpha(Y(t))$. This means that E provides a "training sequence" over X if it implements an infinite sequence of payoff functions and emits the corresponding sequence of context vectors $X^{i1}, X^{i2}, ..., X^{il}$. Each $X^{il} \in X$ and each element of X occurs infinitely often. The termination condition of the associative search problem is solved when, after some finite portion of a training sequence, the ASN responds to each $X^\alpha \in X$ with the output pattern $Y^\alpha = (y_1^\alpha, ...y_m^\alpha)$ which maximizes Z^α. As outlined in [2], the output vectors required from the system are only based on scalar feedback. Other mechanisms that are also able to solve similar problems, such as perceptrons based mechanisms [4], have some counterparts, e.g. they require a separate error feedback. The basic unit of an ASN is the adaptive element and in the simplest version, an ASN can be regarded as constituted by a single adaptive element. Let us indicate with $x_i, i = 1, ..., n$ the context input, z represents the payoff (or reinforcement signal) and y is the output. Every context input x_i is associated with a weight $w_i(t) \in R$. Let assume $W(t)$ is the vector of weights at time t and $s(t)$ is the weighted sum at time t of the contexts inputs. We obtain $s(t) = \sum_{i=1}^{n} w_i(t)x_i(t) = W(t)X(t)$ and the output $y(t)$ is

$$y(t) = sign(t) = \begin{cases} 1 & \text{if } s(t) + noise > 0, \\ 0 & \text{if } s(t) + noise = 0, \\ -1 & \text{if } s(t) + noise < 0. \end{cases} \tag{1}$$

where *noise* is a random variable with zero mean normal distribution. The element's output depends on the value s. If s is positive $y(t)$ will be more likely 1, otherwise it will be more likely 0. The update of the weights is governed by the following equation, at each time step:

$$w_i(t+1) = w_i(t) + c[z(t) - z(t-1)]$$
$$[y(t-1) - y(t-2)]x_i(t-1), \tag{2}$$
$$i = 1, ..., n$$

where c is a constant determining the learning rate. The more the value of n increases the more the accuracy increases too, but also the complexity will increase and, with it, the occupancy of the memory. In this equation, the response latency is considered equal to zero. It is worth noticing that, when the simplest ASN with only a single adaptive element is considered, the search of the optimal action is determined by two possible actions by the ASN. However, in a larger ASN (with more than 1 adaptive element), the adaptive elements exploit their capability of operating in an effective way, with random payoff response characteristics. From 1, we can observe that the change of the payoff signal z is used by the adaptive element for determining weight changes. Of course, if the payoff (or reinforcement signal) changes at every time step and it does not vary smoothly over time, an adaptive element that implements the rules 1 and 2, is not capable to solve an associative search problem.

3   Related Work

The issue addressed in this paper is characterized by different properties, the target localization, the ASN and RSSI-based localization. Target Localization represents the main goal that the robot has to fulfill, the ASN is the main technique used in this work to reach the goal and the Received Strength Signal Indicator is the parameter used to obtain information from the surrounding environment. To the best of our knowledge, combining these three components is new. We thus briefly survey the literature for these three topics independently.

Target Localization. A special category of target localization, named Anchor Based considers a subset of nodes, placed in fixed coordinates, called Anchor Nodes. Through the exchange of messages among those nodes and a target, it is possible to estimate the position of the target inside the monitored area. Such a localization can have different purposes, like [7] where measured RSSI is used as parameter in maximum likelihood estimation algorithm. A more complex use of this technique can be found in [8] where the RSSI is used to determine the position of a robot using a distributed algorithm and to direct it to follow a path. In [11], the authors consider the target localization problem based on range measurement by considering a single mobile robot or several cooperating robots. Similarly to our approach, the authors consider that the robots do not have access to global knowledge about the environment. They do not know their current position, do not share a common sense of direction, etc. The robot is asked to estimate the relative coordinates of the target. Anyway, the approach they consider is totally different, since it is based on a specific filter.

In [12], the authors consider a set of mobile robots able to localize a set of unknown static targets within a known obstacle map. The robots use measurement Probability Hypothesis Density, or PHD, filter to collect the information for localization purpose. The authors do not make reference to RSSI as viable parameter to localize the targets. Moreover, the main difference is that the authors in [12] assume they know the obstacle map. In our case we introduce an explicit mechanism to detect and avoid the obstacles. The purpose is yet different and the aim is to use anchor nodes (if available), to help a robot in the localization process of an active target without a priori knowledge of the map, the geographic coordinates, etc. and without a oracle that manages the right weights associated with the weight matrix to compute the output.

Associative Search Network. ASN has been introduced by Barto and Sutton [2] as a learning process. It interacts with an environment (E) receiving from it a feedback link. Through the analysis of this feedback and a reinforcement payoff signal the ASN is able to learn the best actions to perform in order to maximize the payoff function and reach a goal. This technique has been further analyzed in [9], where the authors define a simulation environment to solve the practical problem called Hill Climbing. In the scenario depicted in this example a robot had to climb to the top of a hill where a tree is placed. The operations of the robot are assisted by the presence of some landmarks. Therein, the authors show how the presence of the landmarks and the use of ASN can improve the efficiency. Our work aims to replicate this scenario in a real environment, rather than a simulated one, to analyze the difference. We were mainly focused to identify the assumption that remains valid and the ones that is necessary to reduce when moving from a simulated scenario to a real one.

RSSI Use in Localization Processes. The Received Signal Strength Indicator (RSSI) is often used as a parameter in target localization algorithms because of its relationship with the Path Loss Model, also known as Friis transmission equation [3]. Thanks to this equation it is possible to calculate the power of a transmitted signal at a fixed distance d from the transmitter. It can be used as well to obtain the distance, from a transmission point, given the power of the received signal. The use of RSSI for distance estimation may present some drawbacks, especially for indoor localization, due to the presence of multi-path fading, shadowing and scattering which affects the transmitted signal as depicted in [10]. Heurtefeux and Valois outline that the great popularity of localization protocols based on RSSI (in Wireless Sensor Networks) is mainly due to the fact that no extra hardware is required and the theory formulates the RSSI in terms of distance function, but the disadvantages can make its use for Localization Target purpose unfeasible. In [13], the authors show the effectiveness of a navigation technique based on RSSI. Similarly to our approach, the orientation adjustment and the motion tracking are performed through the help of other nodes (sensors nodes in their case). The main difference is that they consider sensors distributed in a grid pattern. We also make reference to landmarks that are arranged in the middle of the side of a rectangle, but our approach is able to dynamically adjust and learn about the landmarks even if they are arranged in different positions and are different in number.

4   Target Localization Problem Statement

The main goal of this work is the target localization in an unknown environment, based on the Received Signal Strength Indicator (RSSI). We provide our robots with an ASN and formalize the Target Localization as an Associative Search Network problem. By the definition of the appropriate weights, the robot will move in a weighted space, instead of a physical space. This means that, the robots will perform a specific action based on the ASN implemented on them. We got inspiration from the work of Barto and Sutton [2], where the authors show how a simple network could be used to model a learning approach based on reference points (landmarks). Specifically, the movement rules defined by Barto and Sutton, are based on distinct olfactory gradients (emitted by the reference points).

By considering a payoff function z, that is maximized when the robot reaches the objective and is decreasing while the distance (between the robot and the target) increases, it is possible to show that the robot is able to find the right path and reach the target. Of course, by providing the system only with the payoff function makes the movement of the robot less precise and the overall process longer. In our reference model, the network is constituted by 4 input units and 4 output units. The input unit i can assume the values $North$, $South$, $East$ and $West$, the context input $x_i(t)$ is the signal emitted by the correspondent reference point and y represents the output of the ASN system. Every input unit is completely connected to each output unit j, where $j = North$, $South$, $East$ and $West$. In this way, each input unit can "modulate" or adapt 4 connection weights $w_{ji}(t)$ in the connection matrix by following the equation 2. Each weight encodes a confidence degree in such a way that, when the robot is close to a reference/landmark point i, it should proceed towards the direction j, closer to the target.

The confidential degree $s_j(t)$ (in order to move in direction j) is computed as the sum of the products of the current weights and signals received by the reference points as

$$s_j(t) = w_{0j}(t) + \sum_i w_{ji}(t)x_i(t), \tag{3}$$

where $w_{0j}(t)$ is a polarization term. The weights w_{0j} are updated as follows:

$$w_{0j}(t+1) = f[w_{0j}(t) + c_0(z(t) - z(t-1))y(t-1)], \tag{4}$$

where

$$f(x) = \begin{cases} BOUND & \text{if } x > BOUND, \\ 0 & \text{if } x < 0, \\ x & \text{otherwise} \end{cases} \tag{5}$$

f bounds each w_{0j} to the interval $[0, BOUND]$. c, c_0 and $BOUND$ are positive real numbers. The rule as defined in 5 is necessary to allow the ASN to correctly work also in the absence of landmark information. More details about values and impact of c, c_0 and $BOUND$ can be found in [2].

In our specific case, if our robot is close to the reference point $North$, the output unit $South$ will be activated and next the robot will head to $South$. Furthermore, if the robot is in the quadrant $South - West$, the output units of *North* and *East* will be activated and the next step of the robot will be in the North-East direction. The robot has to learn the appropriate weights by implementing the rule as in Eq. 2. In this case, a connection weight w_{ji} will change if and only if a movement towards direction j, i.e. $(y_j(t-1) > 0)$, is executed and the robot is close to a reference point $i(x_i(t-1) > 0)$. By considering $z(t)$ as a measure of the closeness of the target, we can observe that w_{ji} increases when z increases, yielding that direction j makes the robot to move towards the right direction. In this case, a movement j is likely to occur again. On the other hand, whether w_{ji} decreases, the function z also decreases and the robot will move towards the wrong direction.

5   Our Target Localization Algorithm

This section details our Localization Algorithm, detailing the rules that drive the movement of the robot. The main goal for the robot is to "detect" the target (receive a signal strength with a sufficient level from the target) and to move to reach it without a priori knowledge about the environment.

In order to correctly move, the robot has to implement a behavioral logic, based on the input information it receives (e.g. the RSSI) and the elaboration of the inputs through the ASN.

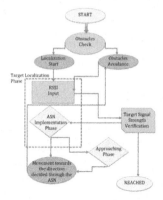

(a) Steps of the behavior of a robot.   (b) Real scenario.

The Localization Algorithm is split in two phases: the 1) ASN implementation Phase and the 2) Approaching Phase, as shown in Fig. 5. During both phases, an underlying obstacle avoidance process, detailed in the next section, is running.

We assume the target to be reached is always turned-on and that the robot is moving in the room where the target is. Based on these assumptions, our algorithm terminates when, based on the inputs received the robot estimates it has reached the target. The robot checks for the list of tasks and implements the first one. It enters the ASN Implementation Phase, which consists in receiving the "signals" from different devices and analyzing them. If the robot does not overhear its target, it moves forward for an arbitrary time Δt (e.g 1 or 2 sec.) by following a Random Way Path (RWP)[5]. It travels a prefixed distance, then it stops and checks for listening the devices. It repeats this process while it does not hear the target device.

Algorithm 1. Localization Algorithm

• **Local variables:** TargetFound = TargetReached = FALSE; List List of tasks;
RSSI-based target localization

1: **while** List $\neq \emptyset$ **do**
2:     $T \leftarrow$ POP(List) {Move to next task/target T in the list}
3:     **while** (TargetReached == FALSE) **do**
4:         **if** TargetFound **then**
5:             Collect x_i {Collect RSSI signal x_i from T and from landmarks L}
6:             DIR←ASN-Localization(x_i); Move in DIR direction
7:             **if** TargetReached==TRUE STOP {task completed;} and Remove task from List
8:         **else**
9:             $\Delta t \leftarrow$ Random(). Move forward for Δt at speed s.
10:        **end if**
11:    **end while**
12: **end while**

ASN-Localization(x_i)

1: Compute s_j $\forall j$ {Solve Eq.2 and 3}
2: Return i such that $s_i = max_{\forall j} s_j$

---

6   Performance Evaluation

In this section, we describe the test-bed considered to assess the performances of the ASN-based target localization. First, we detail the entities considered to realize the proof-of-concept and then we describe the scenario.

6.1   The "Entities" Involved

The reference scenario we implemented is characterized with heterogeneous items. Specifically we have:
1) The target node : TP-LINK Router Wireless N300;
2) 4 landmarks - 1 NETGEAR Wireless Router MR314, 1 ALICE Gate2 Plus Wi-Fi and 2 notebooks HP 630 (hotspots);
3) Rovers (robots equipped with wheels to support mobility).
 We placed the two hotspots in the points $West$ and $East$ of the area, the target in the centre of the area and at $North$ and $South$ we put the other routers. The reference scenario is represented by an area of $15m^2$ ($3 \times 5m$) as shown in Figure 1(b). The received power value has been obtained both from the anchor nodes (landmarks) and the target through the command *Iwlist*, that is available in the Linux platform as part of the *wireless-tools* library. Through this package, it is possible to have a set of commands to control the wireless devices based on the standard 802.11. The *Iwlist* command is used in combination with some parameters to better specify the data requested by a user. It details, for every detected network, a set of data related to the ESSID of the network, the

quality of the signal, the transmission channel frequency, and the Received Signal Strength Indication (RSSI).

To the follow we detail each step of the algorithm as implemented in our Rover and shown in Figure 5.

Obstacle Check and Obstacle Avoidance. Every robot runs an obstacle detection and avoidance based on ultrasound sensors. Once an obstacle is detected, the robot bypasses it. To do so, the robot scans the area on the right side with an angle $\alpha°$. If the obstacle is still there, the robot scans the area with an angle $2 \times \alpha°$ on the left side. If the obstacle is still there, the robot moves backward, turns $\alpha°$ right again and resumes its previous movement (either in searching or approaching phase).

Localization Start. If the robot does not detect any obstacle, it runs the *Localization Phase*, by acquiring the signal inputs. If the robot individuates the target ID among the signals received, it compares the RSSI value with a *threshold* value. If the signal RSSI results greater than a certain *threshold*, the robot estimates the target as reached, otherwise the robot enters the ASN-Localization algorithm.

ASN Implementation Phase This is the core of the algorithm. Based on the received input signals $x_1, x_2, ..., x_n$, the ASN will output a specific action that corresponds to a specific direction towards which the robot will move. The output signals $y_1, y_2, ..., y_m$ will constitute the new RSSI values, deriving from the new position of the robot. The payoff z represents the *closeness* of the robot from the target.

6.2   Results

In order to evaluate the ASN technique proposed, we realized a proof-of-concept based on a testbed as described in 6.1 and a variable number of robots (ranging from 1 to 3). We build this Arduino platform from scratch and we equipped it with a mini-pc, that constitues the *"brain"* of our robot. We performed three types of experiments, every result is the average over more than 30 runs. The parameters we evaluated are the time needed to reach the target (Delay) and how close the robot is positioned from the target when the algorithm exits (Dist). Numerical results are reported in Table 1.

Table 1. Results. Delays are in sec, distances in cm

Robot 1		Robot 2		Robot 3	
Delay	Dist.	Delay	Dist.	Delay	Dist.
61,6	26	–	–	–	–
65,7	25,5	80,5	31,3	–	–
69,6	26,5	82,2	33	93,4	39,7

7 Characterization of Our ASN-Based Target Localization Technique

In this section, we summarize the main features of our ASN system and we discuss some derived properties. Our system is characterized as follows:

- The learning process is no central unit;
- The weights are adjusted locally on current variables (signal, position);
- Weights do not depend on the difference between the desired output and the actual value of the system;
- The transition process runs until the network has reached an equilibrium. In our case, it is achieved when the RSSI-estimated distance is smaller than a threshold value, the robot will not move and then RSSI are unchanged.

Let w_{ij} be the weight value that connects the output of the ith context input with the jth output, $W = w_{ij}$ the weight matrix and $Y = [y_1, ..., y_n]^T$ the output vector. W is symmetric (i.e. $w_{ij} = w_{ji}$) and $w_{ii} = 0$. We consider a discrete Hopfield network used as an auto-associative memory [6] for searching purpose. Based on the premises considered, the evaluation of the stability property of our system can be performed by considering the computational energy function E, which is defined in n-dimensional output space Y as:

$$\Delta E = E(x(t+1)) - E(x(t)) = -\frac{1}{2}Y^T W Y \qquad (6)$$

that is:

$$E = -\frac{1}{2}\sum_i \sum_j w_{ji} x_j(t+1) - \sum_i w_{0j}(t) x_i(t+1) + \frac{1}{2}\sum_i \sum_j w_{ji} x_j(t) + \sum_i w_{0j}(t-1) x_i(t) \qquad (7)$$

where w_{0j} is as defined in Eq. 3. In the theory of stability, if the structure of the matrix is as those defined for our weights matrix W, and the schedule, where only a unit of the network is updated at a time, namely *asynchronous* update, it is possible to show that the system converges to one stable state in finite time. The stability is proved by showing that the energy function always decreases as the state of the processing are changed one by one. Let us consider that the neuron input (context input), that just changes state at step t is neuron p. Therefore, $x_p(t+1)$ is determined as:

$$x_p(t+1) = \begin{cases} 1 & \text{if } s(t) + noise > 0, \\ x_p(t) & \text{if } s(t) + noise = 0, \\ -1 & \text{if } s(t) + noise < 0. \end{cases} \qquad (8)$$

It is worth recalling that X is the input pattern and Y is desired output pattern and in the case of auto-associative memory, we have $X = Y$, and the diagonal entries of the weights matrix W are set to 0, namely $w_{ii} = 0$, with $i = 1...n$. If all the states of the network are to be updated at once (as in our case), then the next state of the system will be represented as: $x(t+1) = y(W^T x(t))$. When the exemplars are orthonormal and we have: $y(x) = x$ and $Y X^T x^r = \sum_i \delta_{ir} y^i = y^i$, with r=1...n and δ_{ir} is the *kronecker delta*, then we obtain: $y(W^T x^r) = y(x^r) = x^r$ that means that each stored pattern (or memory element) is a stable state of the network. Whether $x_p(t+1)$ is determined as 8, for all the other inputs (or context inputs), we have $x_i(t+1) = x_i(t)$ for $i \neq p$. Furthermore, we have $w_{pp} = 0$, and:

$$\Delta E = -((x_p(t+1) - x_p(t))(\sum_j w_{jp}x_j(t)) + w_{0p}(t)) \tag{9}$$

namely,

$$\Delta E = -((x_p(t+1) - x_p(t))s_p(t) \tag{10}$$

It is worth noticing that, if the value of x_p remains the same, then $x_p(t+1) = x_p(t)$ and the $\Delta E = 0$. If they are not the same, either it will be $x_p(t) = -1$ and $x_p(t+1) = 1$ due to the fact that $s_p(t) > 0$, or $x_p(t) = 1$ and $x_p(t+1) = -1$ due to the fact that $s_p(t) < 0$. Whatever the case is, if $x_p(t+1) \neq x_p(t)$ it is in a direction for which $\Delta E < 0$. Therefore, for this type of specific network (discrete Hopfield), we have $\Delta E < 0$. Since the energy function decreases at each state (some fixed amount) and it is bounded, it reaches a minimum value in a finite number of state changes. This can be translated as a convergence to one stable state of the network in finite time. The type of schedule considered here is named *asynchronous* update, since only one unit at each time is updated. Where all the units are updated at once, namely the *synchronous* update, the convergence is not guaranteed, since it may result in a cycle of length two. Of course, some of the stored patterns may not be a stable state. In fact, we are dealing experiments with RSSI in indoor environments, and we experimented cases of components of multi-path that add in some points, resulting in higher values of the target signal. We also faced with some spurious stable states, that is different from the stored patterns. Based on the details we have given in the implementat Section, whether the initial state is set to one of the exemplar (the ASN implementation output says that the robot already reached the target, based on the input signals received), the robot remains there (it does not move). On the other hand, if the initial state is set to some arbitrary input, then the network converges to one of the stored memory elements, depending on the basin of attraction in which $x(0)$ lies.

8   Conclusions

In this work we implemented an Associative Search Network on Arduino-based robots to perform target indoor localization tasks. As input signals, we considered the RSSI parameters for the inherent advantages that it has, such as no extra-hardware required and it is always available. These features can play a very important role when heterogeneous devices are considered and are asked to accomplish the target localization task. The realized ASN is Hopfield-network based, and this allowed us to characterize our system with some main and important features regarding stable states. Even if there are open issues related to the presence of spurious stable states (i.e. optimal states that are different form those stored), we showed that the system is effective and allows the robots to reach the target object. Moreover, the learning technique as implemented is not constrained neither with a specific number of landmarks nor with a specific position in the area, since the system evolves and learns by acquiring the external signals.

References

1. Vempaty, A., Han, Y.S., Varshney, P.K.: Target Localization in Wireless Sensor Networks using Error Correcting Codes. IEEE Trans. Inf. Theory 60(1), 697–712 (2014)

2. Barto, A.G., Sutton, R.S., Brouwer, P.S.: Associative Search Network: A Reinforcement Learning Associative Memory. Biol. Cybern. 40, 201–211 (1981)

3. Shaw, J.A.: Radiometry and the Friis transmission equation. Am. J. Phys. 33(81) (2013)

4. Minsky, M.L., Papert, S.: Perceptron: an introduction to computational geometry. MIT Press, Cambridge (1969)

5. Hyytiä, E., Virtamo, J.: Random waypoint model in n-dimensional space. Operations Research Letters (2005)

6. Hopfield, J.J.: Neural networks and physical systems with emergent collective computational abilities. Acad. Sci. 79, 2554–2558 (1982)

7. Priwgharm, R., Srivilas, K., Cherntanomwong, P.: Indoor localization system using RSSI measurement in wireless sensor network based on ZigBee standard. In: NCIT (2010)

8. Deshpande, N., Grant, E., Henderson, T.C.: Target localization in unknown environments using static wireless sensors and mobile robots. In: IEEE MFI, Salt Lake City (2010)

9. Bota, M., Guazzelli, A.: "The Associative Search Network: Landmark Learning and Hill Climbing. The Neural Simulation Language A System for Brain Modeling. MIT Press, Cambridge (2002)

10. Heurtefeux, K., Valois, F.: Is RSSI a good choice for localization in wireless sensor network? In: IEEE AINA, Fukuoka, Japan (2012)

11. Zhang, X., Li, S., Lin, Z., Wang, H.: Range based target localization using a single mobile robot or multiple cooperative mobile robots. In: Proc. ICCA, June 2013

12. Dames, P., Kumar, V.: Cooperative multi-target localization with noisy sensors. In: IEEE ICRA (2013)

13. Zhou, N., Zhao, X., Tan, M.: RSSI-based mobile robot navigation in grid-pattern wireless sensor network. In: CAC (2013)

14. Gang, L., Wei, Z., Shiyi, M., Shuqin, S.: Sensor selection for target tracking in a wireless sensor network of bearing-only sensor. Inter. J. of Digital Content Technology and its Applications 6-1, 41–48 (2012)

15. Hamdoun, S., Rachedi, A., Benslimane, A.: RSSI-based localization algorithms using spatial diversity in wireless sensor networks. In: Ad Hoc and Ubiquitous Computing (IJAHUC), January 2014

16. Zanca, G., Zorzi, F., Zanella, A., Zorzi, M.: Experimental comparison of RSSI-based localization algorithms for indoor wireless sensor networks. In: REALWSN, Glasgow, UK (2008)

17. Loscrí, V.: Performance evaluation of novel distributed coverage techniques for swarms of flying robots. In: IEEE WCNC, Istanbul, Turkey (2014)

18. Tsetlin, M.L.: Automaton Theory and modeling of biological systems. Academic Press, New York (1973)

19. Narendra, K.S., Thatachar, M.A.L.: Learning Automaton - A Survey. IEEE Trans. Syst. Man Cybern. 4, 323–334 (1972)

Self-organization, Virtualization and Localization

Self-Organizing Access-Centric Storage Optimization in Smart Sensor Networks

Carsten Grenz, Uwe Jänen, Jonas Winizuk, and Jörg Hähner

Organic Computing, University of Augsburg, Augsburg, Germany
carsten.grenz@informatik.uni-augsburg.de

Abstract. Sensor networks are getting much more complex these days. The mixture of various low-cost sensors together with increasing computational power enables for whole new systems running a lot of different analysis and control algorithms concurrently. It is impossible to anticipate their composition and data flows a priori. Although the actual data flows are hardly predictable during design-time, we present a lightweight and self-organizing approach on how shared data stores are used to optimize the storage allocation of data during run-time. While mostly using the existing traffic to disseminate routing information, we show that our distributed algorithm significantly reduces query latencies by placing data according to the access-centric storage paradigm.

Keywords: Distributed Algorithm, In-Network Storage, Routing.

1 Introduction

Classical sensor networks often consist of many homogeneous nodes which are targeted on specific goals like collecting observations from their physical environment and regularly report them to a sink, or occasionally report specific events. Much research has been done on all layers of the protocol stack to optimize these systems for various configurations and environments. However, these systems were mostly optimized during design-time by domain specialists to efficiently and effectively solve their specific tasks.

The ongoing improvements in the fields of sensor hardware and networking capabilities lead to whole new compositions of sensors and their integration into multi-purpose sensor networks. One example are Smart Cameras (SCs) which incorporate a visual sensor, a capable computation unit, and a (wireless) network interface [14]. SCs are able to perform elaborated vision algorithms right on the sensor itself to extract high-level information like the detection and tracking of persons, or identifying objects and situations [6]. One example for a smart surveillance system has been presented in [4] which integrates algorithms from different application domains into a self-organizing ad hoc network. The image sensing and processing is handled by *vision algorithms* running on the SCs. Other algorithms exchange messages over the ad hoc network to track people across the entire camera network. Distributed *control protocols* take care of the reconfiguration and alignment of the cameras' field-of-views to establish the best

© Institute for Computer Sciences, Social Informatics and Telecommunications Engineering 2015
N. Mitton et al. (Eds.): AdHocNets 2015, LNICST 155, pp. 161–172, 2015.
DOI: 10.1007/978-3-319-25067-0_13

recording conditions. Elaborated data processing and fusion algorithms use data from SCs to perform pattern detection and 3D reconstruction [2]. User terminals which are arbitrarily distributed in the surveillance region are also part of the network. All these algorithms exchange data using an ad hoc network.

A main difference to classical sensor networks is the way the data is accessed: While some applications issue periodic queries that may cover whole geographic regions, the number of algorithms and applications that perform random accesses on data in the network is on a rise. This is especially the case for systems whose users want to access the information during run-time. That is why, the latency of queries to data stored in the network becomes a major design goal to be responsive and perform in real-time. Due to the concurrent execution of an increasing number of distributed algorithms, it is impossible to anticipate the actual data flows during design-time.

Our contribution is a routing protocol for a self-organizing storage allocation algorithm which migrates data in ad hoc networks and routes requests to the data accordingly. The primary goal of the data placement heuristic is to minimize the average route lengths for queries taking recent accesses into account. The routing protocol is embedded in our storage middleware implementing migration policies to realize the access-centric storage paradigm [5].

2   System Architecture

The nodes in the network are connected through an ad hoc capable wireless LAN network interface with a transmission range which is small compared to the region the sensors are deployed in. Each node is a smart sensor whose software architecture is depicted in Fig. 1. Our *storage middleware* is located between the *application* and the *network layer*. It is generally applicable to sensors as well as other devices since it makes as few assumptions about the other layers as possible. The *application layer* encapsulates any sensing or control algorithm that stores and retrieves georeference-based data. These algorithms interact with connected sensors or process data from the data stores. This layer also contains applications for user interaction. Each data item gets annotated with a geographic position which represents the *key* of this data towards the storage layer. For evaluation purposes we model certain kinds of applications' behavior in *producer* and *consumer* modules (see Sec. 4). The *storage middleware* contains our self-organizing storage reconfiguration algorithms and offers the interface of a distributed hash table (DHT) for each data store to the application layer. The message types for the interaction between application and storage layer are:

Put(Key k, Value v)   Request to store data item v with position k
Get(Key k)   Request to retrieve date item from position k
Result(Key k, Value v) Returns the data item of a $Get(k)$ request

It contains a *local hash table* which is responsible for certain coordinate ranges which change during run-time. Each data item is accessed using its *key* which represents a geographic coordinate. The *local Lookup table* translates key coordinates to their current storage locations. The *dynamic reconfiguration module*

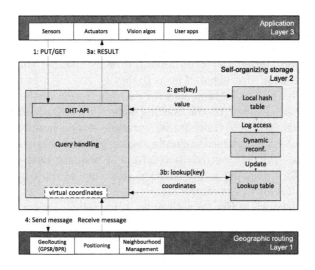

Fig. 1. Node architecture

logs accesses to data a node is responsible for. This log is analyzed and data is migrated when a more suitable storage position has been determined. All nodes becoming aware of new storage locations add a coordinate tuple to their Lookup table which reflects the new positions to optimize the routing process.

The *routing layer* contains a geographic routing protocol, i.e., Greedy Perimeter Stateless Routing (GPSR) [7], which operates on the nodes' positions during packet forwarding. Therefore, each node has to acquire its position, e.g., by using GPS. The nodes exchange beacons to announce their positions and the RNG algorithm is used to planarize the resulting connectivity graph.

3   Algorithm

Our Distributed Access-Centric Storage Algorithm (D-ACS) optimizes the storage positions of data items to minimize the latency caused by queries. This is achieved by migrating data and caching information about known data migrations in distributed Lookup tables. Upon receiving a DHT request ((1) in Fig. 1), the storage layer checks the node's responsibility and migration information. At first, it checks its local hash table (2). If the node is responsible for the data item, the hash table will return the valid data item and it can be handed over to the application layer using a *result message* (3a). Otherwise, it will encapsulate the query into a *storage layer packet* which contains the following header fields:

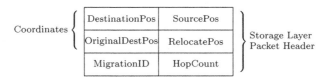

The *DestinationPosition* and the *OriginalDestinationPosition* are set to the key position. Then, it checks its Lookup table (3b) by running the packet update algorithm (see Alg. 1 on page 167). The algorithm ensures that depending on the actuality of the data either the local Lookup table is updated with the packet's header information or vice versa. The actuality of the data is represented by the *migration ID* which is incremented for each migration of the data. Finally, the packet is handed down to the routing layer (4) and is sent towards the current *destination position* (initially its location-centric home node). During packet forwarding, each intermediate node also checks its Lookup table for newer information. This way, the actual *destination* of a query packet may change several times before reaching its destination (the current data node) while the *original destination* always stays the same.

Consider the network in Fig. 2a with node A accessing an data item σ. To access data, an application generates a DHT request, e.g., a *get request*. It contains a *key* which represents the coordinates of the request, i.e., $key = p_r = (x_r, y_r)$, which is the *original destination position*. Since all Lookup tables are empty, initially, the storage layer packet is routed towards position p_r without being rerouted (black arrows). Most often p_r lies between nodes. We make use of the face routing mechanism of the geographic routing protocol to find the node which has the smallest distance to p_r (the *location-centric home node*). This is achieved by exploring the nodes around p_r (the *home perimeter*) [7]. This causes the traversal of the path $E \rightarrow C \rightarrow D \rightarrow C \rightarrow E \rightarrow H \rightarrow I$ determining node E as location-centric home node. This node is the *current data node (CDN)* and adds an entry to the Lookup table which resolves p_r to its own position p_E. Afterwards, it logs the access and sends the response back to the querying node. Therefore, it sets the *destination pos* to the request's *source pos*, but keeps the *original destination pos* at the *key*. Since this is the first access, the *migration ID* is set to 1 and the *relocate pos* is left empty. The response packet is handed down to the routing layer which delivers it to the originating Node A. Fig. 2a shows that the result packet does not necessarily take the same route as the request

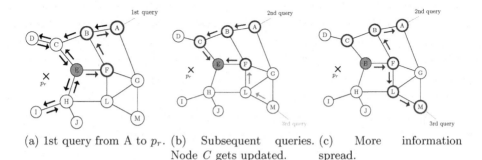

(a) 1st query from A to p_r. (b) Subsequent queries. (c) More information Node C gets updated. spread.

Fig. 2. Initial query routing. With no routing information available geographic routing is used (black arrows). The response leads to dissemination of the data's current location (blue arrows and circles, 2a). Subsequent packets get updated (2b) from the Lookup table and lead to more information spread (2c).

(blue arrows). The nodes on the packet's path add a tuple to their Lookup table containing the key, the CDN's position, and the *migration ID* 1. The knowledge of this information is represented by the blue ring around nodes. The color of the arrow represents the version of migration information the packet carries.

Figure 2b shows how subsequent accesses are updated from the nodes' Lookup tables and the information is spread even further (Fig. 2c). While the query from node A is already updated in step (3b) in Fig. 1, the query issued by node M also reaches the CDN directly since it gets updated by node F. A query is updated by setting the *destination pos* to the one stored in the Lookup table while keeping the *original destination pos* at the key.

3.1   Migration Module

To optimize the storage allocation during run-time, we introduced a *dynamic reconfiguration module* in [5]. This module is part of every node's storage layer and is responsible to periodically analyze the access structure to the data a node stores and identify potential migration pressure representing suboptimal data placement. Therefore, each node keeps short backlogs of accesses to data items. After a key has been accessed ten times, the *dynamic reconfiguration module* optimizes the storage location and performs data migration if the reallocation leads to a decreased query latency, thus, ensuring the access-centric storage paradigm. The *access model* (Acc_{σ_i}) contains a list of the origins of queries in combination with their access frequencies. For each entry $acc \in Acc_{\sigma_i}$ the originating coordinate is accessible via $acc.x$ and $acc.y$, the number of accesses via $acc.n$, and the access type (i.e., the number of message exchanges necessary for a query) via the relativity value $acc.rel$. The optimal coordinates are calculated using the following formula for x (the other coordinates are calculated accordingly):

$$\text{Optimal.x}(\sigma) = \frac{\sum_{acc\ in Acc_{\sigma_i}} acc.x \cdot acc.n \cdot acc.rel}{\sum_{acc\ in Acc_{\sigma_i}} acc.n \cdot acc.rel}$$

This formula calculates the optimal position which would minimize the access latency in hops. Since nodes may be arbitrarily distributed, this method does not guarantee optimal results. However, the evaluation shows that this heuristic produces good results while only imposing very small overhead. For a thorough description of the migration decision process and an evaluation of parameters like the access threshold, the reader is kindly referred to [5].

3.2   Data Migration

The calculated optimal storage position of a data item is denoted by p_r^j with $j \in \mathbb{N}$ indicating the j-th migration. To migrate data, a CDN sends out two types of messages: a *migration message* and a *relocate message*. The *migration message* contains the data and is sent towards the new reference position p_r^j incrementing the *migration ID* to $j + 1$ denoting the newer information. The message gets delivered to the node next to p_r^j. If this node denies the migration, e.g., due to small remaining memory or battery power, the CDN would have to retry. If the node accepts the migration, it stores the data and becomes the new CDN. Subsequently, a *relocate message* is sent to the first (location-centric) home node at p_r (or p_r^0). This ensures that the *home node* can be used as a fallback in cases when queries do not reach the CDN because of missing routing information. By examining these messages, intermediate nodes also learn about the recent migration which increases the information spread.

Figure 3 shows two examples of migrations. The CDN E performs a migration towards p_r^1, which is located next to Node G (see Fig. 3a) and determined by the message traversing the perimeter around p_r^1. For the first migration, no *relocate message* is necessary, since the recent data node (RDN) is itself the original home node. The following queries shown in Fig. 3b are already nearly optimal since the query from Node M is rerouted by Node F. Considering another migration by Node G to p_r^n, both, the migration and the relocate message are sent and Node B becomes the new CDN. Because of the information spread, the access paths from nodes A, M, and I will be optimal although nodes M and I have no or outdated information.

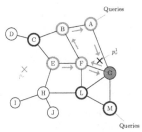
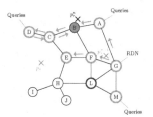

(a) The migration message determines node G as new CDN.

(b) Resulting query paths. The query from M gets updated by node F.

(c) Node G sends a migration message to B and a relocate message to E.

Fig. 3. Data migrations. Node E migrates the data to p_r^1. In (3c) node G performs n-th migration of the data towards p_r^n. New migration information is represented by green and orange circles, respectively.

4   Evaluation

We used extensive simulations to show our algorithm's performance, explore its parameter space, and compare it to location-centric storage (LCS) [3]. Our experiments were taken out in the discrete-event simulator *OMNeT++* [17] together with the *MiXiM* extension which offers models to simulate the characteristics of wireless network interfaces. All nodes are equipped with an IEEE 802.11b/g wireless LAN interface in ad hoc mode which has a transmission range of 160 m and run an implementation of the *greedy perimeter stateless routing (GPSR)* protocol [7]. The requirement for GPSR to operate on a planar graph has been met by implementing the *Relative Neighborhood Graph (RNG)* planarization algorithm proposed by the authors. To focus the evaluation on our algorithms,

Algorithm 1. Update Packet

```
1: procedure ONUPDATEPACKET(StorageLayerPacket msg)
2:     localInfo = retrieve entry from Lookup table for msg.originalDestPos
3:     if No local info found then
4:         Add information to Information Vector
5:         return
6:     if localInfo.MID¹ < msg.MID then              ▷ Packet's information is newer
7:         Update local information from the message header
8:     if msg is of type RELOCATE or RESULT then         ▷ Do not update these
9:         return
10:    if localInfo.MID¹ > msg.MID then              ▷ Local information is newer
11:        Update packet
12:        if msg is of type PUT then         ▷ compensate for (potential) packet loss
13:            Resend RELOCATE to home node
14:    return
```

¹ localInfo.MID is the stored MigrationID

each run has a startup phase of 60s in which the nodes exchange beacon packets and perform the graph planarization (RNG).

Our simulation setups are summarized in Table 1. During startup, the nodes are placed randomly in a simulated area with the size of $1,200 \times 1,200\,\mathrm{m}^2$ and the applications are setup. Nodes run different application models depending on the experiment. To represent the behavior of smart sensors, the *producing application* stores data that is associated with the nodes' surrounding space, i.e., it issues *put* request to keys in its geographic vicinity. The *consuming application* represents any kind of algorithm querying sensor data by issuing *get* requests, e.g., to analyze the data and subsequently store its results, or to process the data and display the results to a user. Each *consumer* randomly chooses five geographic regions of interest upon startup. During run-time, it periodically queries equally distributed geolocations in these regions (see Table 1). The query period is varied randomly by ± 1 second to avoid synchronization effects. To research our algorithms, the number of producing and consuming nodes is varied on startup as well as dynamically during run-time. The following graphs show the average route lengths (quantified by the number of hops) for *put* and *get* queries, respectively.

Table 1. Simulation setup

Parameter	Static access patterns	Dynamic patterns	One data item
Run-time	16,000 s	16,000 s	1,000 s
Repetitions	8	10	9
Number of nodes	100	70 + 5 every 2,000 s	100
Put period	10	10	n/a
Get period	{3s,5s,10s,15s,20s,30s}	{3s,5s,7s,10s,15s,20s}	15s
Put region size	3x3	3x3	n/a
Get region size	8x8	8x8	1

Static Access Patterns

The first set of experiments shows the general performance of our algorithm. Therefore, the parameters of the producing and consuming applications are chosen upon startup and are not changed throughout the simulation run. All 100 nodes create *put* requests with a period of 10 seconds. 30 of these nodes also run consuming applications with fixed *get* request periods which are varied from 3 s to 30 s in the different setups (see Table 1).

Fig. 4a shows the resulting average route lengths for the *put* requests. Obviously, the impact of these types of requests on the network load is very low. This is due to the locality-preserving nature of the modeled sensors, which repeatedly generate sensor events in their direct vicinity. The initial long routes of above 20 hops are due to the home-perimeter runs around previously not addressed positions. Up to 2,000 seconds, one can observe a huge reduction to nearly zero which is mainly caused by nodes storing information about their neighboring nodes in their Lookup tables. Initially, the location-centric storage paradigm leads to the storage of data items either on a producing node itself or a nearby neighbor. Due to migrations of data items towards their optimal position performed by our algorithm, the mean hop count only increases slightly what is invisible in the graph since it is averaged out by the many local storage operations.

The right graph (Fig. 4b) shows the route lengths of the *get* requests and shows a huge reduction in mean hop counts. After the migration threshold of 10 accesses is met, data gets migrated towards its estimated optimal position. The mean hop count is reduced continuously due to the *get* accesses which are equally distributed in the chosen regions of interest. A higher access frequency leads to faster optimizations and also to better results since data gets moved closer to the querying nodes: With a request period of 30s (top line), the mean hop count is reduced by 18.5%, while a request period of 3s (bottom line) leads to a reduction of 57, 8%.

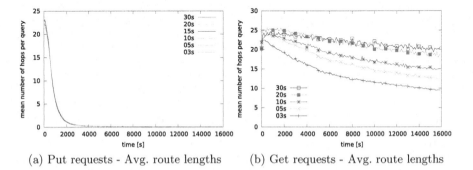

(a) Put requests - Avg. route lengths   (b) Get requests - Avg. route lengths

Fig. 4. Static access patterns with different periods. The data from 100 randomly placed sensors is accessed by 30 nodes running consuming applications each with 5 regions of interest. The graphs show the optimization of queries' route lengths over time. A higher request frequency leads to better results (3s, bottom line).

Dynamic Access Patterns and Comparison with LCS

These experiments show the adaptability and robustness of our algorithm towards changing access patterns. Initially, only 70 nodes produce and store data. After startup, the consuming applications are activated in groups of five nodes every 2,000s until 30 consumers are running at $t = 10,000s$ (marked by dashed lines in Fig. 5a). The first 2,000 seconds in Fig. 5a resemble the prior measurements in Fig. 4b. Each introduction of new access patterns of the five joining nodes leads to an increase in the average route lengths. Our algorithm quickly reacts with data reallocations and optimizes the route lengths again.

Fig. 5b compares the runs with a *get* period of 5 s with location-centric storage (LCS). While the initial storage allocation is similar, our algorithm specifically optimizes the positions of accessed data leading to a huge decrease in access latency by 44%. This significantly decreases network traffic. Furthermore, our algorithm not only shortens the route lengths but also minimizes detours of packages over time which is shown by the standard deviation of the mean route lengths in Fig. 5b. While each change in the applications' behavior leads to a short rise in the standard deviation, it is obvious that the routes stabilize again over time leading to a much lower deviation.

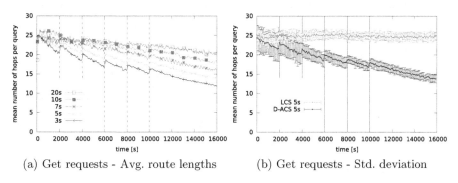

(a) Get requests - Avg. route lengths   (b) Get requests - Std. deviation

Fig. 5. Dynamic access patterns with varying rates. Five consumers are added every 2,000 s (vertical lines). Fig. 5a shows how our algorithm copes very well with changing access patterns by quick reallocations. Fig. 5b adds the standard deviation to the results with a period of 5s and the results of location-centric storage (LCS) as comparison.

One Data Item

This scenario analyses the optimization potential of our algorithm when only exactly one data item is queried by a varied number of nodes. After startup, only a fixed number of nodes (1 to 30) query the same position. Fig. 6 shows that only one querying application leads to a migration onto the node itself which results in an average route length of zero (and resembles local storage). With 2 queriers the data gets migrated between the nodes which leads to an average route length of 8.5. With an increasing number of consumers the optimization potential for our algorithm naturally decreases because the optimal position lies in between these nodes.

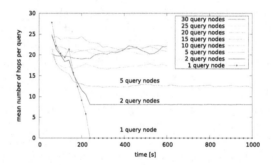

Fig. 6. Different numbers of consumers accessing one data item. The optimization potential depends on the number of queriers. With only one query node it itself becomes the storage node. With more query nodes added the optimization potential decreases.

5   Related Work

Our work originates from the idea of using coordinate translations for fast and transparent access to distributed storage which offers the interface of a distributed hash table (DHT) like Chord [16] and CAN (content-addressable network) [11]. But these approaches form an abstract overlay network which may impose significant detours in the underlying network which is unfeasible for sensor networks with their limited capabilities.

Considering in-network storage algorithms for sensor networks, the authors of [15] proposed a widely adopted data-centric storage (DCS) paradigm. In DCS, a data item is stored on a node which is chosen based on the event's name. In contrast to our work, the authors consider the sensor network to only be queried using one or more fixed access points. Moreover, their approach needs a naming scheme which has to be announced a priori to all nodes before the storage of data can take place. We overcome this drawback with our dynamic reallocation algorithm. The authors propose *Geographic Hash Tables* (GHT) that supports data-centric storage [15,12]. GHT offers a DHT-like interface for key-value-pairs. Data's position is determined by passing the key through a hash function which returns geographic coordinates. Then, GHT uses a geographic routing protocol to route the query to the node that is geographically closest to this position. Their application of a hash function leads to an equal distribution of data on the network nodes, but they do not consider the imposed load on the network. Moreover, the authors only consider queries from a fixed sink. This significantly differs from our application scenarios where we optimize the storage allocation during run-time. The authors of ZGHT [8] try to improve the storage allocation of GHT in nonuniform dense networks by introducing zones, which are responsible for similar amounts of replicated data. By adjusting the size of a zone, they achieve load balancing in terms of storage usage on the nodes. However, the ZGHT algorithm computes all zones centrally with the knowledge of all nodes' positions and floods the calculated hash function into the network. In contrast, our approach offers a fully decentralized storage allocation optimization without a single-point-of-failure. A similar approach is Q-NiGHT [1] which uses nonuniform hash functions to meet the challenge of unequally distributed sensor nodes. Moreover, their algorithm creates a fixed number of replicas of a data item. Another load-balancing approach is presented in [10] proposing a temporally rotating hash function. By changing the storage location in predefined ways during run-time, the system ensures a balanced resource utilization of the nodes. Furthermore, they introduce so-called "potential-based location selection" where nodes report their "internal contribution potential" considering their remaining storage space and energy level [9]. Periodically, potential information is distributed to gain the potential of the cells. This information is then centrally used by a sink to modify the hash-function to point to the more potential nodes. Our approach, in contrast, focuses on the distributed optimization of query routes based on current access patterns to data as primary optimization objective and scales very well. The authors of [13] perform load-balancing by analytically creating a hash function a priori based on expected probability density functions of queries. The online version of their algorithm which optimizes the storage assignments during run-time by collecting load statistics at a central server which then floods the new assignments in the network. This approach becomes unfeasible in large or busy networks.

A fundamental paradigm for in-network storage is location-centric storage (LCS). It combines the expected locality of accesses with the DCS paradigm. Thus, a storage node is determined by evaluating its proximity to a geometric reference location specified by the spatial data which can also be determined using GPSR [3]. We compare LCS to our algorithm.

6   Conclusion and Future Work

We presented a distributed self-organizing algorithm for access-centric storage in smart sensor networks whose primary design goal is the online optimization of in-network storage allocation of georeferenced data. Our novel approach is very lightweight w.r.t. message overhead and achieves a huge decrease in route lengths of up to 57%. This way, the query latency as well as the overall network load is decreased significantly. To function, our algorithm mainly requires some additional storage capacity, which is getting increasingly cheap even for smaller devices, to maintain its local state.

The speed and amount of migrations is a design parameter of our algorithm. Depending on the application domain, different migration policies may lead to much faster optimizations. In this respect, we are going to extend the results of our work in [5]. In the future, we want to investigate the theoretical bounds of access-centric storage w.r.t. its optimization potential compared to the required overhead. Moreover, we want to research different extensions of our algorithm which cover an explicit dissemination of information with CDNs advertising their responsibilities. Another field of our research are suitable replication strategies for access-centric storage.

References

1. Albano, M., Chessa, S., Nidito, F., Pelagatti, S.: Q-NiGHT: adding QoS to data centric storage in non-uniform sensor networks. In: International Conference on Mobile Data Management, pp. 166–173 (2007)
2. D'Angelo, D., Grenz, C., Kuntzsch, C., Bogen, M.: CamInSens - An intelligent in-situ security system for public spaces. In: International Conference on Security and Management (SAM), Las Vegas, Nevada, pp. 60–66 (2012)
3. Dudkowski, D.: Fundamental Storage Mechanisms for Location-based Services in Mobile Ad-hoc Networks. PhD thesis, Universität Stuttgart (2009)
4. Grenz, C., Jänen, U., Hähner, J., Kuntzsch, C., Menze, M., D'Angelo, D., Bogen, M., Monari, E.: CamInSens - Demonstration of a distributed smart camera system for in-situ threat detection. In: Proc. of Int. Conf. on Distributed Smart Cameras (ICDSC) (2012)
5. Grenz, C., Tomforde, S., Hähner, J.: Access-centric in-network storage optimization in distributed sensing networks. In: Human Behavior Understanding in Networked Sensing, pp. 19–44. Springer International Publishing (2014)
6. Hoffmann, M., Wittke, M., Hähner, J., Müller-Schloer, C.: Spatial partitioning in self-organizing smart camera systems. IEEE Journal on Selected Topics in Signal Processing 2(4), 480–492 (2008)
7. Karp, B., Kung, H.T.: Greedy perimeter stateless routing for wireless networks. In: Proceedings of the ACM/IEEE International Conference on Mobile Computing and Networking (MobiCom), Boston, MA, pp. 243–254 (2000)
8. Kumar, B.: ZGHT- A Zonal Hash-Table for Data-Centric Storage. TAMU Comp.Sci, College Station, TX 77840
9. Le, T.N., Xuan, D., Yu, W.: An adaptive zone-based storage architecture for wireless sensor networks. In: IEEE Global Telecommunications Conference (2005)
10. Le, T.N., Yu, W., Bai, X., Xuan, D.: A dynamic geographic hash table for data-centric storage in sensor networks. In: IEEE Wireless Communications and Networking Conference (WCNC), pp. 2168–2174 (2006)
11. Ratnasamy, S., Francis, P., Handley, M., Karp, R., Shenker, S.: A scalable content addressable network. In: Proc. of the Conf. on Applications, Technologies, Architectures, and Protocols for Computer Communications, pp. 161–172 (2001)
12. Ratnasamy, S., Karp, B., Yin, L., Yu, F., Estrin, D., Govindan, R., Shenker, S.: GHT: A geographic hash table for data-centric storage. In: Proceedings of the First ACM International Workshop on Wireless Sensor Networks and Applications, New York, NY, USA, pp. 78–87 (2002)
13. Renda, M.E., Resta, G., Santi, P.: Load Balancing Hashing in Geographic Hash Tables. IEEE Trans. on Parallel Distributed Systems 23(8), 1508–1519 (2012)
14. Rinner, B., Wolf, W.: An Introduction to Distributed Smart Cameras. Proceedings of the IEEE 96(10), 1565–1575 (2008)
15. Shenker, S., Ratnasamy, S., Karp, B., Govindan, R., Estrin, D.: Data-centric storage in sensornets. SIGCOMM Computer Commun. 33(1), 137–142 (2003)
16. Stoica, I., Morris, R., Karger, D., Kaashoek, M.F., Balakrishnan, H.: Chord: A scalable peer-to-peer lookup service for internet applications. In: Proceedings of the Conference on Applications, Technologies, Architectures, and Protocols for Computer Commun., New York, NY, pp. 149–160 (2001)
17. Varga, A., Hornig, R.: An overview of the OMNeT++ simulation environment. In: Proceedings of the 1st International Conference on Simulation Tools and Techniques for Communications, Networks and Systems, Simutools (2008)

Hierarchical Area-Based Address Autoconfiguration Protocol for Self-organized Networks

Mandimby N. Ranaivo Rakotondravelona, Fanilo Harivelo, and Pascal Anelli

Laboratoire d'Informatique et de Mathématiques (LIM)
University of Reunion Island, France
{mandimby.ranaivo,fanilo.harivelo,pascal.anelli}@univ-reunion.fr

Abstract. Node autoconfiguration is one of the main issues in self-organized networks. One class of approaches relies on hierarchical organization of nodes. This kind of structuration aims to deal with scalability issues, especially for wireless networks. But building and maintaining a hierarchy is generally expensive for these resource-limited networks. We propose a low-cost distributed, hierarchical, location-based address autoconfiguration protocol. Each node infers its address from those of its one-hop neighbors and from its relative position to them. In this way we obtain a globally-consistent organization resulting from local interactions only. This reduces the latency and the overhead generated during address configuration. Moreover this scheme is the first step towards the design of a scalable routing protocol taking advantages of the proposed hierarchical addressing.

Keywords: self-organized, ad-hoc, wireless, distributed protocol, address autoconfiguration.

1 Introduction

Self-organized networks consist of hosts that rely neither on a central infrastructure, nor on an external intervention to perform necessary configurations of members. *Wireless Sensor Networks* (WSN), *Wireless Mesh Networks* (WMN) and *Mobile Ad-hoc Networks* (MANET) are typical examples. Internet of things, smart cities, disaster recovery emergency communication systems are possible fields of application of such networks. But to be useful and widely adopted in the real world, they need to scale well. By good scaling capability we mean: bounded configuration time, limited traffic overhead ... in other words, good performance despite an increased size of the network.

In self-organized networks, address autoconfiguration is a major issue as it is one of the fundamental prerequisites for communication between hosts. Address assignment takes place before any routing protocol execution. The routing protocol will gain from a suitable organization of nodes obtained by the addressing mechanism. Many address autoconfiguration protocols have been proposed but

© Institute for Computer Sciences, Social Informatics and Telecommunications Engineering 2015
N. Mitton et al. (Eds.): AdHocNets 2015, LNICST 155, pp. 173–184, 2015.
DOI: 10.1007/978-3-319-25067-0_14

those using hierarchical approaches give the better results in term of scalability as they provide benefits to hierarchical routing protocol [5].

Some mechanisms of existing hierarchical approaches rely on the election of special nodes known as cluster heads. These nodes have more responsibility, such as maintaining the hierarchy, than the rest of the network. For this task, they have to maintain more information, for instance addresses of the nodes in their clusters. Thus their failure is difficult to handle. Other approaches use particular address structure, most of the time, an address tree. The trees are constructed in a top-down approach. But with this way, when the address length is fixed, it is difficult to extend the network with larger addresses. This could lead to rapid address exhaustion. Moreover, in high density networks, granularity problems can occur, again because of the top-down construction. In fact, an a priori distribution of addresses is difficult since the topology of the network is unpredictable. A bottom-up approach doesn't suffer from these drawbacks because it is by nature flexible. For instance, in the granularity problem, the top level of the hierarchy would raise instead of address exhaustion. In this paper, we focus on how to get hierarchical organization without having the cumbersome tasks in maintaining the hierarchy.

We propose a hierarchical addressing scheme for self-organized networks. The nodes are treated equally. Each of them runs the same algorithm: local interactions between nodes result in a hierarchical organization of the network. In other terms we obtain a hierarchy from a bottom-up construction. Moreover address acquired by a node not only indicates the hierarchy branch to which it belongs but also reflects its position in the network. To achieve all of this, we designed an address pattern that is naturally followed by the nodes as they run the proposed protocol. We choose to make a distinction between the identifier and the address as in [2]. The identifier is unique and remains unchanged during the node's lifetime. The address gives only information on node's location.

Our two main contributions are:

- *A hierarchical subdivision and labeling of space.* This is a geographic subdivision of the space. Each smallest area is locally labeled with a binary number following a simple rule. A number of those areas form a bigger area that is locally labeled in its turn and so on. The result is a hierarchy of areas with several levels. The global label of an area is a concatenation of its local label and those of the bigger areas it is member of. Another interesting property of the subdivision is that areas sharing a part of their labels (e.g. same n most significant bits) are geographically close to each other. The details are discussed in Section 3.
- *A distributed address autoconfiguration protocol.* From the previous space partitioning, an address plan is created. In a few words, the labels i.e. the binary numbers representing an area are used as addresses for the nodes. This assignment can be achieved using either the absolute geographic locations of the nodes or their relative positions to each other. In the latter case, only one-hop communications are necessary to determine the address of a new host. By applying the particular labeling of the space to node addressing,

we are able to construct an address hierarchy in a bottom-up way. This protocol is detailed in Section 4.

Performance of the address assignment scheme is evaluated qualitatively and through a simulation realized on ns-3 [1] as described in Section 5. Results show that in the worst case (all the nodes starting at the same time in a connected topology network) the convergence delay, i.e. the time needed for all nodes to get valid addresses, is $O(log(n))$ where n is the number of nodes. The number of configuration packets generated during this process is $O(n)$. The results demonstrate the scalability of the protocol.

2   Related Work

Numerous address autoconfiguration protocols for self-organized networks, mostly for MANETs have been proposed in the literature. They can be classified as stateless, stateful or hybrid. In stateless protocols, nodes have no knowledge about the already used addresses in the network [12,3,11]. The address given to a new node is usually selected randomly from the available set of addresses. Therefore it is necessary to check if the new address is already used. This process is called *duplicate address detection* (DAD). Because nodes don't retain all the used addresses, DAD implies the flooding of the entire network generating high traffic overhead, leading to poor scalability. AROD [8] tries to limit DAD procedures by performing DAD on multiple addresses but broadcast is still necessary.

Stateful schemes tend to be more scalable because there is no need for network-wide DAD. Configured nodes store a state from which addresses for new joining nodes are derived. Usually the protocols rely on some mathematical properties to generate unique sequences of addresses. For instance, Prophet [17] uses a function which generates distinct sequences of addresses according to the seed, each new node receiving a new seed. In [6], properties of prime numbers are used. Other approaches consist in sharing disjoint address pools between configured nodes [18] [13].

The above mentioned addressing protocols produce a flat addressing scheme. Yet according to Hong et al. comparative study [5], hierarchical and geographic routing protocols offer better scalability. And these two approaches are efficient with non flat address structure. Hierarchical addressing can be obtained by clustering the network. Some nodes act as cluster heads like in [7]. A node's address is the sequence of addresses of all its higher levels cluster heads addresses. An adaptation of the IPv6 stateless address autoconfiguration with a hierarchical approach is proposed in [15]. One of the drawbacks of these schemes is that these special nodes potentially become bottlenecks because they have to deal with traffic from lower nodes in the hierarchy. In [2], a hierarchical addressing without clustering is proposed. The link made between positions of the nodes and the branch of the hierarchy to which they belong inspired us. But in this approach, the hierarchy is constructed in a top-down way. So if there are regions with high node density, some nodes can potentially not obtain an address.

With the availability of geographic location information, another way to obtain hierarchical addressing reflecting the positions of the nodes is to partition the network space with structured areas and use the identifiers of these areas as addresses [10]. We propose a similar scheme with elastic partition shape and size depending on the topology and the dynamic of the network.

Finally we want to point out the study in [2] showing that scalability problem in MANETs and in self-organized networks results mainly from the use of the node's address as its identifier at the same time. The authors propose a dynamic addressing in which node's identifier remains unchanged during its lifetime; node's address is only intended for location and routing purposes.

3   Hierarchical Areas Organization

This section deals with how we can partition the two-dimensional space into labeled areas in order to get a hierarchical organization. This structure constitutes the address plan used to configure nodes as seen later in Section 4.

3.1   Hierarchy of Areas

From now on, we consider the two-dimensional space. Let's delimit a square and define it as an elementary area. Then we give it a *label*. A label is a binary number of 2 bits, for instance, 00 (Figure 1(a)). This area is a level-1 area. The remaining available labels are 01, 10 and 11. Let's assign them to the 3 areas of the same size next to the first in a way that the whole forms a larger square area (Figure 1(b)). The latter is in turn labeled with a 2-bits number and constitutes a level-2 area. Again, 4 larger areas are grouped together resulting in a much larger area labeled with a 2-bits number (Figure 1(c)) and so on. The process can be repeated indefinitely. The hierarchy is highlighted on Figure 1(d). The elementary areas are uniquely identified by the *concatenation* of the labels of every larger areas to which they belong. To sum up, a level-n area has a 2-bits label appended to a global label resulting from the concatenation of the labels of level-N to level-$n+1$ areas having it as "child" where N is the level of the largest area.

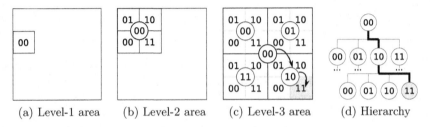

(a) Level-1 area   (b) Level-2 area   (c) Level-3 area   (d) Hierarchy

Fig. 1. Area hierarchy

How about the hierarchy? Each 4 siblings of areas belongs to a particular level of the hierarchy. One area of level n is composed of 4 areas of level $n - 1$ and so on. The equation (1) gives the global labels of any 4 siblings of the space with the desired number of levels of hierarchy represented by n. The two-dimensional space can be considered as covered by a numerical matrix $(M(n))$ whose elements correspond to the global labels of each area.

$$M(n) = \begin{pmatrix} (10 - n\%4)||M(n-1) & (01 - n\%4)||M(n-1) \\ (01 - n\%4)||M(n-1) & (00 - n\%4)||M(n-1) \end{pmatrix} \quad (1)$$

With $M(0) = ()$

Example. On Figures 1(c)(d) we have a hierarchy with $n = 3$ levels. Let's consider the area colored in gray. It is labeled with 11. The larger area to which it belongs is labeled with 10 that is itself part of the largest area 00. Therefore the complete global label of the considered area is the concatenation of these labels from top to down (indicated by arrows on (c)). The result is 001011.

3.2   Properties

The area hierarchy described above has some interesting properties for the design of the address configuration mechanism:

- *Unlimited.* Theoretically, with equation (1), we can partition the entire two-dimensional space with an infinite number of levels of hierarchy.
- *Quasi-isotropic.* If we calculate values of equation (1) with great n, and if we draw the path from label 00 to the highest value, we would get a spiral. In other words, the construction of the structure tends to grow equally towards all directions. Moreover, as there is no privileged direction, the lengths of the labels of two opposite areas with respect to the center of the considered space tend to be the same.
- *Geographic and hierarchical property.* One of the most important property of this area organization is the relation between the geographic location of an area and its hierarchical position. In fact areas with the same parent belong to the same level of hierarchy but are also close to each other. For instance, if we have a look at Figures 1(c) (d), the areas 001011 (the gray one) and 001010 (on "top" of the gray one in (c), on its "left" in (d)) share the same parent level-2 area 0010 but are also geographically in the level-2 area corresponding to this label. In other words, the more bits two areas share (from the high-order bit), the more they are geographically close to each other.
- *Easy neighboring identification.* From equation (1) we know how global labels are geographically distributed to all areas. Hence for a given area, it is easy to find the labels of the surrounding areas (from the elements of $M(n)$ in (1)).

4   Address Autoconfiguration Protocol

In this section we give details about the address autoconfiguration protocol that we designed based on the previous two-dimensional space subdivision. The main idea is to use the labels of areas as addresses for nodes. In other words, the previous labels distribution serves as an *address plan*. This way, the address assignment scheme inherits the above mentioned properties:

- The maximum number of addressable nodes depends only on the maximum supported address length. It is possible to start with a small address length and increase it as the network grows in scale.
- The more bits two addresses share (from the high-order bit), the more geographically close the hosts are.
- Neighbors addresses of a given node can be calculated from its own address. Inversely, a node's address can be deduced from those of its neighbors, provided the information about its relative position to them.

As stated before, we make a distinction between the *identifier* (ID) and the *address* of a node. The ID uniquely identifies the node and the address gives an information about its geographic position. This scheme is interesting for networks of mobile nodes. As a matter of fact it is not easy to keep track of a node whose ID is changing frequently. Hence it is better to keep the ID unchanged. But the ID has then to be resolved into an address. To achieve that, distributed lookup service exists [2] [10]. ID-address separation allows also the assignation of the same address to two or more nodes in the same limited geographic location. This helps to solve granularity problem (case of very high number of nodes in the same location) and spares the address space.

4.1   Basic Idea

We propose a mechanism that assigns addresses to nodes depending on their geographic position in the network. There are two cases:

- If the nodes know their absolute geographic position (using GPS), the entire region where they are located is mapped with our address plan. This leads to a grid partitionning of the space. The size of the elementary squares is chosen to be close to the radio range of the nodes. Each node chooses as address the label of the region where it is located using its absolute coordinates.
- If the nodes have only access to their relative geographic position [16], the address assignement needs communication between nodes. From now on, we will focus on this second case.

A new arriving node gets its address from an already configured node. By configured we mean having a valid address. Thanks to a distributed algorithm, nodes acquire addresses according to the address plan. After the configuration of all nodes in the network, the distribution of the addresses looks like the distribution of the labels of areas as seen previously.

There are two types of configured nodes :

- A *standard* node doesn't respond to address requests from new joining nodes.
- An *Address Agent (AA)* node responds to address requests of incoming nodes with its own address.

It is important to notice that AA nodes aren't elected. They become AA in order to satisfy unconfigured nodes with no AA in their vicinity.

4.2   Conventions and Assumptions

From now on, we will consider a wireless ad-hoc network. The *neighborhood* of a node is the set of nodes within its communication range. In other terms, the neighborhood is formed by all nodes reachable within one hop. The *relative position* of a node to one of its neighbor must be taken in a geographic sense and can be obtained using techniques similar to those surveyed in [16]. We call *prefix* at level n the two bits corresponding to the label of an area of level n. The address of a particular node is then the concatenation of all prefixes of all levels. For example, given the address 1011, the prefix of level 1 is 11 and that of level 2 is 10.

The following assumptions are made and are necessary for the protocol to work properly:

- A node is uniquely identified with a separate identifier than the address (the MAC address, the EUI-64 identifier, ...)
- A node is aware of its neighborhood. Nodes exchange "hello" messages periodically with the neighbors.
- The nodes are aware of their relative position to their neighborhood.
- Each connected group of nodes (or one isolated node) is identified by a network ID.

4.3   Address Allocation

New Node. To join a network, a new node sends an address request. If present, existing AA in the neighborhood provide the node an address. If this is the first node in the network, it assigns itself the address 00 and then becomes an AA while a random network ID is generated.

Becoming an AA. When it "hears" repeated address requests from a new joining node indicating that there is no response, a standard node becomes AA to satisfy the address solicitation. For this purpose, it takes the addresses of all AA in its neighborhood and calculates a new address in accordance with the address plan. This new address will be used to configure incoming nodes.

Example. On Figure 2(a), a node A starts. It sends address requests but receives no reply. So it assigns itself the address 00 and becomes an AA. Later (Figure 2(b)), node B arrives, wants to join and sends address requests. A replies so B is configured as standard node with the same address as A. Then comes node C (Figure 2(c)). We suppose that it is out of the range of A. It sends address requests. B "hears" but doesn't reply as it is not AA. C continues to send requests. B assumes that C has no AA in its vicinity. So B configures itself as AA and uses A's address and its relative position to infer the address 11 (see Figure 1(b)). Finally B responds to C.

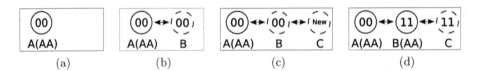

Fig. 2. Joining nodes

4.4 Topology Changes Issues

Mobility. From the moving node point of view, when it reaches a new position, it acts like a new node: it requests new address whether it was a standard node or an AA. From the neighborhood perspective, there is no action to take. A node is aware of its moves (or those of its neighbors) by observing changes in its neighbors table.

Merging. Merging of networks can be detected when nodes with different network IDs are in contact. One solution makes the node with lower (or higher) network ID reach the other network by requesting for new address just like a new node. An optimized solution would compare the size of the two networks: the nodes from the smaller join the bigger. Estimating the size can be done in a distributed way [9]. In any case, the merging process goes gradually, node per node, avoiding a potential explosion of traffic in the network. At the end, the nodes form a single network with the same network ID.

Partitioning. Partitioning of networks doesn't affect the validity of addresses in the resulting partitions. In fact, every partition corresponds to a part of the address plan. Therefore, there is no action to take. And the address space is not reduced because nodes arriving at the previously used partition will use the same addresses as the previous holders.

5 Evaluation

5.1 Qualitative Analysis

To evaluate the quality of an address autoconfiguration protocol, common metrics are considered [14]:

Uniqueness. It used to be the most important criteria for address assignment in ad-hoc networks: two or more nodes aren't allowed to share an address. This is only relevant in the case where addresses serve also as identifiers. In our proposition, addresses are only intended to give location information for routing purpose. The nodes which are located in a nearby area are allowed to share the same address. It is analog to people living in the same house who share the same postal address. This contributes to the savings of address space. It solves also the granularity problem which happens when a level-n of the hierarchy is saturated and can't take more level-$n - 1$. It happens when all possible addresses within a given area are allocated and a new node starts.

Protocol Overhead. How much bandwidth is consumed during configuration processes? As we have seen previously, all the protocol's operations require local communication only. This reduces traffic overhead compared to other mechanisms with multi-hop broadcast communications. But our protocol needs neighboring discovery, so, hello packets are advertised periodically. The bandwidth consumed by these packets increases linearly with the number of nodes in the network. Nevertheless hello protocols can be improved [4], generating less overhead. Comparing to stateful approaches our solution generates fairly the same amount of traffic as these protocols need also periodic updates.

Latency. Latency is the time between the joining of an unconfigured node and when it is fully configured with a valid address. The notion of AA reduces latency. If there is an AA in the neighborhood of a new node, the configuration process ends after the exchange of only two messages (assuming a reliable radio connection). If there is no AA, the latency is increased with the time needed for one of the one-hop neighbors to become an AA. This shows that latency increases as much as the distance to the closest AA. Because all configured nodes had an AA in their vicinity prior their address assignation, the probability to not find an AA is equivalent to the probability that every AA in a given region crashes at the same time. It decreases with the size of the region. Hence the probability to not find an AA decreases with distance (again assuming a reliable radio connection). Therefore latency is bounded at least in a reliable network.

Integration with Routing Protocol. The efficiency of routing process can be improved with a well designed address assignation mechanism. In our scheme, addresses have a hierarchical structure giving advantages for hierarchical routing protocols which are known to scale well [5]. Another property of the address structure is the relation between addresses and geographic position. Therefore, our protocol can be used along with geographic routing protocols that consume fewer bandwidth [5]. A hybrid approach can also be chosen, combining the hierarchical and geographic aspects.

Scalability. Local communication means lower communication overhead and shorter latency leading to good scalability.

Comparison with Similar Approach. Compared to [2] the traffic overhead is merely on the same order. But in our solution, nodes don't have to maintain any address range. [10] assigns addresses to nodes with only geographic position, hence without bandwidth cost. Author make the assumption that every node is aware of the global partitioning of the world, what we don't.

Compatibility with IP Applications. Our approach needs some adaptations in order to run IP applications. This can be done by using nodes identifiers as "IP addresses". This way the autoconfiguration of the nodes addresses (in the sense of our protocol) and the routing through them is hidden to the application layer. Another approach consists in using our addressing scheme for geocasting, i.e, multicasting with groups composed with nodes geographically close to each other. These adaptations are necessary for our protocol to be compatible with IP-based trending protocol stack like 6LowPan.

5.2   Simulation

In this subsection we focus on a quantitative study of the scalability of the proposed protocol. The simulation was done on ns-3 [1] (ns-3.22 release).

Scenario and Metrics. We consider the worst case scenario for the protocol, consisting in unconfigured nodes starting at the same time in a topology connected network. In fact, joining nodes receive addresses quickly when there are already configured nodes in the network. In the case of concurrent starts, address requests are unsatisfied due to unconfigured neighbors. Each node "thinks" that it is alone then assigns itself the 00 address and chooses a random network ID while becoming an AA. After this first configuration, high number of merges occur as each node receives hello packets from different network IDs. At the end of this transient state, the entire network should share the same network ID and addresses should respect the address plan.

To study the scalability of the protocol in this worst case, we chose two metrics and observed their behavior with different network sizes:

- The *convergence delay* which is the amount of time between when the nodes start and when the last node acquires a valid address with respect to the address plan. In other words, it shows the maximum latency for acquiring a network-wide valid address in a concurrent start case.
- The *number of configuration packets* which is exchanged from the start till the end of the configuration of the last node with a valid address. These packets include address requests, address offers etc. The hello packets are not considered because they are periodically exchanged in any situation.

Simulation Parameters. The above metrics are measured with increasing nodes number from 100 to 1000. The nodes are randomly distributed in a square region with a density of 0.375 node per unit × unit, each node having a communication range of 3 units. These values ensure a global connected topology network. The density is kept constant for all simulations. The nodes are also kept in static positions. From the point of view of the protocol, mobility is a crash followed by a start because, as a node moves, it must acquire a new address reflecting its new location. Therefore very high mobility can be considered as a massive concurrent start as studied here. The ns-3 wifi model is 802.11b with non-Qos MAC, disabled rate control and set to ad-hoc mode. UDP is chosen as transport protocol. All the means in the data are presented with their respective 95% confidence interval.

Results. Figure 3 shows the evolution of the average convergence delay for different simulations, each with different number of nodes n. Here n varies from 100 to 1000 nodes. One finds that for a given density, the delay is proportional to $log(n)$. The reason is that each configured node can in turn configure all

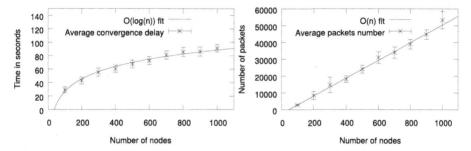

Fig. 3. Average convergence delay   **Fig. 4.** Average number of configuration packets

its neighbors. Thus the number of "configurable" nodes grows exponentially with the number of already configured nodes. In other words, the number of configured nodes grows exponentially in time even if "slowed" by the merges implying reconfigurations.

In Figure 4 we see that the average total number of configuration packets grows linearly with n. In fact, the more we have unconfigured nodes, the more configured packets are sent. This linearity shows that for a single node, the average necessary number of configuration packets it has to exchange doesn't depend on the total number of nodes in the network.

To resume, in the worst case of massive concurrent starts in a global connected topology network, the average convergence delay is proportional to $log(n)$ and the average number of configuration packets to n. These values can be considered as bounds for other less constraining scenarios, showing the scalability of our approach in terms of configuration delay and traffic overhead.

6   Conclusion and Future Work

We propose a hierarchical addressing protocol for self-organized networks. A node's address reflects both the branch of the hierarchy to which it belongs and its geographic position in the network. Address assignment needs only local information from one-hop neighborhood. Qualitative performance evaluation and simulations results show the scalability of the scheme. In the worst case, the average convergence delay which is the time needed for all nodes to acquire a valid address is $O(log(n))$ and the average total number of configuration packets exchanged is $O(n)$.

The addressing scheme has been thought to allow the future design of a scalable routing protocol taking advantages from the hierarchical and geographic addresses. A distributed location service will be also necessary in order to follow the identifier-address separation paradigm. Regarding the addressing scheme, further research will be conducted to adapt the pattern to the three-dimensional space.

Acknowledgments. Mandimby N. Ranaivo Rakotondravelona's PhD study is supported by Région Réunion and European Union (ERDF).

References

1. ns-3: a discrete event simulator. https://www.nsnam.org/
2. Eriksson, J., Faloutsos, M., Krishnamurthy, S.: DART: Dynamic address routing for scalable ad hoc and mesh networks. IEEE/ACM Transactions on Networking 15(1), 119–132 (2007)
3. Fazio, M., Villari, M., Puliafito, A.: AIPAC: Automatic IP address configuration in mobile ad-hoc networks. Computer Communications 29(8), May 2006
4. Giruka, V., Singhal, M.: Hello protocols for ad-hoc networks: overhead and accuracy tradeoffs. In: IEEE WoWMoM, pp. 354–361, June 2005
5. Hong, X., Xu, K., Gerla, M.: Scalable routing protocols for mobile ad hoc networks. IEEE Network 16(4), 11–21 (2002)
6. Hsu, Y.Y., Tseng, C.C.: Prime DHCP: a prime numbering address allocation mechanism for MANETs. IEEE Communications Letters 9(8) (2005)
7. Iwata, A., Chiang, C.C., Pei, G., Gerla, M., Chen, T.W.: Scalable routing strategies for ad hoc wireless networks. IEEE Journal on Selected Areas in Communications 17(8), 1369–1379 (1999)
8. Kim, N., Ahn, S., Lee, Y.: AROD: An address autoconfiguration with address reservation and optimistic duplicated address detection for mobile ad hoc networks. Computer Communications 30(8), 1913–1925 (2007)
9. Le Merrer, E., Kermarrec, A.M., Massoulie, L.: Peer to peer size estimation in large and dynamic networks: A comparative study. In: IEEE Symposium on International High Performance Distributed Computing, pp. 7–17 (2006)
10. Li, J., Jannotti, J., De Couto, D., Karger, D., Morris, R.: A scalable location service for geographic ad hoc routing. In: International Conference on Mobile Computing and Networking, pp. 120–130. ACM (2000)
11. Nesargi, S., Prakash, R.: MANETconf: Configuration of hosts in a mobile ad hoc network. In: IEEE INFOCOM, pp. 1059–1068 (2002)
12. Perkins, C., Malinen, J.T., Wakikawa, R.: IP address autoconfiguration for ad-hoc networks. IETF draft-ietf-manet-autoconf-01 (2001)
13. Sheu, J.P., Tu, S.C., Chan, L.H.: A distributed IP address assignment scheme in ad hoc networks. International Journal of Ad Hoc and Ubiquitous Computing 3(1), 10–20 (2008)
14. Wangi, N., Prasad, R., Jacobsson, M., Niemegeers, I.: Address autoconfiguration in wireless ad hoc networks: protocols and techniques. IEEE Wireless Communications 15(1), 70–80 (2008)
15. Weniger, K., Zitterbart, M.: IPv6 autoconfiguration in large scale mobile ad-hoc networks. In: European Wireless, pp. 142–148 (2002)
16. Zekavat, S.A., Kansal, S., Levesque, A.H.: Wireless Positioning Systems: Operation, Application, and Comparison, pp. 3–23. John Wiley & Sons, Inc. (2011)
17. Zhou, H., Ni, L., Mutka, M.: Prophet address allocation for large scale MANETs. In: IEEE INFOCOM, vol. 2, pp. 1304–1311, March 2003
18. Zimmermann, A., Hannemann, A., Schleinzer, B.: IP address assignment in wireless mesh networks. Wireless Communications and Mobile Computing 11(3), 321–337 (2011)

From the Characterization of Ranging Error to the Enhancement of Nodes Localization for Group of Wireless Body Area Networks

Anis Ouni[1], Jihad Hamie[1], Claude Chaudet[1], Arturo Guizar[2], and Claire Goursaud[2]

[1] Institut Mines-Telecom, Telecom ParisTech,
CNRS LTCI UMR 5141, 46 rue Barrault, 75634 Paris, France
anis.ouni@telecom-paristech.fr
[2] University of Lyon, INRIA, INSA Lyon, CITI-INRIA, F-69621, Lyon, France

Abstract. Time-based localization in Wireless Body Area Networks (WBANs), has attracted growing research interest for the last past years. Nodes positions can be estimated based on peer-to-peer radio transactions between devices. Indeed, the accuracy of the localization process could be highly affected by different factors, such as the WBAN channels where the signal is propagating through, as well as the nodes mobility that bias the peer-to-peer range estimation, and thus, the final achieved localization accuracy. The goal of this paper consists in characterizing the impact of mobility and WBAN channel on the ranging and localization estimation, based on real mobility traces acquired through a motion capture system. More specifically, the ranging error is evaluated over all the WBANs links (i.e. on-body, off-body and body-to-body links), while an impulse Radio Ultra-Wideband (IR-UWB) physical layer, as well as a TDMA-based Medium Access Control (MAC) are playing on. The simulation results show that the range measurement error can be modeled as a Gaussian distribution. To deal with the gaussianity observation of ranging error and to provide high positioning accuracy, an adjustable extended Kalman Filter (EKF) is proposed.

Keywords: Body Area Networks, Group Navigation, Ultra Wideband, Ranging error, localization, EKF.

1 Introduction

The field of Wireless Body Area Networks has attracted much interest during the last years. Recently, these networks are considered for radio-location purposes thanks to their easy deployment. Unlike some costly and geographically restricted video acquisition system (e.g. Kinect, VICON [1]), WBANs are very suitable to work in non-controlled indoor environments over large-scale body movements. In this localization context, several challenges are met, such as the need of high ranging and positioning accuracy. For those purposes, significant works have addressed the localization and navigation problem based on ranging estimation algorithms, while making direct and opportunistic use of the transmitted radio packets over Impulse Radio Ultra Wideband (IR-UWB) links or even Received Signal Strength Indicators (RSSI) over narrowbands links. The last solution is rather based on a prior model, which defines the variation

© Institute for Computer Sciences, Social Informatics and Telecommunications Engineering 2015
N. Mitton et al. (Eds.): AdHocNets 2015, LNICST 155, pp. 185–196, 2015.
DOI: 10.1007/978-3-319-25067-0_15

of the received power as a function of the distance separating the involved devices. However, several studies show that the RSSI is not accurate enough for extracting the distances between devices [2]. On the opposite, IR-UWB benefits from high temporal and fine multipath resolution capabilities, which allow high precision on the estimation of the Time of Arrival (TOA) of the transmitted signal. Thus, the IR-UWB is promoted as a relevant physical layer for the localization applications [3]. Based on the TOA estimation, several ranging protocols lead for estimating the Round trip - Time of Flight (RT-TOF) based on n-way (i.e. 2-Way or 3-Way) transactions.

In this paper, we consider a group of mobile WBANs in navigation application occupied with a set of wireless devices. The positioning of the on-body nodes consists in collecting the range measurements either in a centralized manner (at a central node), or in a distributed scheme (each node collects its range measurements with respect to its neighborhood devices for its own localization). The range estimation through several transactions, as well as of the range collection from devices conducts for latency, which depends on the network size as well as the addressed scheduling [4]. In turn, this latency triggers ranging error, as the body can change its position and its gesture during this elapsed time. Besides, another main source of ranging error is related to the involved WBAN channel, in which the signal may suffer from NLOS propagation effects and dense multipath situation. These errors source, if not properly mitigated, generally yield severe degradation of positioning accuracy. The aim of this paper is twofold. Firstly, we characterize the impact of both mobility and WBAN channel on the ranging error with respect to on-, off- or inter-body links and, secondly, we propose an improvement of the final localization precision.

Due to the high difficulty of using radio-location experiments (i.e. lack of IEEE 802.15.6 integrated devices), most works of literature are focused on theoretical studies using often unrealistic assumptions and inaccurate abstraction of wireless communications, or focusing on a given layer, ignoring the other network layers. In this paper, we use a discrete-event simulator, WSNet [5], which takes into account the real time constraints for maintaining the peer-to-peer ranging transactions along the network and addresses all the layers. We implemented a complete protocol stack by crossing the physical up to the application layer dedicated to WBANs localization applications, particularly, based on IR-UWB physical layer with OOK modulation as defined by IEEE 802.15.6 and TDMA-based access control layer that mimics the scheduled access of a group of WBANs. We use a mobility model resulting from real experiments in which people movements were logged by a professional motion capture system. We considered a navigation group scenario composed of three WBANs. Our simulation results show that the measurement error range due to the nodes mobility can be modeled by a Gaussian distribution. To mitigate the effects of this error source and provide high positioning accuracy, an adjustable extended Kalman Filter (EKF) is proposed. Simulation results are included to show the capability of our improved EKF in increasing the positioning accuracy.

The rest of the paper is organized as follows. Next Section reviews related work. Section 3 describes the system model and gives the problem statement. In Section 4, we evaluate and characterize the ranging error obtained under realistic body mobility.

Section 5, then, presents the core cooperative EKF, as well as our optimization approach and their localization performances. Finally, Section 6 concludes the paper.

2   Related Work

In the context of ranging estimation, [6] presents the issues of ranging error, position update latency and calculation algorithms under mobility. The authors are limited to the impact of MAC allocation resources on the capacity of the tracking system for Wireless Sensor Networks scenarios. In [7], the authors modeled the ranging error in terms of TOA estimation with real IR-UWB channel measurements in order to perform better localization algorithms but without any focus on the statistics of ranging error. [8] realizes a realistic measurement setup to achieve accurate positioning of WBAN nodes and compare the results with a Vicon system. The study, however, requires special attention on the ranging accuracy, i.e., characteristics of the on-body ranging error.

   In the context of localization estimation, various positioning algorithms have been developed in the past few years. [9] has used the Non Linear Least Squares (NLLS) algorithm, which consists in minimizing a global quadratic cost function using the Gradient descent method incorporating the peer-to-peer range measurements. In [4], the problem of scheduling strategies at MAC layer is addressed to enable an Individual Motion Capture application with IR-UWB systems. The authors show that an effective scheduling scheme leads to estimate the nodes position one by one. The study, however, does not take into account the impact of channel noise on the position estimation. [10] and [11] adapt a centralized classical *Multidimensional Scaling* (MDS) for on-body motion capture applications and pose estimation. In [11], the authors introduce additional constraints relying on the prior knowledge of minimal and maximal feasible distances related to the body dimensions (and thus some kinds of geographical limitations). In [12] the centralized Maximum Likelihood estimator has been considered, introducing other constraints relying on the actual positions of on-body mobile nodes. More recently, the problem of cooperative localization based on the extended Kalman filtering (EKF) has been developed which incorporates the cooperative peer-to-peer range measurements with the on-body nodes as well as the anchors [13]. The existing contributions do not exploit the potential information of the lower layers. In this paper, we investigate the robustness of the cooperative EKF in delivering high positioning accuracy for group navigation purposes while exploiting cross layer information, i.e., channel and nodes mobility.

3   System Model and Problem Formulation

3.1   System Model and Assumptions

We consider a group of mobile WBANs and a set of fixed anchors (reference nodes) placed at known positions (position has been hard-coded into each anchor) with respect to a global 3D coordinate system. Each WBAN is defined by a set of on-body wireless devices, which are called on-body nodes. These on-body nodes are attached to the human body that evolves in an indoor and outdoor environment. The positions of all these on-body nodes are unknown and must be estimated relatively to the anchors. Since we assume a mesh topology network, we distinguish three kinds of links: either belonging to one single body network (on-body links), between distinct equipped users at reasonably short transmission ranges (inter-WBAN links), or even with respect to fixed elements of infrastructure (off-body links), as depicted in Figure 1. In this paper, all anchors and on-body nodes use an IR-UWB physical layer and operate with a single-channel frequency. In order to avoid the interference between communications, a TDMA-based MAC layer is used by all the nodes. We assume that the nodes positions are mapped into a stable Cartesian Local Coordinate System (LCS), which is defined by the fixed anchors and can be easily referenced to any Global Coordinate System (GCS). All the on-body nodes are then located in this coordinate system using peer-to-peer range measurements with the anchors or even between them, by performing TOA and 3-Way Ranging (3-WR) handshake protocol transactions. We refer to non-cooperative localization (resp. cooperative localization) when a node perform the 3-WR with the anchors only (resp. with the anchors and the other on-body nodes).

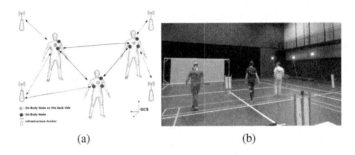

(a)   (b)

Fig. 1. Typical deployment scenario of group of WBANs in navigation application. There are three kinds of links: on-body links (green color), inter-body links (black color) and off-body links (blue color). The on-body nodes (red color) must be positioned relatively to the fixed anchors.

3.2 Mobility Model Derived from Captured Traces

In this paper, we use a real mobility traces obtained from a measurement campaign conducted in the CORMORAN project. A Vicon optical motion capture system provides us the motion of people in a 13mx8m area. This system records all the markers positions thanks to 16 cameras surrounding the scene, and produces a C3D motion capture file containing all markers positions over time. Figure 1 illustrates this process, showing an image from the real scene with three persons in random navigation with the presence of four fixed anchors. Two subjects are equipped with four radios devices each, while the third subject is equipped with three devices (due to the limited number of devices). The devices are placed at the chest left, the chest right, the shoulder and the back. We equipped each wireless device with a marker in order to record its exact position alongside in addition to the movements of each subject.

3.3 Ranging Measurement and Mobility Problem

The peer-to-peer range information is derived from RT-TOF estimation, which relies on 3-WR handshake protocol transactions and unitary TOA estimates for each involved packet [14]. The classical exchange for 3-WR is based on three guaranteed packets to evaluate the TOF between two nodes i and j. Node i starts by sending its request packet inside the assigned packet at time $\widetilde{T}_{i0}$. Once this packet is received by node j at time $\widetilde{T}_{j0}$, node j sends its first response back to the requester node i inside its own dedicated packet at time $\widetilde{T}_{j1}$, after a known delay. Node i will receive this packet at time $\widetilde{T}_{i1}$. To resolve the problem of clock drift, the responding node j transmits a second response packet at time $\widetilde{T}_{j2}$. This packet will be received by node i at time $\widetilde{T}_{i2}$. The resulting estimated TOF can be expressed as follows: $\widehat{TOF} = \frac{1}{2}[(\widetilde{T}_{i1} - \widetilde{T}_{i0}) - (\widetilde{T}_{j1} - \widetilde{T}_{j0})] - \frac{1}{2}[(\widetilde{T}_{i2} - \widetilde{T}_{i1}) - (\widetilde{T}_{j2} - \widetilde{T}_{j1})]$.

The node i can thus estimate its distance to node j as : $\widehat{d_{ij}} = \widehat{TOF}_{ij} * c$, where c denotes the speed of radio waves , i.e. $c = 3*10^8 m/s$. Once all the distances separating the on-body nodes with the anchors and/or with the other on-body nodes are extracted, the on-body nodes positions can be estimated using a localization algorithm.

Given that these procedures have to be realized for each couple of devices, the traffic sent over the wireless medium quickly increases with the number of devices, using a classical peer-to-peer transaction handshake (P2P). To reduce the volume of control traffic, [15] has proposed a procedure called *Aggregate-and-Broadcast* (A&B). They propose to mutualize control packets by letting each node initiates specific ranging transactions by *broadcasting* a request packet to all the other nodes, instead of querying each node separately. Each concerned nodes then aggregate its response and broadcasts a packet, which can play different roles (i.e. response 1, or even response 2). An intermediate solution, peer-to-peer ranging with request broadcasting (P2P-Broadcast), consists in broadcasting requests and transmitting responses one by one.

Another problem is the mobility of the nodes. In fact, as the on-body nodes are moving, it is straightforward that the distance between the nodes i and j can change between the beginning and the end of the 3-WR (between $\widetilde{T}_{i0}$ and $\widetilde{T}_{i2}$), as well as the end of collecting all distances estimation. Therefore, the accuracy of the ranging estimation can be reduced. Besides, another main source of ranging error is related to the involved WBAN channel. Quantifying the ranging error due to the on-body nodes mobility is very beneficial for the phase of the resolution of the localization problem.

3.4 WBAN Simulation Environment

WSNET is a discrete-event simulator providing an advanced and complete simulation environment to evaluate networking protocols and wireless systems. Thanks to its modularity and its flexibility, WSNET offers the opportunity for developing and integrating our own modules and protocols, which could be in compliance with our WBAN context. At the radio layer stage, we implemented an IEEE 802.15.6 PHY UWB with OOK modulation and data rate of 0.4875 Mbps. In order to reduce the TDMA-frame duration, we evolved a dynamic slotted TDMA approach, where the duration of each slot depends on the size of the transmitted packet. To perform a ranging estimation, we added the 3-WR protocol with the possibility of using the A&B or P2P or P2P-B procedure. Finally, we used mobility traces acquired as explained in the subsection 3.2.

4 Ranging Error due to Mobility Problem: Quantification and Distribution

This Section aims to evaluate the impact of nodes mobility on the ranging estimation. The Root Mean Square Error (RMSE), computed as the absolute difference of measured and real distances, is quantified under realistic navigation scenarios. All simulation results are obtained over 20 independent trial runs. Over each run of 100s, the number of ranging updates between each pair of nodes is about 1300 times.

4.1 Preliminary Study: Determining Elements of Mobility

To study the impact of the on-body nodes speed, we deployed 11 nodes in a single body as follows: one at the head, two at the torso, one at the back, one by hand, one by foot, one at the knee and one by elbow. Figures 2(a) illustrates the evolution of the cumulative distribution function (CDF) of the range RMSE of three different on-body links. As expected, the ranging error is more affected when the nodes mobility is considered as fast, confirming the importance of the mobility in the ranging action.
Figure 2(b) shows that the ranging accuracy also depends on the involved handshake transaction protocol. Indeed, we can observe an important gap between the performances of A&B and P2P or P2P broadcast, while the performances between P2P and P2P-Broadcast are closer. These results show that a higher ranging accuracy can be provided by grouping response packets rather than requests, which can be explained by the effect of reducing the required time for performing the 3WR over all nodes.

In the rest of this paper, we consider the group navigation scenario depicted in Figure 1 with A&B protocol. Figure 2(c) illustrate the CDF of ranging error according to three kinds of links, on-, off- and inter-body links. It shows that the on-body ranging error is relatively negligible with respect to that of inter-body and off-body links. This observation refers to the fact that the nodes mobility is bounded at the body scale, but unbounded at the large scale where the body-to-body and the off-body links are involved. This observation is very important for cooperative context, since it leads to promote and enhance the use of on-body cooperation.

4.2 Ranging Error Distribution due to Nodes Mobility

The distribution of the ranging errors of the different kinds of links (on-, off- and inter-body) can be approximated using an empirical statistics analysis. For this purpose, we firstly plotted the histogram and the empirical distribution of all ranging errors measured during 20 independent simulations of 100s each one. Figure 3 shows that the histogram and the empirical distribution closely follow a Normal distribution. The theoretical Normal distribution of each set of links is thus plotted with the mean value

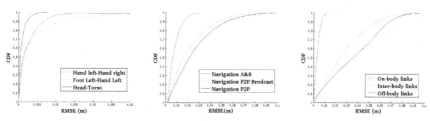

(a) The RMSE for different on-body links. (b) The RMSE for different transaction protocols. (c) The RMSE of on-, off- and inter-body links.

Fig. 2. CDFs of Root Mean Square Error (RMSE) of ranging errors. The impact of mobility on the ranging error depends on nodes speed, handshake transaction protocol and type of links.

and the standard deviation of data. In accordance with the Figure 3 and table 1, the on-body links presents the smallest standard deviation, while the off-body links have the biggest. If we compare the empirical distribution and the theoretical distribution, we observe that the ranging measured errors due to the nodes mobility fits with a Normal distribution model with the specific parameters presented in table 1. These results are very important to improve the localization accuracy, and could be taken into account by the positioning algorithms. Moreover, normality distribution is usually assumed as a model for the ranging error in localization algorithms, like Extended Filter Kalman (EKF).

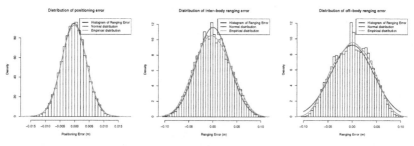

(a) On-body ranging error distribution (b) Inter-body ranging error distribution (c) Off-body ranging error distribution

Fig. 3. Distribution of ranging error for on-body, inter-body and off-body links

Table 1. Standard deviation of Ranging error due to nodes mobility

On-body links	inter-body links	Off-body links
$N(0, 0.0042)$	$N(0, 0.0343)$	$N(0, 0.0433)$

4.3 Impact of Channel Noise on Ranging Error

WBAN Channel Abstraction. In 3-WR, it is supposed that the receiver is able to detect accurately the pulse corresponding to the direct transmission between the nodes. However, depending on the person position, the channel might be multipath, inducing the use of the wrong path. However, modeling accurately the channel is computationally intensive. We therefore abstracted the channel by applying an error model directly to the range estimates. This error model, defined and characterized in [7] derives from UWB on-body and off-body channel measurements carried out in a pedestrian walking scenario. It supposes the use of an IEEE 802.15.6 mandatory band centered around $4GHz$ with a bandwidth of $500MHz$. We assume that the ranging error is added to each distance at time stamp t, as follows:

$$\widetilde{d_{ij}}(t) = d_{ij}(t) + n_{ij}(t)$$

where $\widetilde{d_{ij}}(t)$ and $d_{ij}(t)$ are respectively the measured and the real distance between nodes i and j at time t, $n_{ij}(t)$ is a centered Gaussian random variable with a standard deviation σ_n.

Table 2. Ranging error law due to the channel noise

On-body links	inter-body links	Off-body links
N(0,0.1)	N(0,0.3)	N(0,0.3)

Quantification of Ranging Error With/Without Channel Noise. We evaluate the average RMSE of ranging error in the case of ideal and noisy channel model for each set of links (on-, off- and inter-body). In the first case, Figure 4(a) shows a slow variation of the RMSE, especially, for the off- and inter-body links, while the on-body links presents a quasi-constant evolution with a mean value of 0.6 cm on RMSE. This slow variation of RMSE, can be explained by the limited variation of the on-body nodes mobility. We can also observe that the off-Body links are the most affected by the nodes mobility with a mean value of 3.6 cm. Now by adding a noisy channel model (table 2), Figure 4(b) shows a fast variation of the average RMSE for each kind of links. We can observe that the impact of the channel on the ranging estimation is much higher than the impact of mobility (approximately multiplied by 10), thus the ranging error variation is dominated by the channel variation.

5   Improvement of Extended Kalman Filter Based on Ranging Error due to Mobility

In the last section, the ranging error due to nodes mobility is quantified and shown to follow a Gaussian distribution. To mitigate the effects of this error source and hence increase the positioning accuracy, we focus in this section to improve the performance of EKF algorithm by including the mobility standard deviations over all links.

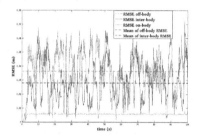 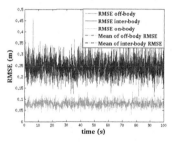

(a) RMSE ranging error with ideal channel. (b) RMSE ranging error with channel noise model

Fig. 4. Average RMSE of the all estimated distances for on-body, off-body and interinter-body links

5.1 Extended Kalman Filter Formulation with Full Cooperative Mode

We assume that positioning measurements are realized every TDMA superframe duration, T, and we will denote by $\{X_i(k)\}_{i\in\{1...n\}}$ the set of the (unknown) 3D positions of the n on-body nodes at time $t = k.T$. Let us also represent by $\{X_i\}_{i\in\{(n+1)...(n+m)\}}$ the set of the 3D positions of the m anchors. Now let us denote by $\widetilde{d}_{ij}(k)$ the value of the range measured at time $t = k.T$ between one on-body node $i \in \{1...n\}$ and another on-body node or anchor, $j \in \{1...m + n\}$. We regroup all the range measurements at step k in a vector $\widetilde{\mathbf{d}}(k) = [\{\{\widetilde{d}_{ij}(k)\}_{j=n+1:n+m}\}_{i=1:n} \ \{\{\widetilde{d}_{ij}(k)\}_{j=1:n}\}_{i=1:n}]$, which has a dynamic length depending on the number of available range measurements.

The TOA-based range measurements are defined as a non-linear functions of the on-body nodes' coordinates, thus we consider applying the well-know EKF solution [16], with the following state-space and observation models:

$$\begin{cases} \mathbf{S}(k) = \mathbf{A}.\mathbf{S}(k-1) + \mathbf{u}(k) \\ \widetilde{\mathbf{d}}(k) = h(\mathbf{S}(k)) + \mathbf{n}(k) \end{cases},$$

where $\mathbf{S}(k) = [X_1^T(k) \ V_1^T(k) \ X_2^T(k) \ V_2^T(k) ... X_n^T(k) \ V_n^T(k)]^T$ denotes the $6n$ dimensional state-space vector at step k, that regroups the three-dimensional positions and velocities of nodes. $h(.)$ is a function that materializes the non-linear relationship between the observed measurements and the state vector variables. The state transition matrix $\mathbf{A}$, assuming locally linear movements in first approximation, is given by:

$$\mathbf{A} = \mathbf{I_n} \otimes \left(\mathbf{I_6} + \left(\begin{pmatrix} 0 & 1 \\ 0 & 0 \end{pmatrix} \otimes \begin{pmatrix} T & 0 & 0 \\ 0 & T & 0 \\ 0 & 0 & T \end{pmatrix} \right) \right),$$

where $\mathbf{I_n}$ denotes the n-dimensional identity matrix and $\otimes$ is the Kronecker product. Hence $\mathbf{A}$ accounts for some a priori information bridging the occupied positions at two consecutive steps k and $k + 1$. $\mathbf{u}(k)$ is the state-space noise vector, whose covariance matrix is $\mathbf{Q}$. $\mathbf{n}(k)$ is the observation noise vector, whose covariance matrix $\mathbf{\Sigma}(k)$. Note that the latter can be adjusted dynamically over time depending on the availability and/or quality of the measurements. The implementation of this cooperative EKF follows a classical sequence of operations which involves the initialization, the prediction and the corrections phases as follows.

Prediction Phase:

$$\begin{cases} \hat{\mathbf{S}}(k|k-1) = \mathbf{A}.\hat{\mathbf{S}}(k-1|k-1) \\ \mathbf{M}(k|k-1) = \mathbf{A}.\mathbf{M}(k-1|k-1).\mathbf{A}^T + \mathbf{Q} \end{cases} \cdot$$

where $\hat{\mathbf{S}}(k|k-1)$ is the predicted state at step k based on the latest available state estimate at step $k-1$ $\hat{\mathbf{S}}(k-1|k-1)$, starting with the initial guess $\hat{\mathbf{S}}(0|0)$. $\mathbf{M}(k|k-1)$ is the corresponding prediction *Minimum Mean Squared Error* (MMSE) matrix.

Correction Phase:

$$\mathbf{K}(k) = \mathbf{M}(k|k-1).\mathbf{H}^T(k). \left(\Sigma(k) + \mathbf{H}(k).\mathbf{M}(k|k-1).\mathbf{H}^T(k) \right)^{-1},$$

where $\mathbf{K}(k)$ is the filter gain and $\mathbf{H}(k)$ is the Jacobian observation matrix:

$$\mathbf{H}(k) = \frac{\partial h(\mathbf{S}(k))}{\partial \mathbf{S}(k)} |_{\mathbf{S}(k)=\hat{\mathbf{S}}(k|k-1)},$$

$$\begin{cases} \hat{\mathbf{S}}(k|k) = \hat{\mathbf{S}}(k|k-1) + \mathbf{K}(k). \left(\tilde{\mathbf{d}}(k) - h\left(\hat{\mathbf{S}}(k|k-1) \right) \right) \\ \mathbf{M}(k|k) = \left(\mathbf{I}_{6n} - \mathbf{K}(k).\mathbf{H}(k) \right).\mathbf{M}(k|k-1) \end{cases},$$

where $\hat{\mathbf{S}}(k|k)$ is the final state estimate at step k based on the current prediction $\hat{\mathbf{S}}(k|k-1)$ and observation $\tilde{\mathbf{d}}(k)$, and $\mathbf{M}(k|k)$ is the related estimation MMSE matrix.

5.2 Adjusted EKF

The last EKF version, takes only into account the range measurement error generated by the channel. However, as the nodes mobility affects the ranging estimation and hence the positioning accuracy, we propose to compensate this ranging errors by adjusting the marginal diagonal elements of the measurement noise covariance matrix $\Sigma(k) = [\hat{\sigma}_{ii}(k)]$. More specifically, our proposal consists in adjusting the covariance matrix, while taking into account the mobility effects over each of on-, off- and body-to-body links. Thus, the mobility standard deviations over all links (i.e. $\hat{\sigma}_{on}$, $\hat{\sigma}_{off}$ and $\hat{\sigma}_{int}$) are incorporated by the system after the correction phase as follows:

$$\hat{\sigma}_{ii}(k) = \begin{cases} (\hat{\sigma}_{ch}(k) + \hat{\sigma}_{on})^2, & on-body \;\; links \\ (\hat{\sigma}_{ch}(k) + \hat{\sigma}_{int})^2, & inter-body \;\; links \\ (\hat{\sigma}_{ch}(k) + \hat{\sigma}_{off})^2, & off-body \;\; links \end{cases},$$

where σ_{ch} is the standard deviation of the ranging error due to the channel component.

5.3   On-body Node's Estimation with Full-Cooperative EKF

In Section 4, we have shown that the ranging errors follow a Gaussian distribution, where each kind of WBAN links (on-, off-, and inter-body links) is characterized by its proper standard deviation. In this subsection, we evaluate the resulting gain from the improvement of Kalman filter, while involving the effects of mobility over all links. Using a full cooperative scenario (on-, off- and inter-body links), Figure 5 shows the CDF of the RMSE resulting from the use of the conventional and the adjusted (improved) EKF. This last figure shows that our proposal permits to improve the localization accuracy, where the average goes from $0.487m$ to $0.442m$ (improvement with a rate of 9.1%). The positive effect of our proposal is also seen by averaging the resulting RMSE of nodes attached to each body. This fact is represented in Figure 6, where the blue bars (resp. red bars) represents the average nodes RMSE over each body, while using the conventional EKF (adjusted EKF). As shown, our proposal improves the localization performances over all the incorporated body in our group of mobile WBAN with a gain of, respectively, 9.88%, 9.28% and 11.22%.

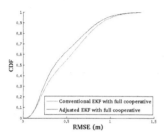

Fig. 5. CDFs of estimated on-body node's RMSE for full-cooperative multi-user navigation scenario

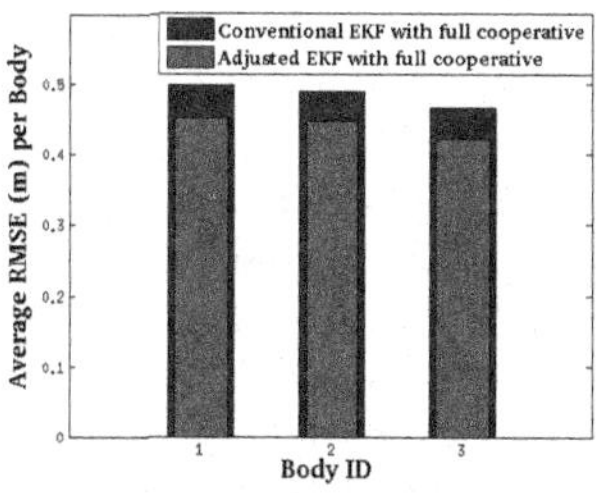

Fig. 6. Average RMSE of the estimated nodes positions per body with full cooperative EKF with and without ranging error mitigation

6   Conclusion

This paper focused on nodes localization problem for group of WBANs, based on peer-to-peer range measurements fed through impulse Radio-Ultra Wideband and time of arrival estimation. We firstly quantified and characterized the error of on-, off- and inter-body distances estimations, based on real mobility model. Based on extensive measurement, our results showed that the ranging errors can be modeled as a Gaussian distribution. To deal with the gaussianity observation of ranging error and to provide high positioning accuracy, we secondly proposed an adjustable cooperative EKF algorithm. Our simulation results showed an improvement between 9% and 11% of localization accuracy.

Acknowledgment. This work has been carried out in the frame of the *CORMORAN* project, which is funded by the French National Research Agency (ANR) under the contract number ANR-11-INFR-010.

References

1. Vicon, http://www.vicon.com/
2. Ieee 802.15 wpan task group 6 (tg6) - body area networks
3. Gezici, S., et al.: Localization via ultra-wideband radios: a look at positioning aspects for future sensor networks. Signal Processing Magazine 22(4), 70–84 (2005)
4. Guizar, A., Ouni, A., Goursaud, C., Amiot, N., Gorce, J.: Impact of MAC scheduling on positioning accuracy for motion capture with UWB body area networks. In: Proceedings of the 9th International Conference on Body Area Networks (2014)
5. Chelius, G., Fraboulet, A., Ben Hamida, E.: http://wsnet.gforge.inria.fr/
6. Choliz, J., Hernandez, A., Valdovinos, A.: A framework for UWB-based communication and location tracking systems for wireless sensor networks. Sensors 11, 9045–9068 (2011)
7. Hamie, J., Denis, B., D'Errico, R., Richard, C.: On-body TOA-based ranging error model for motion capture applications within wearable UWB networks. Journal of Ambient Intelligence and Humanized Computing (December 2013)
8. Bharadwaj, C.G.P.J.B.R., Swaisaenyakorn, S., Alomainy, A.: Localization of wearable ultrawideband antennas for motion capture applications. Antennas Wirel. Propag. Lett. 13, 507–510 (2014)
9. Ben Hamida, E., Maman, M., Denis, B., Ouvry, L.: Localization performance in Wireless Body Sensor Networks with beacon enabled MAC and space-time dependent channel model. In: IEEE 21st International Symposium on Personal, Indoor and Mobile Radio Communications (PIMRC) Workshops, Istanbul, Turkey (September 2010)
10. Shaban, H.A., El-Nasr, M.A., Buehrer, R.M.: Toward a Highly Accurate Ambulatory System for Clinical Gait Analysis via UWB Radios. IEEE Transactions on Information Technology in Biomedicine 14 (March 2010)
11. Mhedhbi, M., Laaraiedh, M., Uguen, B.: Constrained LMDS technique for human motion and gesture estimation. In: 9th Workshop on Positioning Navigation and Communication (WPNC), Dresden, Germany (March 2012)
12. Mekonnen, Z.W., Slottke, E., Luecken, H., Steiner, C., Wittneben, A.: Constrained maximum likelihood positioning for uwb based human motion tracking. In: International Conference on Indoor Positioning and Indoor Navigation (IPIN) (September 2010)
13. Hamie, J., Chaudet, C., Denis, B.: Improved Navigation Capabilities in Groups of Cooperative Wireless Body Area Networks. In: 9th International Conference on Body Area Networks (BodyNets), Oslo, Norway (September 2014)
14. Maman, M., Denis, B., Pezzin, M., Piaget, B., Ouvry, L.: Synergetic MAC and higher layers functionalities for UWB LDR-LT wireless networks. In: IEEE International Conference on Ultra-Wideband (ICUWB 2008), vol. 3, pp. 101–104 (2008)
15. Macagnano, D., Destino, G., Esposito, F., Abreu, G.: MAC performances for localization and tracking in wireless sensor networks. In: 2007 4th Workshop on Positioning, Navigation and Communication (2007)
16. Perälä, T., Piché, R.: Robust extended Kalman Filtering in Hybrid Positioning Applications. In: 4th Workshop on Positioning, Navigation and Communication (WPNC 2007), Hannover, Germany (March 2007)

Cloud, Virtualization and Prototypage

Cloud-Based Network Virtualization: An IoT Use Case

Giovanni Merlino[1,2], Dario Bruneo[1], Francesco Longo[1],
Salvatore Distefano[3,4], and Antonio Puliafito[1]

[1] Università di Messina, Dipartimento DICIEAMA,
Contrada di Dio,
98166 Messina, Italy,
{gmerlino,dbruneo,flongo,apuliafito}@unime.it
[2] Dipartimento DIEEI, Università di Catania, Viale Andrea Doria 6,
95125 Catania, Italy
giovanni.merlino@dieei.unict.it
[3] Dipartimento DEIB, Politecnico di Milano,
Piazza L. Da Vinci 32,
20133 Milano, Italy
salvatore.distefano@polimi.it
[4] Kazan Federal University,
Kazan, Russia
s_distefano@it.kfu.ru

Abstract. In light of an overarching scheme about extending the capabilities of Internet of things (IoT) with Cloud-enabled mechanisms, network virtualization is a key enabler of infrastructure-oriented IoT solutions. In particular, without network virtualization infrastructure cannot really be considered flexible enough to meet emerging requirements, and even administrative duties, such as management, maintenance and large-scale automation, would turn out to be brittle and addressed by special casing, leading to loss of generality and a variety of corner cases. We propose a Cloud-based network virtualization approach for IoT, based on the Open-Stack IaaS framework, where its networking subsystem, Neutron, gets extended to accomodate virtual networks and arbitrary topologies among virtual machines and globally dispersed smart objects, whichever the setup and constraints of the underlying physical networks. This work outlines a motivating use case for our approach, and the ensuing discussion is provided to frame the benefits of the underlying design.

Keywords: IoT, Cloud, OpenStack, network virtualization, WebSocket.

1 Introduction

In the domain of the Internet of Things (IoT) [1], existing solutions are mainly focused on a lower layer, mostly dealing with communication aspects to interconnect network-enabled devices and, generally, *things* to the Internet.

However, from a higher level perspective, specific facilities for management, organization, and coordination of devices, sensors, objects and things are also

© Institute for Computer Sciences, Social Informatics and Telecommunications Engineering 2015
N. Mitton et al. (Eds.): AdHocNets 2015, LNICST 155, pp. 199–210, 2015.
DOI: 10.1007/978-3-319-25067-0_16

required to build up a dynamic infrastructure. To this purpose, on the one hand the capabilities provided by existing solutions in the management of distributed systems, ensuring flexibility and dealing with the complexity of large scale systems, should be exploited to implement basic mechanisms and tools for the resource management, also taking into account IoT solutions. On the other hand, it is necessary to provide and implement advanced solutions and policies able to manage and control the IoT infrastructure, implementing strategies aiming at satisfying higher (applications and end users) requirements, on top of basic facilities provided at a lower level. This two-layer model recalls the *Software Defined Ecosystem* model, where the data plane provides basic, customizable functionalities and the control plane implements advanced mechanisms and policies to control the ecosystem by enforcing strategies on nodes and objects through the lower level basic mechanisms. Thus, the main idea proposed in this paper is to treat the IoT domain as a Software Defined Ecosystem, adopting a two-layer Software Defined model to manage the underlying infrastructure.

To implement such a concept, Cloud computing facilities, applying a service-oriented approach in the provisioning and management of resources, may be exploited. The Cloud-based approach could be a good solution to address IoT-related issues, fitting with the requirements of relevant service users and application providers: on-demand, elastic and QoS-guaranteed, to name a few, all needed properties for an IoT service platform, to be addressed mainly at the control plane.

The contribution of this paper can be summarized as: a requirement analysis for an enhanced IaaS framework able to include and provide facilities for reconfigurable and complex aggregations of IoT devices; an architecture of node-side modules and the corresponding mechanisms needed to empower ubiquitous virtualization of networking functions; a scenario coupled with a related use case, where the approach enables a seamless exploitation of field deployments for IoT devices.

The remainder of this paper is organized as follows: Section 2 describes the reference architecture of a framework implementing the network virtualization for IoT following a service-oriented Cloud model. Then, Section 3 discusses a use case, highlighting pros and cons of the approach. Some remarks and considerations in Section 4 close the paper.

2   Reference Architecture

2.1   Requirements for Cloud-Enabled IoT

The main actors in any IoT scenario are *contributors* and *end users*. Contributors provide sensing and actuation resources building up the "things" infrastructure pool. End users control and manage the resources provided by contributors. In particular, end-users may behave as infrastructure administrators and/or service providers, managing the raw resources and implementing applications and services on top of it. We assume that sensing and actuation resources are provided to the infrastructure pool via a number of hardware-constrained units, from now on referred to as *nodes*. Nodes host sensing and actuation resources and act as mediators in relation to the Cloud infrastructure.

In order to actually accomplish the prospect of a Cloud-based IoT system, a systematic requirement analysis is needed. A subset of requirements are the ones relative to the contributor:

– **Out-of-the-box experience** - letting nodes and the corresponding sensors and actuators be enrolled automatically in the Cloud at, e.g., unpacking time.
– **Uniform interaction model** - resources should be hooked up (or unenrolled, when preferred) with the minimum amount of involvement for the contributor to feed the enrollment process with details about their hardware characteristics.
– **Contribution profile** - each contributor should be able to specify her profile for contribution in terms of resource utilization (CPU utilization, memory or disk space) and contribution period (frame time when the contributor is available for contribution).

and others coming from the end user such as:

– **Status tracking** - monitoring the status (presence, connectivity, usage, etc.) of nodes and corresponding resources, in order to, e.g., track significant outages or load profiles.
– **Lifecycle management** - exposing a set of available management primitives for sensing and actuation resources to, e.g., change sampling parameters when needed or, e.g., reap a pending actuation task to free the resource for another higher-priority duty.
– **Ubiquitous access** - enabled through instant-on bidirectional communication with resources as exposed from sensor-hosting nodes, whichever the constraints imposed by node-side network topology (e.g., NAT) and configuration (e.g., firewall).
– **Ensemble management** - letting nodes and the corresponding sensors and actuators be made available as pools of resources, e.g., to be partitioned in, and allocated as, groups according to requirements.

A certain subset of end user requirements instead needs to be addressed by just providing the facilities for centralized orchestration of virtualized networking instances.

In relation to the latter, the list includes:

– **Service-oriented interfaces** - exposing primitives as asynchronous service endpoint, in order to ease development and third-party software integration.
– **Environment customization** - enabling runtime modifications to the software environment hosted by the node.
– **Topology rewiring** - providing mechanisms for the networking configuration underneath nodes to be modified at any time.

2.2   Sensing and Actuation as a Service for IoT

In the pursuit for integration of IoT infrastructure with paradigms and frameworks for heterogeneous resource management, we are trying to follow a bottom-up approach, consisting of a mixture of relevant, working frameworks and protocols, on the one hand, and interesting use cases to be explored according to such integration effort, on the other.

Indeed, beyond concerns about the scale of the effort, other requirements such as elasticity of the sensing-based services to be provided, as well as registration and provisioning mechanisms of the underlying heterogeneous sensor-hosting platforms deserve an Infrastructure Manager (IM) anyway. To this purpose, Cloud computing facilities, here also implementing a service-oriented [2] approach in the provisioning and management of sensing and actuation resources, are exploited to enable a *Sensing and Actuation as a Service* (SAaaS) paradigm for IoT. In fact, in the SAaaS perspective, sensing and actuation devices should be handled along the same lines as computing and storage abstractions in traditional Clouds, i.e., on the one hand virtualized and multiplexed over (scarce) hardware resources, and on the other grouped and orchestrated under control of an entity implementing high level policies. This way, sensing and actuation devices have to be part of the Cloud infrastructure and have to be managed by following the consolidated Cloud approach, i.e., through a set of APIs ensuring remote control of software and hardware resources despite their geographical position.

A Cloud-oriented solution indeed may fit IoT scenarios, meeting most requirements by default to cater to the originally intended user base, while at the same time also addressing other more subtle functionalities, such as a tenant-based authorization framework, where several actors (owners, administrator, users) and their interactions with infrastructure may be fully decoupled from the workflows involved (e.g., transfer, rental, delegation). Bonus points include recycling existing (compute/storage-oriented) deployments, getting most visualization and monitoring technologies for free, as those are typically already available in such systems, possibly even enabling federation of different administrative Cloud-enabled domains.

In this sense, our choice leans towards OpenStack, as a centerpiece of infrastructure Cloud solutions for most commercial, in-house and hybrid deployments, as well as a fully OpenSource ecosystem of tools and frameworks upon which many EU projects, such as CloudWave (FP-7), are founding their Cloud strategies. Our prototype is thus based on OpenStack and named Stack4Things.

Indeed, choosing an industrial strength solution for infrastructure Clouds lets us eschew at the moment scalability and other generic performance issues, and focus most of the discussion on the challenges which are relevant to centralized management of IoT.

Putting aside the core IaaS framework, as anticipated some additional facilities are needed for our envisioned SAaaS paradigm and the specifics of the domain at hand (IoT), among which here we may describe two classes of mechanisms that are core to the overall approach: those needed to access locally and

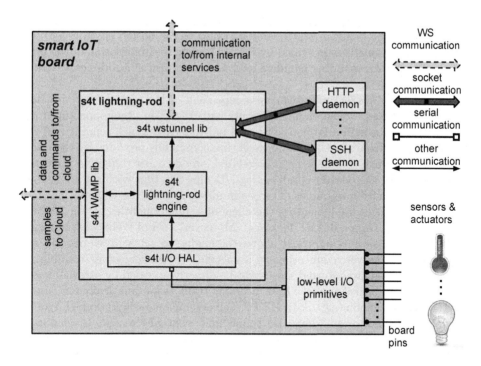

Fig. 1. Stack4Things node-side stack: logical architecture.

transparently remote (I/O) resources, and those to set up arbitrary topologies among nodes.

With regard to the former, in Figure 1 we find a logical architecture of the node-side stack needed for pub/sub or even RPC-style I/O primitives to be exposed to remote hosts through the Cloud. The *Stack4Things lightning-rod*, acting as SAaaS Client, runs on the IoT board and interacts with the OS tools and services of the board, and with sensing and actuation resources through I/O pins. It represents the point of contact with the Cloud infrastructure allowing the end users to manage the board resources even if they are behind a NAT or a strict firewall. This is ensured by a WAMP and WebSocket-based communication between the Stack4Things lightning-rod and its Cloud counterpart. WebSocket is a standard HTTP-based protocol providing a full-duplex TCP communication channel over a single HTTP-based persistent connection. One of the main advantages of WebSocket is that it is network agnostic, by just piggybacking communication onto standard HTTP interactions. This is of benefit for those environments which block Web-unrelated traffic using firewalls. *Web Application Messaging Protocol (WAMP)* [3] is a sub-protocol of WebSocket, specifying a communication semantic for messages sent over WebSocket, providing both publish/subscribe and routed remote procedure call (RPC) mechanisms.

The I/O HAL (*hardware abstraction layer*) is equipped with a set of extensions exposing the board digital/analog I/O pins to the hosted environment. In particular, functionalities provided by the HAL include enumeration of the pins and exporting corresponding handlers for I/O in the form of i-nodes of a virtual filesystem.

The *Stack4Things lightning-rod engine* represents at the core of the board-side software architecture. The engine interacts with the Cloud by connecting to a WAMP router through a WebSocket-based full-duplex channel, sending and receiving data to/from the Cloud and executing commands provided by the users via the Cloud. Such commands can be related, among other things, to the communication with the board digital/analog I/O pins and thus with the connected sensing and actuation resources. The communication with the Cloud is ensured by a set of libraries implementing the client-side functionalities of the WAMP protocol (*Stack4Things WAMP libraries*). Moreover, a set of WebSocket libraries (*Stack4Things wstunnel libraries*) allows the engine to act as a WebSocket reverse tunneling server, connecting to a specific WebSocket server running in the Cloud. This allows internal services to be directly accessed by external users through the WebSocket tunnel whose incoming traffic is automatically forwarded to the internal daemon (e.g., SSH, HTTP, Telnet) under consideration. Outgoing traffic is redirected to the WebSocket tunnel and eventually reaches the end user that connects to the WebSocket server running in the Cloud to interact with the board service. New REST resources are automatically created exposing the user-defined commands on the Cloud side. As soon as such resources are invoked the corresponding code is executed on top of the smart board.

Cloud-Based Virtualized Networking for IoT. Figure 2 shows a conceptual depiction of the tunnel-based layering model employed for Cloud-enabled set up of virtualized bridged networks among nodes across the Internet.

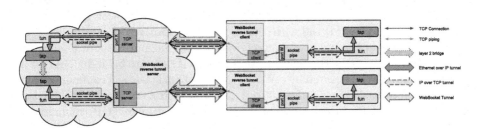

Fig. 2. Stack4Things tunnel-based layering: model.

It is important to remark that the kind of tunneling here mentioned is essential to obtain remote access to IoT resources whichever the constraints of the network nodes reside in, a prerequisite to expose node-hosted resources according to the aforementioned access patterns.

The basic remoting mechanisms are based on the creation of generic TCP tunnels over WebSocket (WS), a way to get client-initiated connectivity to any server-side local (or remote) service. In this sense, we devised the design and implementation of an incremental enhancement to standard WS-based facilities, i.e., a *reverse* tunneling technique, as a way to provide server-initiated, e.g., Cloud-triggered, connectivity to any board-hosted service.

Beyond mere remoting, level-agnostic network virtualization needs mechanisms to overlay network- and datalink-level addressing and traffic forwarding on top of such a facility. Here the novelty of setting up VPNs on top of Web-Socket lies in the decoupled control machinery, and the inherent flexibility of an on-demand mechanism. The former indeed is enabled through a preliminarily activated and always-on WebSocket-based *control* reverse tunnel (rtunnel), acting as an out-of-band channel for command streams.

There are already certain solutions [4] for setting up VPNs on top of WS, but without decoupled control machinery nor the inherent flexibility of an on-demand mechanism.

Focusing the analysis on the instantiation of, e.g., a virtual bridge between two boards, over *data* (in-band) rtunnels, a first step lies in setting up a TCP connection based on a WS-based rtunnel, which consists in exposing, on the server side, a listening socket on a local port, as soon as the rtunnel server accepts a request for a new rtunnel. The TCP connection just established gets piped to the rtunnel that encapsulates TCP segments in a WS-based stream. On the WS rtunnel client side, as soon as the rtunnel is established, a new TCP client is brought up connecting to a local listening port, and such TCP connection gets piped to the rtunnel. A level-3 tunnel is then to be established over this TCP-based tunnel by launching an application that starts up in listening mode on both sides of the socket pipe and, on connection, starts exposing a virtual (TUN) device on either side, both set up with IP addresses of choice, as long as those belong to the same subnet. The workflow could end here if the request was for a layer-3 VPN.

In order to set up instead a level-2 encapsulation over the aforementioned IP-based communication, the system has to bring up a GRE tunnel, where the endpoints are the previously configured TUN IPs and the type of tunnel-hosting virtual device is set to TAP, thus exposing an Ethernet-compatible interface. Adding such interface to a dedicated virtual bridge on the server ends the workflow, in this case exposing a layer-2 VPN. For IP-based tunneling, we resorted to *Generic Routing Encapsulation (GRE)* [5], an IETF standard for a no-frills IP-in-IP tunneling protocol. GRE support is not limited to level-3 encapsulation, but also available for tunneling of level-2 (Ethernet) frames over to the corresponding virtual (TAP) device.

3   Use Case

Once the Cloud-based IoT scenario has been laid out, it is easier to frame the discussion in terms of a focused scenario, such as management of large-scale emergency situations.

A peculiar feature of such scenario lies in the lack of predefined boundaries in terms of the sensing infrastructure, which may span multiple geographical areas and administrative domains. Whichever the footprint of alerting and support activities for civilians, the foremost quality here is the dynamic involvement of infrastructure.

3.1 Opportunistic Exploitation and Transparent Field Upgrade of IoT-Based Facilities

In such a scenario a use case may be identified in the on-demand setup of facilities that are ready to react to certain events which could anticipate an impending emergency, and may avoid or at least contain damages and/or casualties. For instance, a bridge may be considered at risk and put under control by placing the required sensing infrastructure to monitor critical parameters, such as oscillations, load, and torque or compressive stress of certain sections and elements. In terms of actuators, the most fitting example may be gates at either side of the bridge, only involving entry lanes in order not to impact vehicular outflow, to be closed at the occurrence of such kind of event, as a precautionary step to be taken before deeper investigations.

Such potential infrastructure thus needs reactive mechanisms in place, possibly encoded as statements for a Complex Event Processing engine.

The aforementioned use case may indeed be implemented by deploying at least two transducers, a sensor and an actuator respectively, where a board driving an actuator hosts an application that operates it when triggered upon detection of an event of interest. The latter gets generated by a CEP engine every time predefined patterns (e.g., steady-state and/or structural anomalies) get recognized out of measurements by one or more sensors sampling the corresponding phenomena on (possibly other) boards.

Interesting patterns are set by loading rules written in an engine-specific language.

The interactions are here described, when requesting for a number of boards currently enrolled to the Cloud to be booked, mapped to an enumerable set of resources, ultimately exposed for seamless interaction to a CEP engine, and the corresponding rules, deployed in Cloud-hosted VM.

According to the description of our core mechanisms, built on top of the IaaS framework, the first request is a routine one for the framework once extended to include enrollment of IoT nodes, as well as the second and the fourth one even when IoT extensions are not considered. The third request instead requires the framework to deploy (IaaS-context) data into a VM, but then the enumeration may take place only if the WAMP subsystem is available. Exposing remote resources as local I/O needs a wrapper around the same subsystem too.

An opportunistic exploitation of resources yet gets feasible only when expecting to be able to avoid an operator to set up the whole (distributed sensing and actuation) system beforehand in the finest detail, including runtime adaptations such as, e.g., swapping part of the logic and replacing nodes to be involved, when needed.

In particular a useful approach may lie in the field deployment of an array of devices with sensing functions the (aggregate) coverage of which is not necessarily known in advance or perfectly partitioned somehow. As long as this set of resources may be set up as an inter-node addressable ensemble and has a running mechanism in place for the election and maintenance of a master node, event detection may be delegated to the latter. In turn the detection routines would leverage as much information as possible by aggregating data originating from whichever resource is part of the aforementioned ensemble. For such an autonomous system to work, sensors advertisement and discovery services are of course a prerequisite.

The master node may as well be leveraged to invoke one or more actuators (e.g., close the gates) should a predefined emergency event be detected, by also discovering relevant actuating resources through the same mechanisms. Unplanned field deployment coupled with this approach may thus lead to a seamless exploitation of resources, where even replacement for upgrade, or loss of a subset of nodes is not disruptive to the working status of the system.

A side effect of the choice to lift some decisions and duties off the operator may also lie in the ability to make the system fault tolerant by design, especially when employing an approach of redundant deployment on the actuating side, as resilience benefits in this case from the transparent addition or replacement of nodes.

An operator thus only needs to reserve a set of nodes once, roughly by function category or even better by geographical area, and just resort to the SAaaS framework for the corresponding setup (and runtime adjustments) of an inter-node configuration based on **Virtualized bridging for IP-based transport of discovery services**.

As said previously, we are able to get remote access to the boards, for instance for deploying an application, from anywhere a client may connect to any Cloud-enrolled board, whichever its connectivity (e.g., node-side NAT or firewall notwithstanding). We may submit a request for certain nodes on demand as resources, and another to arrange a certain topology among boards by network virtualization, in order to accomodate the requirements of the application itself, by leveraging the (wide-area) *control plane*.

In particular, an interesting case is that of the AllJoyn [6] framework for IoT, a family of standards and reference implementations which comprises at its core a DBus-derived application protocol useful for messaging, advertisement and discovery of services, working via selected mechanisms on available transports. As long as the application is based on AllJoyn, services may be discovered automatically, and thus leveraged according to the logic of the application. The distributed system works by letting these boards interact through AllJoyn over an IP-based network and the corresponding transport implementation, where mDNS and a combination of multicast and broadcast UDP packets are used. A limitation indeed is that the protocol is currently designed to work only as long as the communicating boards are on the same broadcast domain. Therefore, such a case may be covered by being able to leverage the Cloud to instantiate a (virtualized, wide-area) bridged network among the nodes, coupled with the availability of remote access for deployment and execution of the required binaries.

Under the assumption that nodes are not globally addressable or otherwise reachable on whichever port, i.e., behind a firewall/NAT system due to an ubiquitous IPv4 setup, a complex interaction flow is required to provide this kind of abstractions and the underlying connectivity.

Supposing thus the boards to be bridged are already registered to the Cloud, a high-level description of the workflow, from the point of view of the user, comprises the following steps:

1. Book two (or more) managed boards.
2. Request for a bridge among the reserved boards.
3. Request for exposing SSH service on every reserved board.
4. Connect via SSH service to every reserved board for deploying and launching the AllJoyn application.

Focusing on the unique steps of the one under consideration, the first request gets serviced by leveraging the virtualized networking facilities and the second one by tunneled remoting.

The following list of sequences is then expected to take place, with (low-level) operations as depicted and numbered in Fig. 3.

1) The user requests the setup of a bridge between two specific boards, either through the s4t dashboard or, in alternative, through the s4t command line client.
2) The s4t dashboard performs one of the available s4t IoTronic APIs calls via REST, which pushes a new message into a specific AMQP IoTronic queue.
3) The s4t IoTronic conductor pulls the message from the AMQP IoTronic queue and correspondingly performs a query on the s4t IoTronic database. In particular, it checks if the board is already registered to the Cloud and looks up the s4t IoTronic WAMP agent to which the board is registered. At last, it decides the s4t IoTronic WS tunnel agent to which the user can be redirected and randomly generates a free TCP port.
4) The s4t IoTronic conductor pushes a new message into a specific AMQP IoTronic queue.
5) The s4t IoTronic WAMP agent to which the board is registered pulls the message from the queue and publishes a new message into a specific topic on the corresponding WAMP router.
6) Through the s4t WAMP lib the s4t lightning-rod engine receives the message by the WAMP router.
7) The s4t lightning-rod engine sets up a rtunnel with the s4t IoTronic WS tunnel agent specified by the s4t IoTronic conductor, also providing the TCP port through the s4t wstunnel lib. It also brings up a number of sockets to be piped and overlaid over the rtunnel, plus the corresponding virtual interfaces, as described in Sec. 2.2.

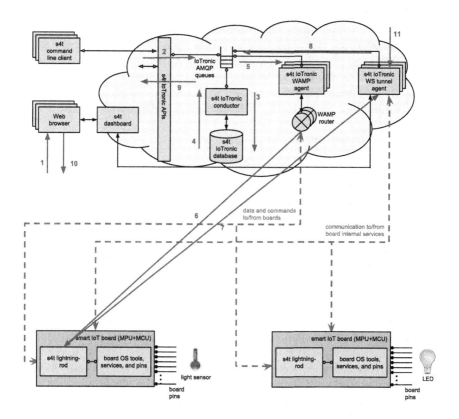

Fig. 3. Workflow and interactions between Cloud and board for the use case.

8) The s4t IoTronic WS tunnel agent follows up with its own set of server-side network virtualization duties, still according to Sec. 2.2. Then, it publishes a new message into a specific AMQP IoTronic queue confirming that the operation has been correctly executed.

9) The s4t IoTronic APIs call pulls the message from the AMQP IoTronic queue and replies to the s4t dashboard.

10) The user gets notified of the success of the operation.

This first sequence has to be replicated for both nodes, as well as the following two. In order not to stretch the description, here only phases which are different from the previous one are outlined. In particular, the second sequence (remote access) steps 2-6,9 remain unchanged, step 1,7-8,10 are changed as follows:

1) The user asks for a connection to the SSH service local to a specific board, either through the s4t dashboard or, in alternative, through the s4t command line client.

2) The s4t lightning-rod engine sets up a rtunnel with the s4t IoTronic WS tunnel agent specified by the s4t IoTronic conductor, also providing the

TCP port through the s4t wstunnel lib. It also opens a TCP connection to the internal SSH daemon and pipes the socket to the tunnel.

3) The s4t IoTronic WS tunnel agent brings up a TCP server on the specified port, and then publishes a new message into a specific AMQP IoTronic queue confirming that the operation has been correctly executed.

4) The s4t dashboard provides the user with the IP address and TCP port that she can use to connect to the SSH daemon running on the board.

And an additional step is present:

5) As the user employs an SSH client to connect to the specified IP address and TCP port, the session is tunneled right to the board.

4   Conclusions

In this paper, we presented a new paradigm that can be considered as an approach to provide a simplified and programmable exploitation of the underlying ecosystem of devices so that innovative and powerful services can be realized. Starting from the well known concept of Software Defined paradigms (e.g., separating control and data planes) a Cloud-based framework is proposed, taking advantage of off-the-shelf technologies (e.g., OpenStack) and extending the computing and storage virtualization concepts also to the sensing and actuating facilities. Architectural aspects have been discussed as well as implementation choices. Future work will include the validation of the whole architecture in a real-world scenario involving hundreds of devices, under the #SmartME project.

References

1. Gubbi, J., Buyya, R., Marusic, S., Palaniswami, M.: Internet of things (iot): A vision, architectural elements, and future directions. Future Generation Computer Systems 29(7), 1645–1660 (2013)
2. Distefano, S., Merlino, G., Puliafito, A.: Sensing and actuation as a service: A new development for clouds. In: 2012 11th IEEE International Symposium on Network Computing and Applications (NCA), pp. 272–275, August 2012
3. Fette, I., Melnikov, A.: The WebSocket Protocol. RFC 6455, RFC Editor, December 2011
4. VPN-WS. https://github.com/unbit/vpn-ws
5. Hanks, S., Li, T., Farinacci, D., Traina, P.: Generic Routing Encapsulation (GRE). RFC 1701, RFC Editor, October 1994
6. AllJoyn. http://allseenalliance.org

OpenMote: Open-Source Prototyping Platform for the Industrial IoT

Xavier Vilajosana[1], Pere Tuset[2], Thomas Watteyne[3], and Kris Pister[4]

[1] Universitat Oberta de Catalunya, Spain
xvilajosana@uoc.edu
[2] OpenMote Technologies, Spain
pere.tuset@openmote.com
[3] Inria Paris-Rocquencourt, EVA team, France
thomas.watteyne@inria.fr
[4] UC Berkeley, EECS, USA
pister@eecs.berkeley.edu

Abstract. This paper introduces OpenMote, the latest generation of Berkeley motes. OpenMote is a open-hardware prototyping ecosystem designed to accelerate the development of the Industrial Internet of Things (IIoT). It features the OpenMote-CC2538, a state-of-the-art computing and communication device. This device interfaces with several other accessories, or "skins", through a standardized connector. The skins developed to date include boards to provide power, boards which enable a developer to easily debug the platform, and boards to allow seamless integration of an OpenMote network into the Internet.

This hardware ecosystem is complemented by a suite of software tools and ports to popular open-source IoT implementations. The OpenMote platform is for example tailored to run the OpenWSN open-source implementation of emerging IIoT standards. The combination of hardware and software ecosystems gives an embedded programmer an intuitive and complete development environment, and an end-user a fully working low-power wireless mesh networking solution running the latest IIoT standards.

1 Introduction

Tomorrow's Smart Factory will be wireless. Industrial process monitoring and automation applications are both "going wireless" and "going IP" to reduce installation cost and simplify Internet integration. Standardization is leading this effort, for example through the IETF 6TiSCH working group [1], which is standardizing tomorrow's "Industrial Internet of Things" (IIoT).

Early experimentation is needed for these standards to be widely adopted, and for the Industrial IoT to take off. Key accelerators for this process are open-source hardware and software projects which provide early access to implementations of those standards, and link pioneering ideas to industrial adoption. In the early 2000's, this happened through the IEEE802.15.4 [2] standard, the TelosB

© Institute for Computer Sciences, Social Informatics and Telecommunications Engineering 2015
N. Mitton et al. (Eds.): AdHocNets 2015, LNICST 155, pp. 211–222, 2015.
DOI: 10.1007/978-3-319-25067-0_17

Fig. 1. An OpenMote-CC2538 and an OpenUSB

hardware platforms and the TinyOS [3] implementation. This combination triggered significant research on Wireless Sensor Networking, resulting in standards such as 6LoWPAN.

This experience has thought us several lessons. First, tight coupling and parallel evolution between hardware platforms and open-source projects benefit the adoption of the standards they implement. Second, a modular hardware design improves the applicability of the hardware to different applications. Third, providing easy-to-use board support packages (BSP) and prototyping tools speeds up time-to-deployment and eventually time-to-market. Fourth, open hardware benefits knowledge transfer and industrial adoption, as companies can take advantage of already proven designs. Fifth, symbiotic alignment between standardization groups and open-source hardware/software projects yields better standards and speeds up their adoption. These lessons learnt where the basis when designing the OpenMote hardware ecosystem.

This paper introduces OpenMote[1], a modular open-hardware ecosystem designed for the Industrial IoT. The OpenMote platform is designed to efficiently implement IIoT standards such as IETF 6TiSCH. It was designed within Berkeley's OpenWSN [4] open-source project, and is therefore perfectly suited for the new wave of IIoT standards such as IEEE802.15.4e TSCH and IETF 6TiSCH. It is an open platform, given users "bare metal" access to state-of-the-art hardware, with current work being done to use it within several additional open-source IoT communities such as Contiki [5], RIOT [6] and FreeRTOS[2].

The remainder of this paper is organized as follows. Section 2 presents other open-source experimentation platforms, and relates them to OpenMote. Section 3 introduces the OpenMote hardware ecosystem and presents the OpenMote platform and its interfaces. Section 4 introduces the tools and software developed around OpenMote. Section 5 presents some results about the performance of the OpenMote hardware. Section 6 reviews use cases and success stories developed using the OpenMote. Finally, Section 7 concludes this paper.

---

[1] http://www.openmote.com/

[2] http://freertos.org/

2   Other Open-Source Experimentation Platforms

The OpenMote is the latest in generation of low-power wireless platforms, and adopts their most useful features and follows "lessons learnt".

The "Berkeley motes" were born with the Smart Dust project in 1997. The MICA family was the first one to establish the idea of a small low-power wireless featuring communication, computation and energy. The widely popular TelosB platform was a milestone "Berkeley mote", which combined an open design, state-of-the-art hardware (in 2004), ease-of-use and commercial availability. After more than a decade of lifetime, the hardware it offers is no longer state-of-the art. Compared to today's off-the-shelf solutions, the TelosB lacks memory space, speed and hardware acceleration for security, while consuming more energy.

During the "TelosB decade" (2004-2014), several companies adopted the open hardware design of TelosB, and developed updated versions of it. This includes the TMote Sky, IRIS and Zolertia Z1 motes. Other designs departed from the TelosB constrained design and developed more powerful motes. This includes Sun Microsystems' SunSpot (which embeds a Java virtual machine), the Arduino, or the COU motes [7]. These platforms are targeted mainly at educational use, and lack the reliability and low-power operation required for industrial applications.

Most chip vendors have now switched to 32-bit microcontroller architectures (e.g. ARM's Cortex-M series), which offer more computational power for a lower-power consumption. Systems-on-Chip (SoCs) are available which combine a microcontroller and a radio in a single chip. These SoCs reduce complexity and costs of new designs, while offering higher performance and lower power than their equivalent 2-chip solutions.

The OpenMote is the latest generation "Berkeley mote". It is designed to capture this exciting state-of-the-art technology, while maintaining the simplificity and elegance of a platform such as the TelosB.

3   The OpenMote Hardware Ecosystem

A prototyping platform is not just a single communicating "mote"; it must also encompass accessories it can plug into (including sensors), and tools to help firmware development. This section presents this hardware ecosystem.

The driving idea of the OpenMote ecosystem is to separate the communication/computation module from interface boards, resulting in a simple, modular and elegant solution. The OpenMote-CC2538 (Section 3.1) is the heart of this ecosystem, and provides computation and communication capabilities. Its standardized pin-out enables it to interface to the other elements of the ecosystem using digital and analog interfaces (GPIO, I2C, SPI, UART), through high-level connectors such as Ethernet, USB, Phidgets and Grove sensor connectors. The boards the OpenMote-CC2538 can interface to today include the OpenBattery (Section 3.2), the OpenBase (Section 3.3) and the OpenUSB (Section 3.4).

Fig. 2. The OpenMote hardware ecosystem: (from left to right) OpenMote-CC2538, OpenBattery, OpenBase, OpenUSB.

3.1 OpenMote-CC2538

The OpenMote-CC2538 (Fig. 2) sits at the core of the OpenMote hardware ecosystem. It is the brain of the platform, and the element a developer programs. The first generation OpenMote, the OpenMote-CC2538, features a TI CC2538 SoC. The design of the "OpenMote" is, however, generic and future revisions can integrate other SoCs, possibly featuring different communication technologies.

The CC2538, at the core of the OpenMote-CC2538, is a SoC from Texas Instruments with a 32-bit Cortex-M3 microcontroller and an IEEE802.15.4-compliant radio. The microcontroller has a clock speed up to 32 MHz, embeds 32 kB of RAM and 512 kB of flash memory, and features several peripherals (including GPIOs, ADC, I2C, SPI, UART and timer modules). The radio operates in the 2.4 GHz band and is fully compliant with the IEEE802.15.4-2006 standard.

The power subsystem is driven by a step-down DC/DC converter (TPS62730) with two operational modes: bypass and regulated. In bypass mode, the DC/DC converter directly connects the input voltage from the battery (typically 3 V) to the system. In regulated mode, the DC/DC converter regulates the input voltage down to 2.1 V. The benefit of such approach is that the efficiency of the system can be improved under both low and high load conditions (when the system is sleeping or when the radio is transmitting/receiving).

A 32 MHz crystal clocks the radio, and has a drift of up to 30 ppm (parts per million) from -20 C to +70 C. This crystal remains off when the radio is asleep. To achieve tight time synchronization – a fundamental requirement of new industrial communication protocols – a second 32 kHz crystal clocks the microcontroller's RTC (Real Time Clock). This ultra low-power RTC allows the OpenMote to keep track of time, even when in deep sleep. This second crytal is rated at 10 ppm from -40 C to +85 C (the industrial temperature range).

The OpenMote-CC2538 board features 4 LEDS, 2 programmable buttons, a chip antenna and an SMA connector for an external antenna. The form factor and pin-out is the same as other popular low-power wireless board, such as the

XBee and WaspMote. This means that an OpenMote can interface with any accessory built for those boards, and can be a swap-in replacement.

The OpenMote-CC2538 is the core of the OpenMote hardware ecosystem. The modular design separates it from different development interfaces – "skins" – to provide a versatile set of tools to the developer. This design also enables a user to replace today's OpenMote-CC2538 with future versions of the board.

3.2 OpenBattery

The OpenBattery (Fig. 2) is a skin for the OpenMote-CC2538 which provides power and basic sensing capabilities. It is composed of a battery holder for 2 AAA batteries, a socket for the OpenMote-CC2538, an on/off switch, and three sensors: a temperature/humidity sensor (SHT21), a 3-axis accelerometer (ADXL346) and a light sensor (MAX44009). All sensors are interfaced with the OpenMote-CC2538 using an I2C bus. The temperature sensor (and updated version of the one on the TelosB) can be used in a wide set of applications, including network synchronization [8]. The 3-axis accelerometer can be used for dynamic or static motion detection. The light sensor can be used for a wide range of applications, from presence detection to touch-less switching.

3.3 OpenBase

The OpenBase (Fig. 2) is a skin for the OpenMote-CC2538 which offers all the interfaces needed for efficient firmware development. It features a socket for the OpenMote-CC2538, a 10-pin JTAG connector for in-circuit debugging of the OpenMote-CC2538, a circuit to monitor the current draw of the OpenMote-CC2538, pins to interface the OpenMote-CC2538 to external devices, a USB connector to re-program and debug the OpenMote-CC2538, and a 10/100 Mbps Ethernet connector[3] to connect the OpenMote-CC2538 directly to a LAN.

This wealth of interfaces means that the OpenBase can serve several purposes. Through the JTAG interface, it can be used during code development to place breakpoints and inspect variables. Through the USB interface, it can be used to reprogram the OpenMote-CC2538 with pre-compiled binary images, and receive status information from that firmware over a serial interface. Through the 10/100 Mbps Ethernet interface, the OpenMote-CC2538 can be connected to the Internet without requiring a computer.

3.4 OpenUSB

The OpenUSB (Fig. 2) is designed for ease-of-use by ends users, and for using OpenMote-CC2538 boards in a testbed. It features a USB "male" connector, a 10-pin JTAG connector, a battery holder for 2 AA batteries, the same 3 sensors as the OpenBattery, and a Grove connector[4] to connect to dozens of sensors.

---

[3] The Ethernet connector is based on a Microchip ENC28J60 chip and a standard RJ-45 connector that includes both the magnetics and the circuit protection.
[4] http://www.seeedstudio.com/

An end-user uses the OpenUSB much like he/she uses a TelosB today: re-program the board with precompiled firmware, debug either through `printf` statement or through the JTAG interface, and deploy battery-powered nodes. In the contex of a testbed, the OpenMote-CC2538 connected to an OpenUSB (see Fig. 1) is a drop-in replacement of a TelosB. Similar to a TelosB, it can be connected to a small single-board computer (such as the Raspberry Pi) which can reprogram it. This makes it an ideal solution for a testbed.

3.5   Interfaces and Accessories

One of the main requirements for an OpenMote is to be able to interface to other devices and boards. Thanks to its form-factor, numerous "shields" already exist, for example to the Arduino.

Fig. 3. The Raspberry Pi adapter for the OpenMote.

As part of its continuous push to expand the OpenMote ecosystem, the Open-Mote team has developed an adapter board for the Raspberry Pi version 1 and version 2 (see Fig. 3). With this setup, the Raspberry Pi can be programmed with the OpenPi image[5], an OpenWSN-ready distribution for the Raspberry Pi, turning the Raspberry Pi+OpenMote into the gateway of an OpenWSN network.

4   The OpenMote Software Ecosystem

The OpenMote hardware ecosystem is empowered by the OpenMote software ecosystem, a collection of tools to simplify development (Section 4.1) and ports to popular operating system (Section 4.2). Section 4.3 further details the end-user experience of using OpenWSN on the OpenMote ecosystem.

---

[5] https://github.com/openwsn-berkeley/openpi

4.1   Tools

The OpenWSN project contains an Eclipse-based development environment for the OpenMote-CC2538, including JTAG debugging. The OpenWSN build system contains the necessary scripts to upload pre-compiled binaries onto the board, when in-circuit debugging is not needed.

The OpenMote community has developed firmware to turn an OpenMote-CC2538 into a IEEE802.15.4 packet sniffer[6]. When connected to an OpenBase (resp. OpenUSB), the OpenMote-CC2538 publishes captured packets onto the Ethernet (resp. serial) interface. In both cases, packets can be analyzed using Wireshark, a popular packet analysis software.

4.2   Operating Systems

The OpenMote team believes in community-driven open-source hardware and software.

OpenMote can be seen as the hardware spin-off of Berkeley's OpenWSN project [4]. A number of OpenMote prototypes were developed in that project to identify the components which are most suitable for implementing IIoT standards such as IEEE802.15.4e TSCH. OpenWSN promotes the Industrial Internet of Things by providing an open implementation of standards such IEEE802.15.4e TSCH [9], IETF RPL [10], IETF CoAP [11] and the standards promoted and developed by the IETF 6TiSCH working group [12].

It is also possible to use the OpenMote with other open-source projects such as FreeRTOS, RIOT and Contiki. The latter has adopted the OpenMote as its prototyping platform through Thingsquare, Contiki's commercial offering.

The OpenMote community has also developed the first low power implementation of the Distributed Queuing (DQ) protocol [13], demonstrating that the concept of DQ can be implemented on off-the-shelves hardware.

4.3   End-User Experience

The OpenMote team aims at providing an integrated hardware/software platform for end-users to use cutting IIoT standards.

For a developer, it enhances user experience by facilitating tasks such as debugging, having access to GPIOs and hardware interfaces leveraging the burden of bare metal programming. When developing on OpenWSN, OpenMote provides all the necessary tools to develop an application or contribute to a protocol implementation. The OpenBase and the OpenUSB provide external pins to debug peripheral buses such as SPI, UART and I2C, using a logic analyzer.

---

[6] https://github.com/OpenMote/firmware/tree/master
/projects/ieee802154-sniffer

For an end-user, reprogramming an OpenMote-CC2538 with the latest release of the OpenWSN stack is as simple as running a single command line:

```
scons board=OpenMote-CC2538 bootload=/dev/ttyUSB0 oos_openwsn
```

One OpenMote-CC2538 can be connected to a Raspbarry Pi running the OpenPi distribution (Fig. 3) to turn it into the gateway. The other motes can be connected to OpenUSB boards (Fig. 1) and deployed in the field. The out-of-the-box experience is that the Raspberry Pi becomes the 6LoWPAN "Low-power Border Router" (LBR), connecting the OpenWSN network of OpenMotes to the Internet.

5   Performance

This section presents performance results measured on the OpenMote-CC2538.

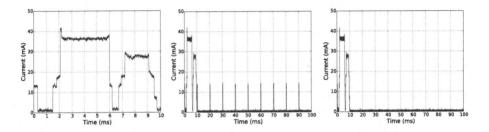

Fig. 4. Current draw of the OpenMote-CC2538 running the OpenWSN protocol stack. (left) The 10ms active slot; the mote transmits and receives an acknowledgment. (center) The active slot followed by 9 inactive slots; the mote wakes up at each slot, the default OpenWSN behavior. (right) Same result, but the node stays asleep during inactive slots (optimization).

Current Draw. To measure the current draw of the OpenMote-CC2538, we program two boards with the latest OpenWSN firmware, and connect both to a computer using OpenBase boards. We configure one node to be DAGroot, the other a regular node.

The data is acquired using a Rigol DS1000E digital oscilloscope and a uCurrent Gold current probe. The current probe is connected in series to the OpenBase current sense pins, and transforms the current flowing into the OpenMote-CC2538 board into a voltage through a low-noise operational amplifier circuit. The current probe is connected to the digital oscilloscope, which acquires and digitizes the analog voltage. The oscilloscope has a vertical resolution of 8 bits and the vertical range is set to 10 mV/div, which yields 195 uA/LSB. The sampling frequency is set to 1 MHz, the acquisition time to 10 ms. Results are show in Fig. 4.

In an active slot, the node transmits a data packet to the DAG root and waits for the acknowledgment (ACK) packet from the DAG root. The data packet is 127 bytes long (≈4 ms duration); the ACK is 32 bytes long (≈1 ms). In an active slot, the transmitting mote waits 1.5 ms, then turns on its radio to transmit the data packet. 200 μs after the data packet is fully transmitted, the mote start listening for the ACK.

The OpenMote's CPU is clocked by a 32 MHz external crystal, rather than the 16 MHz internal crystal. When the CPU is on, the OpenMote-CC2538 consumes 13 mA.

During packet transmission and reception, the CPU consumes around 1.5 mA. This consumption adds up to the radio transceiver current consumption. When transmitting at +7 dBm, the OpenMote-CC2538 consumes 34 mA. When receiving a signal at -50 dBm, it consumes 20 mA. These values match the datasheet.

RF Signal. We capture the transmission of a packet on a spectrum analyzer to measure the power radiated by the radio front-end. Results are shown in Fig. 5. The signal is well centered, demonstrating the good performance of the radio front-end.

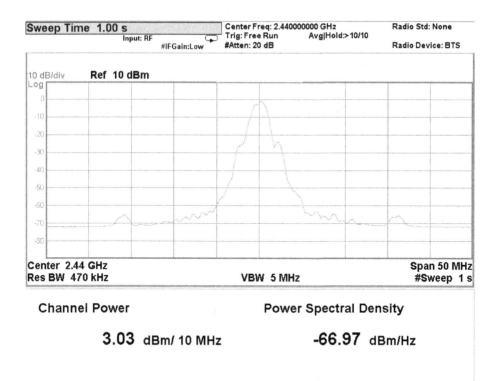

Fig. 5. Power spectral density of OpenMote-CC2538 transmitting at 2.44 GHz

6 Example Use Cases

This section contains examples of projects in the industrial, standardization, robotics, medical and mobile network fields where the OpenMote is used today.

Industrial. In [14], the authors build a energy consumption model of the OpenMote-CC2538 running the OpenWSN protocol stack to predict the networks battery lifetime in critical industrial environments. In [15], the authors study the dependability of low-power wireless networks, and use the OpenMote-CC2538 as the state-of-the-art hardware for industrial applications. In [16], the authors study the applicability of the OpenWSN implementation running on the OpenMote-CC2358 to run wireless control loops in industrial applications

Standardization Support. Standardization of communications protocols is a fundamental step to enable massive adoption of technologies. The initially fragmented IoT communication ecosystem is converging towards several IoT standards, most of them with a common network layer. The IETF is leading this effort by bringing IP to different link-layer technologies, including IEEE802.15.4 and Bluetooth. The IETF 6TiSCH working group is standardizing a protocol stack which combines the industrial performance of IEEE802.15.4e with the ease of use of IP.

In this complex process, the OpenMote helps accelerating the adoption of these emerging standards. Most open-source operating systems, including OpenWSN but also Contiki and TinyOS are adopting 6TiSCH technology and taking advantage of the tools provided by the OpenMote platform. Recently, ETSI organized an interoperability event around 6TiSCH technology [17] in which the OpenMote-CC2538 running OpenWSN was selected are the reference device to test interoperability against.

Robotics. Grieco *et al.* [18] survey the interaction between the fields of robotics and IoT, and identify the OpenMote-CC2538 as the state-of-the-art platform for this type of applications.

Medical. In [19], the authors implement a system capable of real-time on-demand monitoring of patient in hospitals using the OpenMote-CC2538.

Mobile Networks. Weekly *et al.* [20] uses the OpenMote-CC2538 in indoor environmental sensing applications using networks of mobile sensors.

7 Conclusion

This paper introduces the OpenMote prototyping environment. The goal of this modular, versatile, open-hardware platform is to support development and prototyping of tomorrow's Industrial IoT communication technologies. OpenMote has been designed to address the lessons learnt in the past decade of IoT research and early development. OpenMote is supporting and collaborating with most open-source initiatives and standardization efforts around the IoT, including Berkeley's OpenWSN project – the birthplace of the OpenMote – , but also Contiki, RIOT and FreeRTOS.

The hugely popular OpenMote has become the de-facto low-power wireless experimentation platform. Its very active community is constantly supporting new technologies and building a wider hardware ecosystem for the IIoT.

Acknowledgments. The development, testing and commercialization of the OpenMote has been a community effort. The authors would like to thank Kevin Weekly, David Burnett, Mark Oehlberg, Qin Wang and Tengfei Chang for participating in the design and testing of what became the OpenMote, to Ariton Xhafa and his team at Texas Instruments for their help with the CC2538 platform, and to the people at the UC Berkeley Swarm Lab for their constant support. We also thank the members of the OpenWSN community and the Thingsquare team for providing the requirements of the platform from a user point of view. A special thanks to the hundreds of OpenMote customers for believing in open-hardware for the Industrial IoT.

References

1. Dujovne, D., Watteyne, T., Vilajosana, X., Thubert, P.: 6TiSCH: Deterministic IP-enabled Industrial Internet (of Things). IEEE Communications Magazine 52(12), 36–41 (2014)
2. IEEE802.15.4-2011: Low-Rate Wireless Personal Area Networks (LR-WPANs), IEEE Computer Society Std., Rev. IEEE Std 802.15.4-2011, September 5, 2011
3. Levis, P., Madden, S., Polastre, J., Szewczyk, R., Whitehouse, K., Woo, A., Gay, D., Hill, J., Welsh, M., Brewer, E., Culler, D.: TinyOS: An operating system for sensor networks. In: Ambient Intelligence, pp. 115–148. Springer, Heidelberg (2005)
4. Watteyne, T., Vilajosana, X., Kerkez, B., Chraim, F., Weekly, K., Wang, Q., Glaser, S., Pister, K.: OpenWSN: A Standards-Based Low-Power Wireless Development Environment. Transactions on Emerging Telecommunications Technologies (ETT) 23(5), 480–493 (2012)
5. Dunkels, A., Gronvall, B., Voigt, T.: Contiki - A lightweight and flexible operating system for tiny networked sensors. In: International Conference on Local Computer Networks (LCN). IEEE (2004)
6. Baccelli, E., Hahm, O., Gunes, M., Wahlisch, M., Schmidt, T.C.: RIOT OS: Towards an OS for the internet of things. In: Conference on Computer Communications Workshops (INFOCOM WKSHPS), pp. 79–80. IEEE, Turin, April 14-19, 2013
7. Vilajosana, X., Llosa, J., Vilajosana, I., Prieto-Blazquez, J.: Arp@: Remote Experiences with Real Embedded Systems. Computer Applications in Engineering Education 22(4), 639–648 (2014)
8. Stanislowski, D., Vilajosana, X., Wang, Q., Watteyne, T., Pister, K.S.: Adaptive Synchronization in IEEE802.15.4e Networks. IEEE Transactions on Industrial Informatics 10(1), 795–802 (2014)
9. IEEE802.15.4e-2012: IEEE Standard for Local and Metropolitan Area Networks–Part 15.4: Low-Rate Wireless Personal Area Networks (LR-WPANs) Amendment 1: MAC sublayer, IEEE Computer Society Std., Rev. IEEE Std 802.15.4e-2012, April 16, 2012
10. Winter, T., Thubert, P., Brandt, A., Hui, J., Kelsey, R., Levis, P., Pister, K., Struik, R., Vasseur, J., Alexander, R.: RPL: IPv6 Routing Protocol for Low-Power and Lossy Networks, IETF Std. RFC6550, March 2012

11. Shelby, Z., Hartke, K., Bormann, C.: The Constrained Application Protocol (CoAP), IETF Std. RFC7252, June 2014
12. Thubert, P., Watteyne, T., Palattella, M.-R., Vilajosana, X., Wang, Q.: IETF 6TSCH: Combining IPv6 connectivity with industrial performance. In: Innovative Mobile and Internet Services in Ubiquitous Computing (IMIS), pp. 541–546, July 2013
13. Tuset-Peiro, P., Vazquez-Gallego, F., Alonso-Zarate, J., Alonso, L., Vilajosana, X.: LPDQ: A Self-scheduled TDMA MAC Protocol for One-hop Dynamic Low-power Wireless Networks. Pervasive and Mobile Computing 20, 84–99 (2015)
14. Vilajosana, X., Wang, Q., Chraim, F., Watteyne, T., Chang, T., Pister, K.: A Realistic Energy Consumption Model for TSCH Networks. IEEE Sensors 14(2), 482–489 (2014)
15. Fairbairn, M.L.: Dependability of Wireless Sensor Networks. Ph.D. dissertation, University of York, September 2014
16. Pimentel, V.: Estimating the Safety Function Response Time for Wireless Control Systems. Master's thesis, University of New Brunswick, March 2015
17. Watteyne, T., Robles, I., Vilajosana, X.: Low-power, Lossy Network Plugfest Demonstrates Running Internet of Things Code. IETF Journal 10(2), 18–20 (2014)
18. Grieco, L., Rizzo, A., Colucci, S., Sicari, S., Piro, G., Di Paola, D., Boggia, G.: IoT-aided Robotics Applications: Technological Implications, Target Domains and Open Issues. Computer Communications 64, 32–47 (2014)
19. Mathur, A., Newe, T.: Secure wireless sensor network for medical applications. In: NUIG-UL Alliance Conference, April 2015
20. Weekly, K.P.: Applied Estimation of Mobile Environments. Ph.D. dissertation, University of California, Berkeley (2014)

Security and Fault Tolerance in Wireless Mobile Networks

Lightweight, Dynamic, and Flexible Cipher Scheme for Wireless and Mobile Networks

Hassan Noura and Damien Couroussé

Univ. Grenoble Alpes, F-38000 Grenoble, France
CEA, LIST, MINATEC Campus,
F-38054 Grenoble, France
`hassan.noura@cea.fr`, `damien.courousse@cea.fr`

Abstract. The security of Wireless and Mobile Networks (WN, and MN, respectively) is crucial for effective deployment in various areas and applications such as military and business. The existing security solutions are based on static block /stream cipher to ensure Data Confidentiality (DC). These solutions require multi-round function, and consequently a high computing complexity and energy consumption. However, WN or MN has limited resources that prevent their efficient deployment for a long period. To overcome the previous challenge, a new kind of cipher scheme based on a dynamic permutation packets cipher is presented in this paper to ensure the DC requirements with low computation complexity. Theoretical results show that the proposed algorithm has a reduced computational complexity, which can lead to reduce the energy consumption. It is equally important to note that our proposed solution could be adapted for other kinds of networks that employ packet transmission such as vehicular network.

Keywords: Data Confidentiality, dynamic and lightweight cipher, flexible permutation layer, security analysis.

1 Introduction

Wireless Sensor Networks (WSNs) are used for many purposes, such as monitoring and collecting data as well as accessing and evaluating such information. Indeed, WSNs are appearing in enormous disciplines such as: smart houses, building, environment monitoring, traffic monitoring, military surveillance, health monitoring, or even in bodies as patient monitoring.

Typically, WSN are consisted of small devices that have the capability to gather information about their physical environments. WSNs realize the communication among the nodes by a multi-hop routing protocol. Usually, users of WSNs are divided into two different types (see Fig. 1): Base Station (BS) or **carrier** and sensor node. However, the major problem that threatens WSN is the security, since they are susceptible to several kinds of attacks such as passive and active attack [1], [2]. The former can seriously impair the confidentiality of the network, by trying to extract the content of transmitting packets, while the

© Institute for Computer Sciences, Social Informatics and Telecommunications Engineering 2015
N. Mitton et al. (Eds.): AdHocNets 2015, LNICST 155, pp. 225–236, 2015.
DOI: 10.1007/978-3-319-25067-0_18

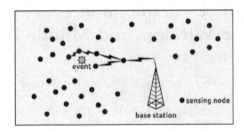

Fig. 1. An example of WSNs scheme

latter can damage the network authentication, by inserting, deleting or modifying the packet contents. One solution to overcome the passive attack, is to encrypt the transmitted packets among sensor nodes.

Hence, it is necessary to ensure that the transmitted data is secure enough from any unauthorized access (DC), as well as that data exchange is occurring only between legitimated parties. With state-of-the-art, low resources, limited computing power, limited power as well as limited battery lifetime are the main characteristic of any WSN architecture. Indeed, these limitations pose several problems from the cryptographic view point and attract many researchers since existing solutions suffer from the limited battery lifetime, where the battery of a sensor is depleted rapidly, and consequently terminates the network lifetime.

A block cipher such as AES [3] is used in real implementationwith secure operation modes such as (OFB) and Counter (CTR) [4], which are more suitable schemes for WSN, where the ciphering process is independent of plain-text, and can be considered as a stream cipher. However, despite its high level of security, AES has a high computational complexity since it uses multi-round structure. The presented implementation in [5] shows that AES decreases rapidly the lifetime of nodes and networks such as in ZigBee [6], WirlessHART [7]. As a conclusion, AES is not suitable for WSN platform, since its average performance has been higher on a range of sensor standard platforms. First, a security Protocol for Sensor Networks (SPINS) based on a block cipher (AES) in Counter mode (CTR) is presented in [8]. SPINS offers several security services such as DC, in addition of low communication overhead (8 bytes per packets). Then, in [9], a new protocol is presented to replace SPINS, while providing similar security services and denoted by TinySec [10] and it is the TinyOS security platform. Furthermore, TinySec suggests to replace AES by other block cipher based on its performance on WSN nodes such as Skipjack [11], or RC5 [12]. Moreover, Skipjack is used in the majority of well-known security platforms for WSN in addition, such as in SenSec [13] and TinyKey-Man [14]. The traditional approach uses the multi-round r function, which can be categorized into two classes: Feistel Networks (FN) and Substitution-Permutation Networks (SPN). Indeed, for each round, several simple iterated functions are applied, which require an important overhead. However, the security level depends on the number of rounds r, which leads to a trade-off between high security level and required computational complexity and consequently overhead energy consumption.

These WSN protocols ensure secure data transmission over the network, but with a **low network performance**. Hence, the limitations existed in WSN prevent the traditional security tools to achieve the security aspect efficiently. Recently, a new dynamic cipher kinds using dynamic diffusion layers in the integer Galois field were defined in [15]. After that, an enhanced scheme is defined in [16] by using binary diffusion matrix that is based on binary bmixing operation compared to the multiplication operations in integer field that are complex and large in size, slow in speed, and consume much power.

Furthermore, to achieve a secure WSN, a trade-off between security and performance is presented in existing protection techniques. The security in WSN suffers from various limitations and vulnerabilities, which encourages to implement new kinds of packet encryption to achieve a secure data transmission among sensor nodes with low computation complexity.

To overcome this problem, especially in constrained resources WSN, a new efficient cipher must involve. From here, comes the idea of our secure cipher scheme that achieves DC in an efficient manner and with the respect of WSN characteristics, in particular the throughput and energy consumption. In this paper, the proposed cipher consists of a dynamic permutation layer for the packet payload. The permutation process is realized using our modified version of GRP, which is our second contribution. The rest of this paper is organized as follows. Section 2 starts by describing our design goals & rationale then presents the proposed secure scheme, and then defines a new construction technique of key dependent and a flexible permutation layer based on our modified scheme of GRP algorithm [17]. Performance and security of the proposed scheme are analyzed in Section 3. Finally, Section 4 presents our conclusion.

2   The Proposed Secure Scheme

The proposed scheme has been designed with the following goals in mind:

1. **Simplicity:** As our approach is designed to be applied on sensor nodes, then it has to cope with the limitations as well as the requirements of the various kinds of WSN which are often fastest and lowest memory using. Our approach was also designed with as simple as possible computational operations in mind, suitable for sensor devices. One round of dynamic permutation operations makes our proposal efficient on a larger number of software platforms. The absence of S-box, diffusion, and key expansion makes our proposal small and efficient in hardware as well.
2. **Security against Attacks:** In fact, the cipher should provide strong resistance against exhaustive search attacks. A relatively large key size (128 bits) was therefore chosen for our approach.

In this section, a new efficient and secure permutation scheme is discussed. Usually, the term efficiency means achieving the security conditions of WN with

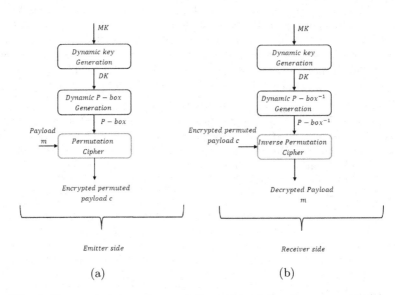

Fig. 2. Proposed cipher scheme at the emitter (a) and receiver side (b)

a little amount of time. The proposed scheme overcomes the disadvantages presented in the previously discussed techniques, and defines new kinds of cipher. In addition, it ensures a simple implementation when operating with constrained devices.

Table 1. Dynamic keys generation

1: **procedure** KEY_UPDATE(Mk, SK_{c1}, $adin$, i, $c1$, $c2$)
2:     **if** $(Ctr_2 \% w == 0)$ **then**
3:   ▷ Update the session key
4:
5:         $Ctr_1 \leftarrow Ctr_1 + 1$
6:         $SK_{Ctr_1} \leftarrow SHA - 512(MK||c1||adin)$
7:     **end if**
8:   ▷ Produce the dynamic key
9:
10:     $O_{Ctr_2} \leftarrow SHA - 512(SK_{Ctr_1}||Ctr_1||Ctr_2)$
11:     $DK_{Ctr_2} \leftarrow LSB(O_i, 4 \times l)$
12:     **return** $DK_{Ctr_2}, SK_{Ctr_1}, Ctr_1, Ctr_2$
13: **end procedure**

First, an extension for the packet header is introduced to express the sequence number of packets as NP with length equal to 1 byte (optimal value in order to reduce the trade-off between security and communication overhead). This header, similar to the sequence number used in IPSec, is involved in the proposed key derivation function to provide robustness against replay attacks. Indeed, a key exchange is supposed to be realized.

2.1   Secure Scheme at Emitter Side

In practical WSNs scenarios, a source node needs to transmit some data denoted by M. First, at the source side, the required data to be transmitted is divided into different packets M_1, M_2, ..., M_n. The different steps of the proposed scheme at the emitter side are described below in details:

Dynamic Key Generation. The dynamic key is produced using HASH-CTR DRBG, where its theoretical security analysis was analyzed in [18] and its robustness and performance have been proved. **Dynamic** key approach is used in our scheme instead of a static key approach in order to overcome the fixed key problem.

This process is presented in the following pseudo code as in Table 1 and seen in Fig. 3. In this section, the process of dynamic key generation is deeply explained starting with the generation of the session keys and ending with the reconstruction of dynamic keys from each session key.

First, a secret key is agreed between the sensor nodes and the sink. This single private key called 'Master Key' is designed by MK. Besides, Ctr_1 is a counter that is incremented for each w packets ($w = 251$). The Master key MK_{c1}, $c1$ value and some additional information related to the source/sink node $adin$ are concatenated together, then hashed using SHA-512 in order to perform at the end the session key required for the Ctr_1^{th} interval, denoted by SK_{Ctr_1}. Then, for each d (with $d \leq w$, $d = 251$) packets, the session key value SK_{Ctr_1} is combined with Ctr_1 and Ctr_2 values to perform O_{Ctr_2} value. Finally, a dynamic key, denoted by DK_{Ctr_2} is obtained directly by truncating $4 \times l$ -bits of Least Significant Bit (LSB) of O_{Ctr_2}. Noting that the size of the Master MK_{c1} and session SK_{c1} keys are 512 bits, while the dynamic key DK has a variable size.

Encryption Cipher Based on Dynamic, Flexible P_box. After the dynamic key generation, a key dependent permutation layer is fulfilled. The GRP permutation algorithm is defined in [17], can be considered as simple, flexible, and efficient in software and hardware implementation that is the reason why it chooses. In the following, the GRP permutation algorithm, used as a basic element of our permutation scheme, is described: As in Fig. 4, $R1$ is the source array or the original vector, CR is the configuration vector (control register) and $R3$ is the destination vector. The basic idea of the GRP instruction is to divide the index into two groups according to the pseudo-random bit sequence (CR). If the bit in CR is 0, this index is moved into the first group. Otherwise, this element is put into the second group.

A modification scheme of GRP is proposed here and described in Table 2. This modification was done in order to enhance the level of random of permutation but with acceptable computation. It consists of iterating two times the GRP's

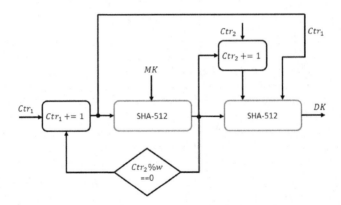

Fig. 3. Proposed key derivation function

algorithm for each round of permutation rp. CR and the bitwise complement of CR, are used as a control register permutation for the first and second time, respectively. The final permuted vector P_box is obtained after rp (round of permutation). Another contribution is to use different CR for each iteration of *Perm* round function.

Table 2. Proposed permutation algorithm

```
1: procedure PERM(DK, l, rp)
2:                                        ▷ L is the length of input vector
3:
4:      P_box ← 1 to l
5:
6:      for i ← 1 to rp do
7:          CRᵢ ← DK[(i − 1) × l : (i − 1) × l − 1]
8:          P_box = GRP(P_box, CRᵢ)
9:          P_box = GRP(P_box, CRᵢ‾)
10:     end for
11:                                       ▷ P_box is a dynamic Pbox
12:
13:     Return P_box
14: end procedure
```

Where i and $(P\_box[i])$ are the original and permuted positions of the input packet, where l represents the size of a packet. This transformation is iterated 4 times to ensure a good cryptographic performance (see Fig. 6). Hence, as result 4 control registers are needed to be used to calculate *Pbox*. In this context, the dynamic key DK of size $4 \times l$ bits is divided into 4 components $CR = CR_1$, CR_2, CR_3, CR_4 each of size of l bits, and used for its corresponding iterations. Indeed, this transformation requires for each iteration a control parameter CR_i, $i = 1, 2, \ldots, rp$ and each one can be obtained directly from

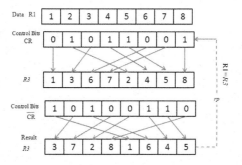

Fig. 4. Example of the proposed permutation $PERM$ algorithm with $l = 8$

DK. After producing the $Pbox.$, each element of the packet contents is permuted by using its correspondent permuted index and the permutation process is applied byte-by-byte as seen below:

$$c[i] = m[P\_box[i]] \tag{1}$$

where $m[i]$ and $c[i]$ are the $i-th$ original and encrypted (permuted) byte of packets respectively. $Pbox[i]$ is a permutation coefficient for the ith elements. After applying the permutation process, the output encrypted payload C is the permuted encrypted packets.

2.2 The Proposed Secure Scheme at the Receiver Side

The different steps of the proposed scheme at the receiver side are described below:

1. The receiver buffering model sorts the packet stream into packets according to their NP.
2. then, DK is generated using the same approach, that was investigated at the emitter side.
3. After that, the destination produces the inverse secret permutation process P_box^{-1} by using the same permutation scheme but applied in reverse order of control parameters.

After producing the $Pbox^{-1}$, each element of the encrypted packet contents is permuted by using its correspondent inverse permuted index as seen below:

$$d[i] = m[P\_box^{-1}[i]] \tag{2}$$

where $c[i]$ and $d[i]$ are the $i-th$ encrypted (permuted) and decrypted byte of packets respectively. $Pbox^{-1}[i]$ is an inverse permutation coefficient for the ith elements. After applying the process of inverse permutation, the output decrypted payload D is the original content of packet.

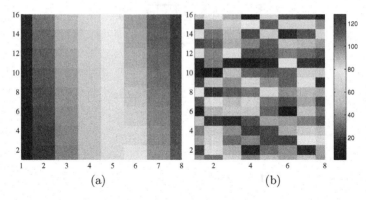

Fig. 5. Original and Permuted indexes for a random produce dynamic P-box in a matrix form with $l = 128$

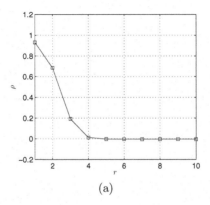

(a)

Fig. 6. Variation of the average of ρ of the recurrence of producing P-boxes versus rp for 1000 random dynamic keys

3   Cryptographic Strength and Performance

3.1   Cryptographic Performance of the Proposed Dynamic Permutation Layer

The performances of the proposed dynamic permutation scheme should be quantified in order to demonstrate its safe implementation. Indeed, a new criterion, which is the coefficient correlation (described in [19]) between the recurrence of permuted vector $((P\_box(t), P\_box(t+1), t = 1, 2, \ldots, l-1)$ is used in order to quantify the round number of permutations rp. These tests were applied for $nk = 2^{15}$ random dynamic keys. Fig. 6 shows the average of the coefficient correlation between the recurrence of permuted index versus rp for $l = 116$, which is the maximum length of the payload in WSN. It is clear that for $rp \geq 4$, the coefficient correlation becomes close to zero (ideal value). Consequently, rp should be 4, and the choice of this value is justified.

3.2 Key Sensitivity

Sensitivity refers to a huge change in the cipher-text, responding to a slight change in the keys K. The sensitivity of K is analyzed for 1000 random keys, using the percent Hamming distance PH that is calculated between two vectors X and Y with the same length l as following:

$$PH = \frac{\sum_{j=1}^{l} Byte2Bin(X_j \oplus Y_j)}{l \times 8} \times 100\% \tag{3}$$

In this case, the sensitivity of K becomes as follows:

$$KS_w = \frac{E_{K_w, IV}(M) \oplus E_{K'_w, IV}(M)}{l \times 8} \times 100\%$$

$$= \frac{\sum_{j=1}^{l} Byte2bin(C_j^w \oplus C_j^{w'})}{l \times 8} \times 100\% \tag{4}$$

where C_w, C'_w are the corresponding cipher packets using K_w and K'_w respectively. All the elements of K'_w are equal to those of K_w, except one element, which is the random Least Significant Bit (LSB), which was flipped to show the sensitivity of the scheme with a little change in key. Fig. 8, show the sensitivity of the secret key and its distribution, where only a LSB is changed on the secret key versus 1000 random keys for initial and enhanced scheme.

Additionally, Fig. 7-b shows the percent of hamming distance PH between original and permuted packet. From these figures, it can be seen that the majority of samples are close to the optimal value in bit level (50%). Therefore, we can consider that the proposed cipher block is strong enough to make the chosen/known plain-text attacks ineffective, while a dynamic key is used for each input packet.

3.3 Cryptanalysis

A cryptographic scheme is considered secure if it can resist attacks. The cryptographic security of our scheme relies on two properties:

- The use of a dynamic key (using counter mode).
- The unpredictability and high sensitivity of the secret permutation layer P.

However, all the packet contents are permuted via the dynamic secret permutation layer $Pbox$, at the source node before transmitting, and the intermediate nodes have no knowledge about DK. Thus, making the reconstruction of the original packet content very difficult.

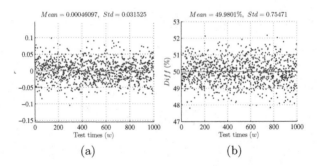

Fig. 7. The variation of the coefficient correlation between the original and encrypted contents packets (a) and PH between plain and cipher-packet (b) versus 1000 random dynamic keys respectively, with $l = 116$

Moreover, in Fig. 7-a, the average coefficient correlation between the original and encrypted packets for 10000 different secret permutation layers is shown. These results indicate that no detectable correlation exists between the original and its corresponding cipher packets which indicates that our proposal ensure security against statistical attacks. This discussion is presented in order to prove that the cryptographic security of our proposal is similarly powerful like traditional cryptographic solutions, and moreover, it ensures computational difficulties for a global attack to recover any meaningful information. Additionally, the proposed scheme works on dynamic manner, which means that the use of special encrypted packets will not lead to obtain any useful information about dynamic key and consequently about the session and master key respectively. Therefore, the key space of the master or the dynamic key of our scheme is sufficiently large to make the brute-force attack unfeasible. Moreover, the key space of the master keys is 2^{128}.

Besides, using the dynamic key method will limit the ability of the attackers to break our proposed scheme. The sensitivity of the master and dynamic keys is proved since our proposed scheme uses the cryptographic keyed hash function $SHA - 512$.

3.4 Flexibility and Execution Time

Our proposed scheme ensures the flexibility against the packet length l, while it is able to extend (increase/decrease) the length of the payload. On the other hand, the execution time is a very important factor for any cipher algorithm, since less computational time means low computation complexity, and consequently less energy consumption and minimum resource requirements for ciphering/deciphering process. This is considered as paramount for practical importance, especially for recent kinds of networks, where huge amounts of data are transmitted. The computation complexity of the proposed permutation cipher is $O(l)$ in addition to the process of generation of P-box, which is also linear ($O(l)$).

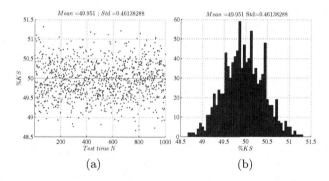

Fig. 8. The sensibility results for change a random LSB bit of the secret key versus 1000 random keys (a) and its corresponding density function (b)

Let us note that an iteration of unkeyed hash function SHA-512 (with small input block 512 bits) is also required for each input packet (high level of security), or for a set of packets (depend on the configuration). This shows that the proposed method is sufficiently fast for applications and especially for real time constraint applications.

4   Conclusion and Perspectives

Security in MN and WN becomes more and more crucial, due to the vastness use of this field such as WSN. The existing schemes using cryptographic algorithms cannot achieve a low execution time for high security level such as AES. In fact, a new security scheme has been proposed and realized to ensure safe data exchange, while providing less complexity and consequently less energy consumption. After that, simulation results are discussed and analyzed to validate the robustness of the proposed packet encryption scheme, its degree of randomness, and its key sensitivity as well as its cryptographic strength against different traditional and physical attacks (dynamic keys). These results indicate a significant improvement compared to AES, which leads to achieve the required security level with lower computational complexity. Indeed, our proposed scheme can be well deployed in any kind of networks, and also it appears to be adequate for the use with real time application with constrained devices.

References

1. Huang, Y.: Research of efficient security scheme in wireless network. In: Liu, X., Ye, Y. (eds.) Proceedings of the 9th International Symposium on Linear Drives for Industry Applications, volume 4. LNEE, vol. 273, pp. 717–724. Springer, Heidelberg (2014)
2. Karygiannis, T., Owens, L.: Wireless network security. In: NIST Special Publication, vol. 800, p. 48 (2002)

3. Daemen, J., Rijmen, V.: The Design of Rijndael: AES - The Advanced Encryption Standard. Springer, Heidelberg (2002)
4. Dworkin, M., Dworkin, M., Gallagher, P.D., Director Nist Special Publication -f : Recommendation for block cipher modes of operation: Methods and techniques (2001)
5. Lee, H., Lee, K., Shin, Y.: Aes implementation and performance evaluation on 8-bit microcontrollers. CoRR, abs/0911.0482 (2009)
6. Evans-Pughe, C.: Bzzzz zzz [ZigBee wireless standard]. IEE Review 49(3), 28–31 (2003)
7. Raza, S., Slabbert, A., Voigt, T., Landernäs, K.: Security considerations for the wireless hart protocol. In: Proceedings of the 14th IEEE International Conference on Emerging Technologies & Factory Automation, ETFA 2009, pp. 242–249. IEEE Press, Piscataway (2009)
8. Perrig, A., Szewczyk, R., Tygar, J.D., Wen, V., Culler, D.E.: Spins: security protocols for sensor networks. Wirel. Netw. 8(5), 521–534 (2002)
9. Karlof, C., Sastry, N., Wagner, D.: Tinysec: a link layer security architecture for wireless sensor networks. In: Proceedings of the 2nd International Conference on Embedded Networked Sensor Systems, SenSys 2004, pp. 162–175. ACM, New York (2004)
10. Karlof, C., Sastry, N., Wagner, D.: Tinysec: a link layer security architecture for wireless sensor networks. In: ACM, pp. 162–175 (2004)
11. Skipjack, N.: KEA algorithm specifications (1998)
12. Rivest, R.L.: The rc5 encryption algorithm. In: Preneel, B. (ed.) FSE 1994. LNCS, vol. 1008, pp. 86–96. Springer, Heidelberg (1995)
13. Li, T., Wu, H., Wang, X., Bao, F.: SenSec design. Institue for InfoComm Research, Tech. Rep. TR-I2R-v1, vol. 1 (2005)
14. Du, W., Deng, J., Han, Y.S., Varshney, P.K., Katz, J., Khalili, A.: A pairwise key predistribution scheme for wireless sensor networks. ACM Transactions on Information and System Security (TISSEC) 8(2), 228–258 (2005)
15. Noura, H., Martin, S., Agha, K.A.: E3sn - efficient security scheme for sensor networks. In: SECRYPT, pp. 615–621 (2013)
16. Noura, H., Martin, S., AI Agha, K., Grote, W.: Key dependent cipher scheme for sensor networks. In: 2013 12th Annual Mediterranean Hoc Networking Workshop (MED-HOC-NET), pp. 148–154, June 2013
17. Lee, R.B., Shi, Z., Yang, X.: Cryptography efficient permutation instructions for fast software. IEEE Micro 21(6), 56–69 (2001)
18. Campagna, M.J.: Security bounds for the nist codebook-based deterministic random bit generator (2006), matthew.campagna@pb.com 13453 received November 1, 2006. http://eprint.iacr.org/2006/379
19. Thirteen Ways to Look at the Correlation Coefficient. The American Statistician 42(1), 59–66 (1988)

Improving Security Issues in MANET AODV Routing Protocol

Mahsa Gharehkoolchian[1], A.M. Afshin Hemmatyar[2], and Mohammad Izadi[2]

[1] School of Science and Engineering, Sharif University of Technology, International Campus, Kish Island, Iran
Gharehkoolchian@gmail.com
[2] Department of Computer Engineering, Sharif University of Technology, Tehran, Iran
{Hemmatyar,Izadi}@sharif.edu

Abstract. Mobile Ad-hoc Networks (MANETs) are forming dynamically by joining or leaving the nodes into/from the network without any fix infrastructure. It is also possible that each mobile node act as a host or router. This kind of wireless network is prone to various security threats or attacks due to its unique characteristics like dynamic topology, open medium, lack of central monitoring, etc. So security is a vital scope in MANET to protect communication between mobile nodes. Ad-hoc On-demand Distance Vector (AODV) is one of the on-demand reactive routing protocols in MANET that initially was improved without considering security protection. Significant attempts have been done to secure AODV routing protocol in MANET but there are still critical challenges to overcome. In the present study, after reviewing secured protocols of some previous researches, an improved protocol is proposed to enhance the security of AODV routing protocol against black hole attack. For this purpose, we used a different level of trust for MANET nodes and imposed the limitations based on the nodes' trust level, in order to detect the compromised nodes and malicious behaviors inside MANET; which leads to the low delay and high performance in the network. Finally, we simulated the proposed protocol with NS-2 simulator as a means to validate it and evaluate the results. In fact, the results, demonstrate the efficiency of the presented protocol and its resistance to the black hole attack in comparison to AODV routing protocol.

Keywords: AODV protocol, Black hole attack, MANET, Secure routing, Trust-based technique.

1   Introduction

Accessing network resources from any location makes the wireless networks the most popular networks all over the word. On the other hand, this key feature can increase many problems regarding data security. By increasing the number of mobile hardware and devices, wireless networks' security becomes a big concern issue. MANET is a class of wireless networks that include mobile users which are connected by wireless

© Institute for Computer Sciences, Social Informatics and Telecommunications Engineering 2015
N. Mitton et al. (Eds.): AdHocNets 2015, LNICST 155, pp. 237–250, 2015.
DOI: 10.1007/978-3-319-25067-0_19

links with no fixed infrastructure (access point) and are formed on ad-hoc basis. Lack of fixed structures makes MANET more vulnerable to different kinds of attacks in comparison with other types of networks.

MANET does not have typical routers for routing in the network. Instead, each node in the system should function as a router for the other nodes. As a result, malicious behavior from any node can destroy network's function.

One of the most well-known routing protocols in MANET is Ad-hoc On-demand Distance Vector (AODV) protocol, a class of the reactive protocols that finds a route on demand by flooding the network with Route Request packets. This protocol is vulnerable to security threats and attacks. Overall, significant attempts have been done regarding security in MANETs but security issues in a wireless networks still exist.

In this article, first we are going to discuss different security threats and vulnerabilities in MANET and AODV. In next subsections different type of attacks, security attributes and MANET routing protocols are described. Then, the related works, the proposed protocol and achieved results are mentioned.

2   Routing Attacks and Threats in MANET

2.1   Some Attacks against MANET

Networks usually threat by the attackers, different types of attacks are known as flooding attack, gray-hole attack, Denial of Service (DoS) attack, impersonation attack, black hole attack, modification attack, etc. At the following section some of them are explained [1], [2]:

1) Wormhole attack: This attack creates a tunnel by attackers who placed themselves in the strategic position of the network; declaring the tunnel as a shortest path of transmission in order to record the traffic or ongoing packets.

2) Black Hole attack: A malicious node realizes a neighbor initiates to send a RREQ packet, it RREP the fake packet with the highest value of sequence number and lowest hop count. Consequently, neighbor node assumes that this malicious node has the best route to the destination. Thus, the source node discards all other RREPs; malicious node drops all the packets as well. In other words, it stops forwarding packets to the right destination [3], [4].

3) Flooding attack: The attacker set up a path between network's nodes to disseminate its unpleasant packets and congest the network.

4) Gray Hole attack: attacker acts as a both malicious and normal node in the network with aim of misleading network, being detected hardly and preventing them to reach the destination [5].

5) Modification attack: both Impersonation and misrouting attacks are including modification attacks.

6) Denial of Service (DoS) attack: a malicious node with the increase of fake RREQs, floods the network. Subsequently, non-malicious nodes cannot work well in the network while false RREQs imposed the network load. Wastage of bandwidth, extra overhead, network resource exhaustions (like memory or battery exhaustion) are some instances of adverse effects in the network [6].

2.2   MANET Weaknesses

MANET often suffers security attacks more than wired networks because of its nature features such as dynamic topology and open medium. In this section, some of the MANET weaknesses are mentioned.

1) *Lack of centralized administration:* there is no central control, management to monitor the traffic and nodes' functions especially in large scale of networks.
2) *No Boundaries:* nodes can easily join or leave the network, while in a wired network, it is needed to pass firewall or gains physical access to visit the network.
3) *Limited power supply:* selfish problem can be occurred. Selfish nodes don't cooperate with other nodes to provide services while it has enough battery power.
4) *Unpredictable scale:* the protocols and management services should be updated due to frequent change of the network scale.

3   Routing Protocol

3.1   AODV Routing Protocol

AODV protocol is a class of reactive routing protocols or on demand routing protocol, which means that, only by requesting a route – while there is no route to the desire destination – AODV tries to find the best and shortest path to the destination. AODV protocol has three main kinds of control messages during routing processes over UDP, route request (RREQ), route reply (RREP) and route error (RERR) messages.

3.2   AODV Mechanism

The operation of AODV routing protocol can totally be divided into two main stages: route discovery and route maintenance [7]. In route discovery step, source node tries to discover a path to the destination. In the route maintenance mechanism, nodes should be notified if a route is not valid any more due to dynamic network topology.

In MANET, when a source node needs to communicate with a desire destination, which is not existing in routing table, the source node broadcasts RREQ to all its neighbors; each of neighbor nodes rebroadcasts the RREQ as well. This flow is continuing until to finds the destination node or an intermediate node with fresh route to the destination. When the intermediate node gets a RREQ message, it does not need to send RREQ anymore and can have faster replies as it has a valid path into the destination. This RREQ is not only for finding path to the destination, but also it is used for reverse route and informing other nodes about this route to the destination [8]. In continuing, that founded node – destination/ intermediate node – sends a unicast RREP message to the source node in order to establish the desire route between source and destination. Moreover, In AODV, each node maintains a sequence number in order to identify the freshest route of information; Sequence number counter is increased before dispatching RREQ or RREP messages. So in AODV, nodes update their routing tables' information by finding the highest sequence number. Sequence number is unique 32 bit unsigned integer number, which leads to the great feature of loop-free in AODV routing. Hop-count also should be considered in routing updates, that shows the distance between the source and destination [9].

4   Related Work

In this subsection, several previous researches of securing routing protocol are mentioned and discussed.

Generally, the offered routing algorithm of securing AODV protocol classified into two main types: cryptographic and trust-base technique. Most of the presented secured protocols rely on cryptographic techniques, which can provide the confidentiality and integrity services. One of the cryptographic techniques offered an efficient secure AODV routing protocol named as SAODV [2], [8], [10]. This protocol authenticates non-mutable fields and mutable information (hop count) of the message, using digital signature and hash chain, respectively [10]; They have proven that their proposed routing algorithm has a better level of security and performance in terms of overhead and end-to-end delay; furthermore, SAODV can prevent tampering of control messages and data dropping attacks [2], [8]. However, SAODV only provides the authenticity of the message, not the dependability of the route information or route quality.

Some other articles presented the secured protocols which using cryptographic and trust base technique. Liu et al. is one of the researchers who have done research in this area [11]. Jared Cordasco and Susanne Wetzel have done a high quality of search for comparing SAODV and TAODV, including performance comparison on actual resource-limited hardware. The article addresses routing security based on cryptography and trust techniques [12]. Although their researches are valuable, they are not efficient enough because it needs consecutive monitoring neighbors' nodes and has high cost to implementation.

Some other articles that present trust based technique (such as TCLS, LLSP and RSRP), provide a reliable relation among non-malicious nodes and subsequently lead to low or even no requests for verifying certificates [11], [13], [14]. TCLS protocol uses trust counter and digital signature, to count the forwarded packet and verify the packets in the reverse route process respectively. LLSP protocol uses monitoring techniques to provide the security services at the data link layer. And the RSRP presented an efficient broadcast authentication technique to facilitate instant authentication [13]. Usually, trust based techniques rely on monitoring and packet analyzing mechanism with complicated computation; which leads to significant overhead in networks.

Meka et al. proposed trust-based solution (named as Trust AODV or TAODV), which is isolating malicious nodes, penalizing uncooperative nodes and allowing making decision to identify the best route to the destination by consideration of both node's trust and route trust metrics [11].

In another article trusted routing protocol is suggested against the security problem and selfishness issues. This kind of protocol which is named as TAODV protocol is designed based on trusted frame work and intrusion-detection system (secure protocol). In this model, routing table can be extended with trust information gathering directly from monitoring nodes. Hence great decrease of overhead and routing procedure trustiness can be guaranteed as the results from this model [14]. TAODV still is not completely a perfect protocol because of its some flaw's points. When multiple paths cross each other, it cannot support the trust level synchronization setting on different nodes.

Some researchers have tried to improve the performance of MANETs such as Tactical On-Demand Distance Vector (TAODV) routing protocol [15] and Without Black Hole AODV (WBHAODV) [16]. The introduced protocols significantly reduces the network traffic and increases the performance of network. Although these protocols are well performed, they could be faster and more efficient.

In another work, an optimized protocol is introduced in order to solve the problem of routing in dynamic topology. B-AODV is an example that improves the routing discovery and routing repair of AODV; as a result, it decreases the end-to-end delay and routing overload [17] but extra network traffic could be arisen when nodes have low movements.

In Some researches, solutions for determining the malicious nodes, are presented against black hole attack [1], [3], [4], [18]. In an article [3] a solution of Detection, Prevention Reactive AODV (DPRAODV), unto Black Hole attack is offered; in this protocol, the malicious node can be detected and isolated from data routing by using alarm messages to notify its neighbors. This result in normalize overhead of routing and the minimum increase of the average end to end delay. One of the other given approaches secures nodes by identifying the node's sequence number. Consequently, the routing table information won't be forwarded through the network anymore; so the network will be secured against black hole attack [4]. Another proposed protocol to secure AODV protocol against black hole attack is ERDA (Enhance Route Discovery for AODV). In such a work, ERDA introduces new condition in the routing table update that leads to improvement of network performance. The protocol can isolate the malicious node and decrease the effectiveness of black hole attack with no changes in AODV routing protocol scheme [18]. This protocol can be improved in trusted base for better privacy protection.

In this work, another trust-based solution for black hole attack will be presented using level of trust, which can give more appropriate ideas along implementation, in comparison to previous presented protocols.

5   Proposed Protocol

The present study tries to improve the security performance of the AODV routing protocol against black-hole attack using different level of trust for MANET nodes and impose the limitations based on the nodes' Trust Level (TL) in order to distinguish the reliable and unreliable nodes of network.

In the proposed protocol, each node has a list of its neighbors with their TL values. TL indicates that how much a node can be trusted; higher trust level range of a node represents the more reliability. The range of TL value is determined from -1 to 2. Each node initially has the TL value of 1 by joining to the network, and then maybe gain higher value by acting normally. On the other hand, if a node acts maliciously it would be set to the blacklist immediately with 0 TL value. The detail of each value is shown at the following table.

Table 1. Description of Trust Level values

TL Value	Description
-1	When a node is permanently blocked
0	When a node is in blacklist
1	Initially joined to network or released from blacklist
2	A node can reach to this rate after one trust testing

The improving protocol is described as the following steps:

First step is in the RREQ scope which the source node is broadcasting the RREQ to discover a destination node or an intermediate node with fresh enough route toward a desired destination; this part is same as the original AODV protocol.

Second step is in the RREP scope which uses the TL table, and the trust test technique to distinguish the reliable and unreliable nodes and encouraging or penalizing them respectively. When each node receives the RREP message, initially checks its own TL table. If the sender node of RREP is not a Suspicious Node (SN), TL exists with high enough value (TL= 2) in the TL table of the receiver node (Examiner Node). In this case, EN would evaluate the sender node as a trusted valid node. Then the process would be continued in the fourth step.

Otherwise, when the trust level value of the sender node in the trust level table of EN is equal to 1, then EN has to use trust test technique explained in third step. If the TL value is equal to -1 or 0, then SN has been black listed previously and known as an invalid or malicious node. Hence the RREP of SN would be dropped and never reach the originator.

In third step, we have the trust test technique. In this technique, the receiver node of RREP, sends a test RREQ message with a distinct RREQ ID to SN containing originator IP address (that can be any IP address) and destination IP address, which should be its own IP address; As a result, the reply message of this request would be received by EN itself. If the destination sequence number of the reply packet has the same value with the one that is existing in EN's routing table, SN could be a reliable node. (because as mentioned earlier, the malicious node replies the fake packet with a higher destination sequence number to persuade the originator node to change the route to itself); In this case, lower hop count between them must be chosen, which leads to have a shorter route. Subsequently, the TL value of the reliable node should be increased in the EN's trust level table; and it continues to the next step.

On the other hand, if the destination sequence number of the reply packet does not have the same value with the one that is existed in EN's routing table, SN would be an unreliable node. In other words, SN fails in trust testing. In this case, SN would be known as a blacklist node and the TL value of SN would be decreased. If TL value becomes 0, the node would be blocked temporary. After a certain time (blacklist timeout) the node would be released, and the TL value would be set as 1. If the node acts maliciously more than 3 times, the node would be blocked permanently as well as changing TL to -1. Blacklist timeout would be doubled at each time, until the node is blocked permanently and not to be able to communicate any more or establish wrong routes.

As an example, Fig. 1 and Fig. 2 assume that EN has no information about SN regarding TL value. So, initially the SN's TL value would be set as 1 in EN's table. Fig. 1 shows that the EN found the SN as a non-malicious node after a trust test, hence the TL value of SN would be increased to 2 and then the RREP would be forwarded toward the source node.

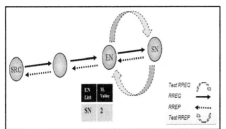 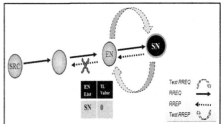

Fig. 1. After testing a non-malicious node   **Fig. 2.** After testing a malicious node

Fig. 2 shows that EN found the SN as a malicious node, hence the TL value of SN would be decreased to 0 and block the node for the certain block time. The EN node would drop the packet and prevent to establish wrong routes. After block time the SN will be released, and its TL would be set to 1. As mentioned, if SN acts maliciously again, corresponding TL would be set to 0 for the second time, and node should be blocked once more for longer time (doubled time). After releasing, if the node shows malicious behavior for third time, the node will be blocked permanently by changing TL value to -1 therefore, it will not be able to communicate with other nodes anymore.

In fourth step, the receiver node of RREP passes the message to the next hop of its reverse route until RREP reach the source node. So data can be transferred through forwarding tables, which has been made during unicasting RREP message. This action is the same as original AODV.

The general trend of the improved protocol in counter with black hole attack is described by the flowchart shown in Fig. 3.

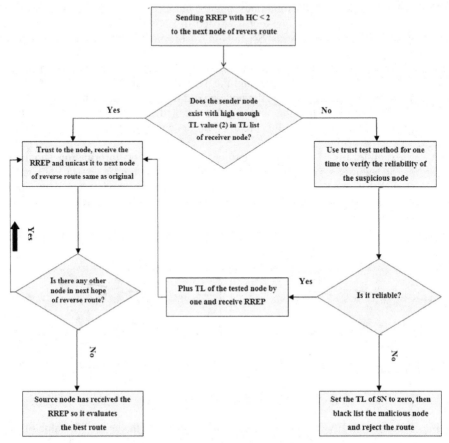

If the TL founded with 0 or -1 value it should be known as a temporary or permanent black list node respectively.

Fig. 3. Flowchart of RREP in the proposed protocol

6   Simulation Results

In this section, the performance of the proposed protocol is evaluated by NS-2 simulator in order to reveal its efficiency.

The following graph compares the total received throughput of network in the proposed protocol and the AODV protocol. Mobility of nodes, forces the AODV protocol to change its route continuously, which leads to give an opportunity to the attacker nodes to disrupt routing. This can cause a significant fall in the received throughput of network (Fig. 4); however, the proposed protocol has a high received throughput. This advantage is achieved because the proposed protocol can detect the attacker at the initial time of route discovery.

In the proposed protocol, we have to use extra packet controls for trust test technique, which cause the overhead to increase. Although the proposed protocol overhead enhanced initially due to the trust test technique at the start of finding reliable routes through new nodes in a network, after a while the overhead could be reduced to the lowest value as TL values are existing in TL tables and there is no need of trust test technique. Therefore, as graph shows (Fig. 5) the proposed protocol overhead has an upward trend by increasing nodes number, and it almost stays at the higher level of pure AODV protocol.

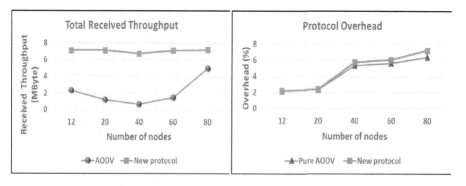

Fig. 4. Total received throughput of network against attackers in different number of mobile nodes (speed 5 to 10 m/s)

Fig. 5. Protocol overhead of network in different number of mobile nodes

For AODV protocol, the probability of facing to attacker nodes in sparse networks is higher than the dense networks; therefore, networks with a lower number of nodes have lower PDR. However, the proposed protocol detects the attacker nodes in any situation, which leads to appropriate PDR (Fig. 6).

Fig. 7 compares the average end-to-end delay of the proposed protocol and AODV against attackers, whether the network nodes have mobility or not (Mobility speed: 5 to 10 m/s). Regarding to the graph, the average delay of the proposed protocol is almost always stayed at lower rates than the AODV protocol against attackers in either mobile networks or non-mobile networks.

Although by increasing the number of mobile nodes in a network the Average delay of the proposed protocol takes an upward trend, it is much lower than the AODV protocol; and in fact, all the average delay values of the proposed protocol are still lower than the AODV rates which fluctuate greatly.

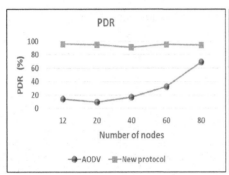

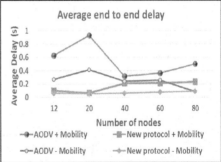

Fig. 6. PDR of network against attackers in different number of mobile nodes

Fig. 7. Comparing average end-to-end delay of the proposed protocol with AODV against attackers in different number of nodes in network

The following graph compares the rate of the average end to end delay of the proposed protocol with pure AODV protocol (no attacker) in a different number of mobile nodes (Fig. 8) in networks. The only main extra delay in the proposed protocol is when the network needs to use trust test technique. As the graph shows, the average delay of the proposed protocol is slightly greater than the pure AODV protocol.

In addition, it can be clearly seen that, increasing number of nodes cause rising of the average end to end delay of network.

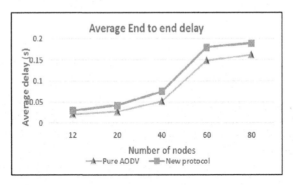

Fig. 8. Average end-to-end delay in different number of mobile nodes in network (Speed of 5 to 10 m/s)

The delay and PDR of some related works are shown in the Table 2. As it is clear, the proposed protocol has an almost better delay in comparison to another trust based techniques (i.e. TCLS, LLSP and RSRP [13]) which is evident in Fig. 9. The PDR of the proposed protocol is much better based on simulation results. This is because of the complicated mechanism of other protocols to find out its reliability. While in the proposed protocol, the unreliable node could be detected at the initial time of routing, which leads to much higher PDR. In comparison to other protocols, it can be clearly seen that the proposed protocol performance is much improved.

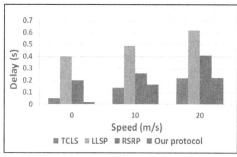

Fig. 9. comparing delay of some trust based
techniques vs. speed

Table 2. Comparing different protocols delay
and PDR when speed is about 10 (m/s)

Routing Protocols	Delay	PDR (%)
TCLS	0.14	62
LLSP	0.49	50
RSRP	0.26	55
The proposed protocol	0.16	94

Furthermore, there are several substantial advantages in using the proposed protocol comparing with some previous works such as monitoring, packet analyzing and cryptographic techniques. In addition, the comparison of present protocol with some other particular researcher's protocols is given in Table 3.

Monitoring or administration techniques usually cooperate with some extra monitor nodes with intention of collecting all other nodes' reports and subsequently decide in a complex manner about the malicious nodes. This is true that this monitor technique tries to enhance the security, but it causes changing the nature of MANET by adding central manager nodes. In comparison, the proposed protocol does not need any extra nodes whilst supporting the MANET features.

Another offered secured protocol is based on packet analyzing, which always has to suffer the overhead of complex computing. Whereas, in the improved proposed protocol, overhead can be decreased using the trust level technique.

In cryptographic techniques, there is mostly a large packet size because of digital signatures. In contrast, the proposed protocol packets do not use any digital signature and have a default field of AODV packets in trust test.

In some offered previous researches, after sending data packets toward a desired destination, it is found that an error had been occurred by an unreliable node (as the number of received packets is less than it expected), hence it starts to find the problem and detects the malicious node following by sending data packets again. Instead, the proposed protocol detects the malicious node as long as it starts a communication, before sending any actual data packets.

One of the significant advantages of the proposed protocol is that only two trust test packets are done and a TL table, with the aim of evaluating a node as reliable or unreliable. After a while, nodes do not need any more trust test packets with respect to the TL table, which leads to low overhead and faster operation. The efficiency of a network can reach the maximum when each reliable node gets the highest value of TL, and the malicious nodes blacklisted with the lowest TL. In other words, the proposed protocol initially has a light overhead and delay, but after some time, overhead and delay reach the lowest value in comparison to other protocols.

Another advantage of this proposed protocol is that it can stand against mass of attackers, because each node has its own TL table and can decide about the reliability of each node.

Another prominent achievement of the proposed protocol is that it can detect the malicious nodes, whether the attacker playacts as a destination or pretends to have a route to the desired destination. In other words, the attackers would be detected by the proposed protocol, whether the malicious node acts to have the normal RREP or the gratuitous one. At the end, the advantages of the proposed protocol in comparison with some other protocols are demonstrated in Table 3.

Table 3. The advantages of the proposed protocol in comparison with some other protocols

Routing protocol	Technique	Problem	The proposed protocol advantages
SAODV [8],[19]	Cryptographic techniques	Message size is significantly large, mostly because of digital signatures.	It does not need any digital signature
A-SAODV [14]	Threshold mechanism	Large packet size	Packets has an original size, does not need threshold mechanism
B-AODV [17]	BRREQ replace of RREP	Extra network traffic when nodes have low movements	The traffic is lower even in networks with fixed nodes
RAODV [14]	Adding two type of control packet	Used the extra packet controls Still has some flaw points	We just use the original control packets
ARAN [20]	Preliminary certification process	High power consuming and large size of the routing messages at each hop.	Messages obey the original packet size

7 Conclusion

In this article, we have focused on securing AODV routing protocol in combat with black-hole attack in particular. Since the AODV is a weak protocol in a countermeasure to this attack, the performance of network stays at a low level. In consideration of this problem, we proposed an improved protocol as means to enhance the security of AODV routing protocol and revised its flaw points. In the proposed protocol, we used the trust test technique and the TL tables to identify reliable or unreliable nodes in a network. In fact, TL tables considerably help the network performance with the intention of reducing trust-test packets' traffic, which leads to lower delay and higher performance in a network. The efficiency of a network can reach to the maximum when each reliable node gets the highest value of TL, and the malicious nodes blacklisted with the lowest TL. In other words, the proposed protocol initially suffers a light overhead and delay, but after a while it reaches to the lowest value. Lastly, the analysis result of simulation demonstrated that the proposed protocol tends to outperform the AODV routing protocol against black-hole nodes in all cases of performance metrics.

References

1. Agrawal, S., Jain, S., Sharma, S.: A Survey of Routing Attacks and Security Measures in Mobile Ad-Hoc Networks. Journal of Computer 3(1), 41–48 (2011)
2. Wadbude, D., Richariya, V.: An Efficient Secure AODV Routing Protocol in MANET. International Journal of Engineering and Innovative Technology (IJEIT) 1(4), 274–279 (2012)
3. Venkatraman, L., Agrawal, D.P.: Strategies for enhancing routing security in protocols for mobile ad hoc networks. Journal of Parallel and Distributed Computing 63(2), 214–227 (2003)
4. Raj, P.N., Swadas, P.B.: Dpraodv: A dyanamic learning system against blackhole attack in aodv based manet. arXiv preprint arXiv:0909.2371 (2009)
5. Vasava, M., Patel, H.: Comparison of Different Methods for Gray Hole Attacks on AODV based MANET. International Journal of Engineering Development and Research 2(1), 60–66 (2014)
6. Sanyal, S., Abraham, A., Gada, D.: Security Scheme for Distributed DoS in Mobile Ad Hoc Networks, School of Technology and Computer Science, Tata Institute of Fundamental Research, India, Mumbai University, India (2010)
7. Sarkar, P., Chaki, R.: A cryptographic approach towards black hole attack detection. In: Meghanathan, N., Nagamalai, D., Chaki, N. (eds.) Advances in Computing & Inform. Technology. AISC, vol. 176, pp. 273–278. Springer, Heidelberg (2012)
8. Goswami, J., Dafda, A.: Security aspects with AODV in WMANETs. In: National Conference on Power Systems, Embedded Systems, Power Electronics, Communication, Control and Instrumentation. Department of Electronics & Comm. Engg., L.D. Collage of Engg. Ahmedabad, Gujarat, January 2012
9. Perkins, C.: (RFC) Request for Comments – 3561. Category: Experimental, Network, Working Group, July 2003
10. Zapata, M.G., Asokan, N.: Securing ad hoc routing protocols. In: Proceedings of the ACM workshop on Wireless Security. ACM (2002)
11. Meka, K., Virendra, M., Upadhyaya, S.: Trust based routing decisions in mobile ad-hoc networks. In: Proceedings of the Workshop on Secure Knowledge Management (SKM (2006)
12. Cordasco, J., Wetzel, S.: Cryptographic versus trust-based methods for MANET routing security. Electronic Notes in Theoretical Computer Science 197(2), 131–140 (2008)
13. Simaremare, H., et al.: Secure AODV routing protocol based on trust mechanism. In: Wireless Networks and Security, pp. 81–105. Springer, Heidelberg (2013)
14. Sharma, P.: Trust based secure aodv in manet. Journal of Global Research in Computer Science 3(6), 107–114 (2012)
15. Uddin, M., Rahman, A.A., Alarifi, A., Talha, M., Shah, A., Iftikhar, M., Zomaya, A.: Improving Performance of Mobile Ad Hoc Networks Using Efficient Tactical On Demand Distance Vector (TAODV) Routing Algorithm. International Journal of Innovative Computing, Information and Control 8(6), 4375–4389 (2012)
16. ShafieeNejad Ghahroud, H.: Detection of Malicious Node in Black in Black-Hole Attack on AODV Protocol, Shiraz University of Technology: Hamid Shafiee Nejad Ghahroud (2012)
17. Liu, S., Yang, Y., Wang, W.: Research of AODV Routing Protocol for Ad Hoc Networks1. AASRI Procedia 5, 21–31 (2013)

18. Jali, K.A., Ahmad, Z., Ab Manan, J.-L.: Mitigation of Black Hole Attacks for AODV Routing Protocol. International Journal of New Computer Architectures and their Applications (IJNCAA) 1(2), 336–343 (2011)
19. Masdari, M., Pashaei Barbin, J.: Distributed Certificate Management in Mobile Ad Hoc Networks. International Journal of Applied Information Systems (IJAIS) 4, 33–40 (2012)
20. Sanzgiri, K., et al.: A secure routing protocol for ad hoc networks. In: Proceedings of the 10th IEEE International Conference on Network Protocols. IEEE (2002)

Bug-Tolerant Sensor Networks: Experiences from Real-World Applications

Marcin Brzozowski and Peter Langendoerfer

IHP, 15236 Frankfurt (Oder), Germany
{brzozowski,langendoerfer}@ihp-microelectronics.com

Abstract. Typical sensor networks include large number of motes deployed outdoors. The users expect these networks to work several months or years without maintenance. As a result, every mote must operate reliably for a long time, and it puts a high stress on both hardware and software. Therefore, programs running on motes cannot suffer from software bugs, and the developers must fix them before the deployment.

In this work, we summarize the major techniques for fixing software errors in protocols and applications for sensor networks. However, some bugs are hard to find in the lab, as they do not occur in testing conditions. Therefore, our motes include self-healing techniques, which detect and deal with software problems in the runtime. By doing so, motes keep working reliably for a long time, even when developers did not fix all bugs before the deployment. For instance, we failed to fix a few software errors in the MAC protocol, but the self-healing approach allowed motes to work several weeks outdoors.

Keywords: sensor networks, reliability, software.

1 Introduction

In recent years, our research work focused on wireless sensor networks, and included mainly communication protocols, operating systems, middleware, and security mechanisms. Further, we worked also on hardware platforms, designed our motes, and several hardware accelerators for efficient protocol processing or private/public key cryptography in sensor networks.

Apart from research activities, we deployed several sensor networks in various scenarios. For example, firefighters wore our motes in a pilot run to monitor body parameters at very high temperatures, hundreds Celsius degrees. Further, thirty of our motes managed solar power plants, and others monitored the water level in the forest.

We learned that most users expect the sensor network to work reliably for a long time. It means that software cannot include even minor software errors, as they will lead to problems sooner or later. However, finding software bugs in software for sensor networks is not trivial and requires good experience. For example, software bugs may depend on certain interactions between motes, or exist only in specific hardware configurations. Based on our experience, we know

© Institute for Computer Sciences, Social Informatics and Telecommunications Engineering 2015
N. Mitton et al. (Eds.): AdHocNets 2015, LNICST 155, pp. 251–262, 2015.
DOI: 10.1007/978-3-319-25067-0_20

we can fail to spot some bugs in the testing phase, and motes may suffer from them in the runtime. Therefore, our software includes self-healing instructions, which detect software bugs during the runtime and perform a reset of affected motes.

In this work, we present these two major means to deal with software bugs in sensor networks: efficient debugging and self-healing during the runtime. The latter demands more effort from developers, as they must add extra assertions in the time of implementation. However, this extra effort will pay off, especially in long-living applications of sensor networks. For example, although our software included some bugs in the communication protocols, the motes worked without serious problems for several weeks. Further, after fixing these bugs, we started the application again, but the motes suffered from other errors. However, they worked for 1.5 years without maintenance, as the self-healing code performed a reset on bug detection, once in two months on average. Without self-healing techniques, motes would have stop working after about two months in this case.

The rest of this paper is organized as follows. Section 2 gives an overview on debugging techniques and experiences with real-world applications of sensor networks. Then, in section 3 we explain both efficient debugging techniques and self-healing solutions tailored for motes. Section 4 introduces briefly our last two applications with self-healing solutions applied to motes. Then, in section 5 we present four important lessons learned from these scenarios. Finally, section 6 concludes this work.

2   Related Work

A few research works focused on debugging of software for wireless sensor networks (WSN). For example, EnviroLog [6] and another tool [10] store events in the non-volatile memory, and allow the developer to trace bugs. We included this feature in run-time assertions, and each time motes perform a reset after detecting an error, they store the error condition in the flash memory. Another debugging tool, NodeMD [5], catches software errors early enough to prevent the system is not working. After catching the error, NodeMD sends diagnostic information to developers.

In our previous work [2] we showed several techniques to efficiently debug WSN software, from hardware drivers to applications. Further, we evaluated various debugging techniques in terms of memory footprint and their impact on the execution time. This paper continues our previous work, and we show the next step of debugging: self-healing techniques in run-time applications. The need of self-healing solutions arises from problems observed in several outdoor scenarios. In the following, we show the major research works about real WSN.

In ref. [1] the authors share the experience of the entire process of WSN deployments. They noticed that the deployment is the time to face unexpected problems. One important observation made by the authors is KISS (*"Keep it Small and Simple"* or *"Keep it Simple Stupid"*), and we fully agree. Also, the authors stressed that some bugs are hard to spot before the real deployment, because they do not occur under testing conditions. The same happened to use and was the major reason to include self-healing code in our software.

In the work [7] authors introduced lessons learned from deploying a large-scale sensor network to monitor a potato field. They confessed they neglected software testing, and the mote suffered from many problems in the runtime. They stressed the need of thorough testing of the sensor network, mainly using a testbed. We followed some ideas of the authors and put a lot of effort in offline debugging before deploying the network. We also changed our attitude towards potential problems in the deployment and assumed the worst-case - it helped us to fix most errors in the lab, and the remaining bugs were handled with self-healing code.

The "potato-field" application was started again a year later [4]. This time, the authors followed the KISS principle and make the design much simpler than before. For instance, motes include only a minimal MAC and no routing at all, meaning they sent data directly to the sink. With such a simple design, the sink gathered about 51% of sensor readings, whereas it got only 2% readings in the year before, with much complex design. These observations confirmed our approach in the early stage of the development: make the whole system simple and robust.

3   Bug-Tolerant Software

In this section, we introduce two major means to deal with software bugs: *offline bug fixing* and *self-healing*. The former includes techniques to find bugs before deployment, whereas the latter detects software errors during runtime.

3.1   Introduction

Motes, like other computer systems, may suffer from software bugs. However, as sensors networks work outdoors, performing a reset on motes cannot be easily done. Similarly, motes usually cannot be updated remotely. Therefore, developers must take great care of finding and fixing all bugs before deployment. Otherwise, the affected motes may stop working, and it cannot be easily fixed.

The authors [1] mentioned that some bugs are hard to spot before starting the application, for example, because the testing conditions differ from the real-world scenario. We fully agree on this, and therefore we claim that long-living applications for sensor networks needs more than only bug fixing. Such software must include self-healing solutions, which recover from software errors on runtime. In this way, motes can work for a long time, even when developers did not fix some bugs before deployment.

Although we find self-healing solutions important, we do not underestimate offline bug fixing. On the contrary, we consider fixing bugs before deployment the major step in building reliable software for sensor networks. However, only the combination of both, offline bug fixing and self-healing solutions, guarantee long-living applications of sensor networks.

3.2   Offline Bug Fixing

Finding bugs before deployment includes mainly testing with network simulators and also on real hardware, on motes. In the following, we introduce the major techniques we apply to find and fix software bugs in WSN protocols and applications:

1. *Cross-Platform Software*
   We implement WSN protocols, mainly MAC and routing protocols, as Cross-Platform software, which we can execute on various operating systems and in network simulators. Therefore, we can fix software errors on the PC in network simulators, before running programs on motes, leading to more efficient bug fixing. In recent years, we managed to fix major bugs only in PC simulations, and on motes we worked mainly on hardware-specific problems.

2. *Assertions*
   An assertion stops software execution when a given condition is not met. For example, a program stops when the radio is not in the RX state. With assertions developers examine the failure just after it happened, narrowing down the root cause of the problem. Further, assertions support us also in testing new program versions.

3. *Debug messages*
   With debug messages testers get run-time information while executing programs. We used such messages not only in PC simulations but also when executing software on motes. In this case, the motes sent messages to the PC, which stored them in log files. Such log files help us to find bugs in interactions between motes, for instance, in routing protocols.

4. *Testbed*
   WSN Testbed consists of several motes connected to a backbone network. Developers can program each mote remotely, and also get data from it, mainly debug messages. It is an intermediate step between PC simulations and real-world deployment.
   With our testbed, we can program all motes within a few seconds and get output from the programs running on them. We use the testbed, coupled with debug messages, mainly to find hardware-related bugs that were not found during PC simulations.

5. *Debugger*
   This tool allows to examine running software by checking variable values, setting breakpoints, etc. There are also debuggers for embedded systems, and we can easily debug program running on motes in this way. However, we applied a debugger only when other techniques failed to find bugs.

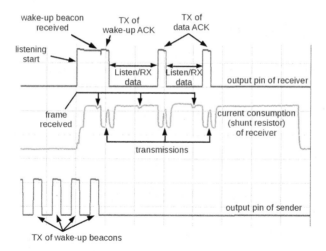

Fig. 1. Example debug session of Low Power Listening with an oscilloscope; this figure shows output pins of the receiver (top) and of the sender (bottom), and the current consumption of the receiver (middle); it allows to discover timing problems of low-level protocols or hardware drivers

6. *LED*

   To get a feedback from the running mote, mainly when implementing low-level drivers, we use a light-emitting diode (LED). For instance, to check if the mote is still running, we observed if the LED kept blinking.

7. *Scope / Logic analyzer*

   We connect General Purpose Input/Output (GPIO) pins of a micro-controller to the scope and debug low-level software problems, mainly hardware drivers. With the scope we get information how long a certain event lasted and how many times it occurred. Further, we can analyze several events at the same time. For example, we examined our MAC protocol by connecting both the sender and the receiver to the scope (see Figure 1). In this way, we were able to trace timing problems of a few milliseconds only. Without using the scope it would be extremely hard to spot this error.

8. Shunt resistor

   A shunt resistor is inserted between the power source and the node. In this way, we measure the voltage drop across it, get the time-current relation by applying the Ohm's law (see Figure 1). For example, with a shunt resistor we can estimate the exact time a message was sent or received.

   To efficiently debug software for embedded system, we couple several techniques. For example, we execute programs with assertions on testbed, and check logs with debug messages. We may continue debugging process by running the debugger and setting breakpoints at specific code regions. Our previous work [2] gives more details about debugging techniques for WSN software.

```
void ps_tx_wake_up_success(addr_t rx) {
        ps_ignore_all_rx();
        if (rx != os_get_broadcast_address()) {
                CHECK_FATAL_ERROR( VAR(ps_state) != TX_ALIVE_MSG,
                        "Bad state %u in wake up\n", VAR(state));
```

Fig. 2. Assertion example. We include assertions in CHECK_FATAL_ERROR macros. If the condition is met, the mote performs the system reset in the runtime, and writes the error notice to the flash memory.
In this case, the mote resets the system if the internal state is not TX_ALIVE_MSG

3.3   Self-healing

As stated before, programs running on motes in real-world deployment can suffer from software bugs, even after thorough debugging. Therefore, WSN applications must include extra instructions that will deal with overlooked software errors, dubbed self-healing. In our applications, we included two following solutions to tackle run-time software problems:

1. *Watchdogs*
   are standard features of common micro-controllers to deal with software problems. In short, the micro-controller expects the software to clear a *watchdog flag* periodically. If software does not clear the flag, the MCU assumes that software does not work correctly, and the running program restarts.
   In our application, we clear the watchdog flag in the MAC protocol, when performing a periodic channel check.

2. *Assertions*
   We already introduced assertions previously in *offline bug fixing*. In that case, the running program stops when a condition specified in the assertion is not met (see Figure 2). Clearly, stopping the program in the outdoor application does not help at all. Therefore, when an assertion detects a run-time problem, it restarts the running program. In our opinion, it is better to start the program again instead of keeping it running in a wrong state.
   In the running system motes write the cause of assertion into the flash memory. In this way, we can trace software problems after collecting motes.
   Clearly, it is up to the developers to put reasonable assertions in the source code. We tend to put rather more assertions than too few, as a single assertion needs only about 30 bytes of memory [2], and a few extra bytes for the corresponding debug message.

In both cases, watchdogs and assertions, the mote performs the reset, and set all program variables to their initial values. However, it may lead to various problems, when the variables should keep their values after reset. For example, motes cooperate to find routes in multi-hop networks, and each mote writes partial route information locally in the routing table. In case of assertion, the

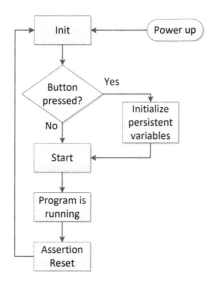

Fig. 3. With assertions motes find software problems in the run-time, perform the system reset, and sets default values to variables. However, some variables, dubbed persistent, should preserve their values on reset. To allow the mote detection of the start condition, reset or power up, we press a button when powering it up. Only in this case the persistent variables are initialized.

mote performs the reset, clears the routing table and cannot forward frames coming from neighbors. It leads to delays in packet forwarding, and to extra traffic caused by finding of missing routes. In this case, the mote should keep its routing table after performing the system reset.

To preserve values of some variable on assertion, the mote must determine whether it was powered up or restarted. Among various solutions, we selected the one based on the *"keep it simple"* principle. That is, when we want the mote to initialize all the variables, we keep the button pressed during power up. In this case, the mote detects the button is pressed, and initializes all variable (see Figure 3). Clearly, when the mote performs the reset caused by assertion, it notices the button was not pressed, and preserves the value of some selected variables.

In previous outdoor applications we learned how powerful and important assertions are. We could even run a sensor network for several weeks knowing there are still software errors in our MAC protocol.

To benefit from self-healing solutions, developers must think already during the implementation what may go wrong in run-time systems, and add appropriate assertions. However, this extra effort will surely pay off, as we experienced in previous outdoor deployments.

4 Application Background

In this section, we introduce briefly our last two real-world applications. Before starting them, we fixed bugs in WSN software in our lab, and also included self-healing techniques. In the next section, we show how well these solutions worked.

4.1 Application One: Tree Growth

During this research project, biologists examined the impact of various phenomena, such as soil quality or solar irradiance, on the tree growth. To carry out this study, they had to collect environmental data in a forest over a long period. We installed the pilot run in the forest about 100 km north of Berlin in Germany.

Our motes provided environmental data from four locations, which were located about 100 meters away from the sink. In theory, motes should send data directly to the sink without problems. However, as there were several trees between motes and the sink, they attenuated the radio signal, and the direct communication suffered from packet losses. We measured the signal strength (RSSI, Receiver Signal Strength Indication) at the sink and found out it was almost as low as the RX sensitivity level of the radio. As it caused the risk of packet losses, we put two relays between the data sources and the sink. These relays forwarded sensor readings to the sink in case there were problems with the direct connection.

After the preliminary run, we fixed some bugs and verified software with our WSN testbed again. After several weeks of in-lab testing, we deployed the sensor network outdoors. The network works already 1.5 years, and it is still operational. However, after about 6 months we replaced all motes, since they were destroyed by a lightning strike.

4.2 Application Two: Water Monitoring

In this project, the sensor network monitors water resources, such as reservoirs, rivers, and channels. By doing so, it provides crucial information for preventing floods, and for management of water quality and energy. The project considers water resources in the south of Spain, close to the city Malaga.

The project started in 2014, and the first year we worked only in our lab. We developed adapters needed to connect water-monitoring sensors, and also worked on communication protocols. During this time, we tested software running on motes with the testbed.

At the beginning of 2015, seven motes were deployed in the demonstrator area, in the south of Spain. Based on our previous experience with real-world deployments, we wanted to keep the network simple to avoid many problems that arise from complexity. Therefore, we deployed data sources close to the sink, and allowed direct communication between them, without relays.

Similarly to the previous application, motes in Spain sent data from sensors to the gateway, which forwarded it to the Internet server.

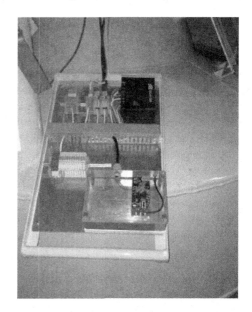

Fig. 4. Our motes used in outdoor applications. On the left, two motes with twelve sensors each for measuring the surface tension of the ground. On the right, the mote installed in a buoy, it measures the water quality in a reservoir.

4.3 Mote Architecture

In both projects we used our proprietary hardware platform for motes, named FWnode [9]. Figure 4 show motes in two above-mentioned applications.

In short, we based the FWnode on 16-bit MSP430 micro-controller, and on three transceivers (CC1101, CC2500, and CC2520), which support 868 MHz and 2.4 GHz frequency bands. In both scenarios, we used the 868 MHz frequency band, since it provides a larger communication range.

To provide long lifetimes, motes need not only a large battery but also suitable protocols that support low duty cycles. Therefore, we applied a low-duty cycle MAC protocol based on preamble sampling [3]. Further, to support multi-hop communication using relays, the motes includes also the AODV [8] routing protocol.

5   Lessons Learned

Before deploying the sensor network, we expected the motes to be the major source of problems. However, as we put a lot of effort to test software running on motes, and included self-healing solutions, the motes worked reliably. The major problems arisen from the Internet gateway. In this section, we shortly share our experience with real-world applications of sensor networks, and emphasize the need of debugging and self-healing solutions.

5.1   Keep it Simple, Or You Are in Trouble

Before starting the projects, we used mainly our schedule-based MAC protocol. It includes many solutions and workarounds to deal with clock problems, leading to high complexity. Further, we discovered some problems during PC-based simulations and fixing them would need a lot of effort. We decided to write from scratch another, much simpler MAC protocol, based on preamble sampling. We hoped that the simpler MAC would lead to smaller maintenance efforts, such as bug-fixing or adding new features. Indeed, it took us only a few weeks to write the complete MAC protocol, which was running in PC simulations and on our motes. Further, finding and fixing bugs of such simple protocol took much less time than working with the complex schedule-based MAC.

Once again we realized that following the "keep it simple" principle brings great benefits.

5.2   PC Simulations Are Essential

As stated before, we implemented the MAC protocol from scratch, and also updated several hardware drivers, mainly for the radio. Therefore, we must thoroughly test new software before deploying it outdoors. Apart from hardware drivers, we tested protocols and applications with the OMNet++ [11] network simulator, and fixed most software problems. After that, we ran tests on real hardware and fixed bugs in hardware drivers. We claim that developers of protocols for sensor networks cannot avoid testing in PC-based simulations. Otherwise, they have to test protocols directly on hardware, and finding bugs related to interaction between many motes is very inefficient and time consuming.

5.3   Self-healing Needed for Maintenance-Free Applications

During the test phase we found and fixed most software errors. However, a few bugs in the communication protocols were hard to spot, as they occurred rarely, once a day, and we could not reproduce them. The affected motes could not send and receive data, and we had to start them again. Nonetheless, we started the preliminary run outdoors, and hoped that self-healing solutions will restart motes when the problem occurs. Indeed, the assertions discovered the software problems and restarted motes several times. As a result, the sensor network worked for a month, until the battery ran out.

After this preliminary run, we fixed the software bug in the MAC protocol and started the final run. Unfortunately, there were still some bugs in software. The self-healing code performed a reset on motes once every 2 months on average. The above example shows the power of self-healing code. That is, motes without it would suffer from software bugs, leading to failures. With the self-healing code, however, the motes ran for long time without maintenance, apart from replacing batteries in case of power-hungry sensors.

5.4   Think about the Whole System, Not Only about the Sensors

We admit that we put a lot of effort to provide reliable software for sensor networks but neglected other parts of the whole application. Before the deployment we assumed that data transmission from the sensor network to our Internet server, using a cellular modem, works without problems. To deal with potential connectivity problems, we added some scripts that monitored the cellular connection. Sadly, our Internet server stopped receiving data from the sensor network a few times, and we realized the need of testing all parts of the running system, not only the sensor network. In the following, we give an example of unexpected problems with the Internet gateways.

5.4.1   GSM Modem Vanished

Once a while the cellular gateway did not send any data to our server due to connection problems. It should not happen, as there was a script running that monitored restarted the connection once a while. In this case, however, the gateway could not detect the cellular modem, as if the modem was removed from the USB slot. After resetting the gateway, it discovered the modem again and got connected to the Internet. To deal with the above mentioned problem, we added a workaround that performed a gateway reset.

5.4.2   SD Card Not Seen by the OS

Another time our server received connection logs from the gateway but the sensor readings were missing. We thought the mote working as the sink was broken. Finally, we came to the demo area and found out that the gateway could not detect the SD card used for storing data from the sink. In this case, the gateway tried to store data into the internal flash memory, but it was full. Surprisingly, after re-inserting the SD card, the gateway detected it and kept saving new data from the sink. We faced the following problem only once, but it may happen again. In this case, we will use extra USB flash drive, and store data on both SD card and USB flash drive.

6   Conclusion

In this work, we presented two major steps to deal with software bugs in WSN applications: offline debugging and self-healing code. We claim that the combination of both solutions allow long-living, reliable applications of sensor networks.

Although we put a lot of effort into software debugging, there were still a few software bugs in the running sensor network. However, as our motes included the self-healing code, they detected the error and performed a reset once in two months on average. By doing so, they worked for 1.5 years and are still operational. Further, we started the preliminary run knowing there are still some software bugs in the running programs. However, the motes detected these bugs at runtime, and continued working for several weeks. It shows the power and importance of self-healing solutions: motes work with software bugs for a long time and do not need maintenance.

We presented briefly two last deployments of sensor networks. These applications taught us to carefully test the complete system, and not only the sensor network. That is, whereas the motes worked reliably over the whole project, the major problems arise from the Internet gateway. In the end, the sensor networks did not suffer from problems, but the users did not get data because of gateway failures.

Acknowledgment. The research leading to these results was partly funded by the European Community's FP7 Programme under grant agreement n° 619132 (project SAID).

References

1. Barrenetxea, G., Ingelrest, F., Schaefer, G., Vetterli, M.: The hitchhiker's guide to successful wireless sensor network deployments. In: Proceedings SenSys (2008)
2. Brzozowski, M., Langendoerfer, P.: Overview and benchmarks of pragmatic debugging techniques for wireless sensor networks. In: Profeedings SoftCOM (2013)
3. Brzozowski, M., Langendoerfer, P.: Multi-channel support for preamble sampling MAC protocols in sensor networks. In: Proceedings SoftCOM (2014)
4. Haneveld, P.K.: Evading murphy: A sensor network deployment in precision agriculture (2007).
   http://www.st.ewi.tudelft.nl/~koen/papers/LOFAR-agro-take2.pdf
5. Krunic, V., Trumpler, E., Han, R.: Nodemd: Diagnosing node-level faults in remote wireless sensor systems. In: Proceedings MobiSys (2007)
6. Luo, L., Zhou, G., He, T., Gu, L., Abdelzaher, T.F., Stankovic, J.A.: Achieving repeatability of asynchronous events in wireless sensor networks with envirolog. In: Proceedings INFOCOM (2006)
7. Langendoen, K., Baggio, A., Visser, O.: Murphy loves potatoes: Experiences from a pilot sensor network deployment in precision agriculture. In: Proceedings IPDPS (2006)
8. Perkins, C.E., Royer, E.M.: Ad-hoc On-demand distance vector routing. In: Proceedings WMCSA (1999)
9. Piotrowski, K., Sojka, A., Langendoerfer, P.: Body area network for first responders-a case study. In: Proceedings BodyNets (2010)
10. Sundaram, V., Eugster, P., Zhang, X.: Lightweight tracing for wireless sensor networks debugging. In: Proceedings MidSens (2009)
11. Varga, A.: The OMNeT++ discrete event simulation system. In: Proceedings ESM (2001)

Author Index

Printed in the United States
By Bookmasters